Emerging Markets and Financial Globalization

Emerging Markets and Financial Globalization

Sovereign Bond Spreads in 1870–1913 and today

Paolo Mauro, Nathan Sussman, Yishay Yafeh

OXFORD
UNIVERSITY PRESS

OXFORD

UNIVERSITY PRESS

Great Clarendon Street, Oxford OX2 6DP

Oxford University Press is a department of the University of Oxford.
It furthers the University's objective of excellence in research, scholarship,
and education by publishing worldwide in

Oxford New York

Auckland Cape Town Dar es Salaam Hong Kong Karachi
Kuala Lumpur Madrid Melbourne Mexico City Nairobi
New Delhi Shanghai Taipei Toronto

With offices in

Argentina Austria Brazil Chile Czech Republic France Greece
Guatemala Hungary Italy Japan Poland Portugal Singapore
South Korea Switzerland Thailand Turkey Ukraine Vietnam

Oxford is a registered trade mark of Oxford University Press
in the UK and in certain other countries

Published in the United States
by Oxford University Press Inc., New York

British Library Cataloguing in Publication Data
Data available

Library of Congress Cataloging in Publication Data
Data available

Typeset by Newgen Imaging Systems (P) Ltd., Chennai, India
Printed in Great Britain
on acid-free paper by
Biddles Ltd., King's Lynn, Norfolk

ISBN 0–19–927269–7 978–0–19–927269–3

10 9 8 7 6 5 4 3 2 1

Preface

This book is the outcome of our long-time fascination with what Stefan Zweig called the *World of Yesterday*, a world in which people, capital, and goods could move freely from Europe to far corners of the world: "Before 1914, the earth had belonged to all. People went where they wished and stayed as long as they pleased. There were no permits, no visas, and . . . frontiers were nothing but symbolic lines" (1943 English edition, p. 311). This period of globalization, which reached a peak between the mid-nineteenth century and the outbreak of the First World War, provides a rare opportunity to look at the globalization we are experiencing today in a historical mirror. What features remain the same? What has changed? And what explains the differences? The present study focuses on financial globalization and international capital flows, and attempts to provide some answers to these questions.

We have made an effort to make the book appealing and accessible to a wide audience, consisting of both academics and others, avoiding excessively technical discussions. Economic historians will hopefully be interested in the discussion of international capital flows in 1870–1913, and in the analysis of the economic institutions of the time. Other economists might be more interested in the comparative analysis of the determinants of borrowing costs for emerging markets before the First World War and today, as well as in the study of mechanisms whereby investors sought to mitigate the consequences of the debt crises of the past. All of these issues are of major importance for academic research in international macroeconomics. We also believe that there are important lessons from the past for policy makers in governments and international organizations, and that the long-run perspective we offer will be interesting and useful for investors focusing on emerging markets.

In the spirit of globalization, work on this book was carried out in numerous institutions in different countries: the Hebrew University of Jerusalem (Sussman and Yafeh), Université de Montreal (Yafeh), and the International Monetary Fund. We are grateful to the Guildhall Library in London for access and assistance in research on the Annual Reports and documents of the Corporation of Foreign Bondholders; to the National Library (Jerusalem, Israel) for access to microfilmed copies of the *London Times* for the historical period; and to the London Stock Exchange Project at Yale University for electronic access to the *Investors' Monthly Manual*.

The collection of historical financial data is no easy task. We would not have been able to undertake the research for this book without the invaluable help of many talented students and research assistants: Alexandre Dubé, Guy Green, Avital Gutalevich, Yosh Halberstam, Shai Harel, Priyadarshani Joshi, Priyanka Malhotra, Martin Minnoni, Tamar Nyska, Erran Oren, Omer Schwartz, Hadas Yoked, and Shalva Zonenshvili. This research was supported by the Israel Science Foundation (Sussman and Yafeh, Grant No. 871/02).

Our friends and colleagues around the world have also contributed many helpful comments and suggestions. We are especially grateful to Barry Eichengreen, Niall Ferguson, Eugene Kandel, Kobi Metzer, Richard Portes, Raghuram Rajan, Zvi Sussman, Alan Taylor, Mike Tomz, Jeff Williamson, Zvi Wiener, Jeromin Zettelmeyer, and participants in the 2003 meeting of the American Economic Association and seminars at the International Monetary Fund, the New York Fed, the World Bank, Brown University, Harvard University, Hitotsubashi University, Queen's University, Rutgers University, Stanford University, Tel Aviv University, and the University of Toronto.

Finally, the views expressed in the book are those of the authors and do not necessarily represent the views of the International Monetary Fund or its policies.

Paolo Mauro (International Monetary Fund)
Nathan Sussman (The Hebrew University of Jerusalem and CEPR)
Yishay Yafeh (The Hebrew University of Jerusalem and CEPR)

Contents

List of Figures

List of Tables

List of Tables

1

International Capital Flows in the Previous Era of Globalization: An Overview and Outline of the Book and its Objectives

The international financial environment in which emerging markets operate today is in its infancy and shows many signs of teething pains. Capital flows toward emerging markets are large, but have been considerable only since the 1970s. International bonds, currently the main form of finance for sovereign borrowers, have only been used by emerging markets on a significant scale since the mid-1990s. And capital flows have been subject to sudden reversals, leading to crises and their disastrous consequences for borrowing countries and, occasionally, international investors. The Mexican crisis of late 1994 and early 1995, the Asian crisis of 1997, and the Russian crisis of August 1998 spread to several other emerging market countries, seemingly regardless of whether the economies they affected were fundamentally sound. The Argentinean crisis that began in 2001 and the associated default—by some measures, the largest default in history—will be long remembered by domestic residents, policy makers, and many investors.

The frequency and virulence of such recent financial crises have led to calls for reform of the current international financial architecture. Several observers have wondered whether globalization in international financial markets has gone too far. To learn more about the international financial environment we live in today, we turn to a similar, earlier era of globalization and sovereign bond finance starting around 1870 and ending with the onset of the First World War.

Not only was the pre-First World War period an era of unprecedented, and in some respects, unsurpassed globalization, characterized by large international capital flows toward "emerging markets" (a term not in use at the time), it was also a period in which international sovereign bonds were a key source of finance for emerging markets. Indeed, although today's size and form of capital flows toward emerging markets had not been observed for several decades, they would not have surprised British investors and other market participants operating before First World War. And while the large volume of sovereign bond issues by emerging markets starting in the early 1990s is a phenomenon not seen for nearly three-quarters of a century, it pales in comparison to the size of the London market during its heyday.

Globalization then, casual observation suggests, was comparable to today's. Even though financial instruments have become more sophisticated, in some respects we may yet have to match the extent of international movement of capital, goods, and labor that the world experienced around the turn of the twentieth century.[1] A vivid depiction of that era was provided by Keynes in 1919; by then, it had already become clear that globalization would cease for many years to come:

The inhabitant of London could order by telephone, sipping his morning tea in bed, the various products of the whole earth, and in such quantity as he might see fit, and reasonably expect their early delivery upon his doorstep; he could at the same moment and by the same means adventure his wealth in the natural resources and new enterprises of any quarter of the world, and share, without exertion or even trouble, in their prospective fruits and advantages; or he could decide to couple the security of his fortunes with the good faith of the townspeople of any substantial municipality in any continent that fancy or information might recommend. He could secure forthwith, if he wished it, cheap and comfortable means of transit to any country or climate without passport or other formality, could despatch his servant to the neighboring office of a bank for such supply of the precious metals as might seem convenient, and he could then proceed abroad to foreign quarters without knowledge of their religion, language, or customs, bearing coined wealth upon his person, and would consider himself greatly aggrieved and much surprised at the least interference. But, most important of all, he regarded this state of affairs as normal, certain, and permanent, except in the direction of further

---

[1] Bordo, Eichengreen, and Kim (1998) describe the period between 1870 and the First World War as an era of global finance in which very large amounts of foreign securities were actively traded in England; they point out, however, that many more types of securities are traded today.

improvement, and any deviation from it as aberrant, scandalous, and avoidable. (1919, pp. 9–10, cited in Obstfeld, 1986)

The following caricature (from *Punch*, dated 4 January, 1890) illustrates, perhaps more realistically, a contemporary investor here seen reading *The Times*, and his global view of economic, political, and strategic developments in other countries (in this case including Brazil, Crete, Egypt, and Germany):

SOME NEW YEAR'S PROBLEMS.

Source: Edward Linley Sambourne, 1890. Reproduced with the permission of Punch, Ltd.

Not surprisingly, the interest in—and nostalgia for—the previous era of globalization did not end in 1919, and the turbulent 1990s have attracted renewed attention to the potential lessons to be drawn from the earlier period of globalization of 1870–1913. A growing academic literature has investigated various characteristics of the period. In particular, a number of studies of the international capital flows of the past have established that global economic integration reached a peak in the late nineteenth and early twentieth centuries, and collapsed with the world wars and the intervening Great Depression. Integration then gradually increased again after the collapse of the Bretton Woods system, to attain levels similar to pre-1914 only in the 1990s.[2] During the pre-First World War era, capital outflows from Britain to contemporary developing economies were extremely high, and barriers to movement of capital and labor were virtually absent (O'Rourke and Williamson, 1998). Large volumes of capital outflows were directed to countries where capital was more productive—that is, countries where natural resources, fertile land, and human capital were abundant (Clemens and Williamson, 2004).[3]

The present book thus attempts to shed light on today's international financial environment by comparing it with that of 1870–1913.[4] Our focus is not only on financial globalization but more specifically on sovereign bond finance for emerging markets in the two periods. The overarching objective is to enrich the current debate on the design and reform of the international financial system and architecture, by drawing on the evidence from an earlier period of globalization.[5]

---

[2] Obstfeld and Taylor (2003a and 2004) examine an impressive array of measures of globalization and financial integration such as flows and stocks of foreign assets and liabilities, co-movement of real and nominal interest rates, savings–investment correlations, and the degree of persistence of current account deficits. Their estimates suggest that only in the 1990s did international financial integration return to the levels experienced in the era of the classical gold standard. A similar conclusion is reached by Sachs and Warner (1995).

[3] Several other studies (such as Edelstein, 1982; Davis and Huttenback, 1986; Offer, 1993; and Ferguson and Schularik, 2004) have analyzed the capital outflows from Britain to the Empire and elsewhere, discussed the economic cost and benefits of the Empire, and asked whether "irrational" capital flight precipitated Britain's relative decline.

[4] While most of the material we present in this book is new, and has not been published elsewhere, the issues we examine follow from our own previous research on international capital flows and emerging market sovereign debt "then" and "now." Sussman and Yafeh (1999a) examine the impact of crises on Chinese and Japanese sovereign spreads in the nineteenth century. Sussman and Yafeh (1999b) discuss the co-movement of Japanese and other sovereign bonds before and after Japan adopted the gold standard (1897). Sussman and Yafeh (2000) investigate the determinants of sharp changes in the spreads of Japanese government bonds between 1873 and 1913. Finally, Mauro, Sussman, and Yafeh (2002) compare the behavior of emerging market bond spreads in 1877–1913 and in the 1990s, and measure the extent of co-movement and the nature of crises in the two periods.

[5] Other studies have addressed issues related to sovereign bond finance and/or globalization in the two periods. Fishlow (1985), Lindert and Morton (1989), and Kelly (1998) study sovereign default; Bordo et al. (2001) and Bordo and Eichengreen (2002) examine

Our comparative study of the markets for international sovereign bonds issued by emerging markets "then" (1870–1913) and "now" (from the early 1990s to the present) is based on archival and financial data, some of which have been hitherto unexplored. More specifically, the present book is based on three newly constructed data sets. These include information on (nearly all of the) news articles on borrowing developing countries published in the *London Times* during a period of over 40 years (1870–1913), and a parallel data set drawn from the *Financial Times* for the modern period. The second data set consists of the monthly yields on sovereign bonds issued by several emerging markets for the historical period (collected by hand and corrected for a number of special bond features). The third relatively unexplored archival source used in this book is the Annual Reports of the Corporation of Foreign Bondholders, an association of British investors holding bonds issued by the emerging markets. The Annual Reports help us explore ways in which investors attempted to deal with sovereign defaults.

In Chapter 2, we portray the markets for sovereign debt in the pre-First World War period and in modern times. The size, liquidity, and sophistication of the market "then" leave no doubt that comparisons between then and now are warranted and potentially informative. The chapter also describes in detail the data sets used in this study and their construction.

We then turn to an in-depth investigation of three important features of the markets for sovereign debt in the historical and contemporary periods. The first feature, which we analyze in Chapters 3 through 5, relates to the determinants of the cost of borrowing for emerging market countries. Why were some countries able to borrow more cheaply than other countries? What institutional changes and policy measures made it possible for countries to reduce their borrowing costs? Throughout the book, the cost of capital is measured using sovereign bond spreads, where spreads are defined as the yield on sovereign bonds (denominated in pounds sterling in 1870–1913 and in US dollars in the modern period) issued by emerging market countries, minus the yield on sovereign bonds issued by the major core country—the United Kingdom in 1870–1913, and the United States in

financial crises over time. A few studies have analyzed a variety of potential determinants of the cost of borrowing, including the gold standard, affiliation with the British Empire, and economic growth (Bordo and Rockoff, 1996; Ferguson and Schularik, 2004, 2005; Flandreau and Zumer, 2004; and Obstfeld and Taylor, 2003b).

the modern period. In particular, we gauge the importance of a number of factors that could affect spreads both before the First World War and in modern times: macroeconomic variables and policies, investor-friendly institutional changes and reforms, and political stability.

The main conclusion that emerges from the analysis is that stability and the absence of violent events are crucial factors distinguishing low risk borrowers from high risk borrowers: financial markets penalized unstable borrowing countries involved in domestic or external wars, which typically had an immediate effect on their cost of foreign debt. In contrast, for the most part, financial markets did not respond in the short run to the establishment of a variety of new institutions in many reforming countries, either because it took years for new institutions to attain the necessary credibility, or because their establishment was followed by renewed turbulence.

Chapter 3 seeks to characterize the events that caused dramatic changes in the cost of capital of borrowing countries using a case study approach. We focus on the case of Meiji Japan (1868–1912) and make some comparisons with Czarist Russia. While this period in Japan constitutes one of the most dramatic examples of institutional reform in history, broad institutional reforms were not nearly as notable in Russia. Interestingly, however, a specific but important change—the adoption of the gold standard—happened to take place in both countries in 1897, with differing consequences in the two cases. We also briefly digress from our core interest in 1870–1913 to revisit the experience of Britain in the aftermath of the major reforms that followed the Glorious Revolution of 1688, a case that received considerable attention in a number of previous influential studies.

The overall conclusion drawn from the cases discussed in this chapter is that the adoption of investor-friendly institutions did not lead to an immediate decline in the cost of capital. In contrast, variation in the cost of capital was primarily driven by the emergence and resolution of violent conflict. While we believe that institutions and the protection of property rights are helpful, we argue that the adoption of the "right" (investor friendly) institutional setup is not rewarded by foreign investors until the credibility of the institutions is established and it becomes clear that the reforms are being implemented. Only then will spreads fall, making it possible for the country to reap the ensuing benefits.

Chapters 4 and 5 reinforce these conclusions on the basis of a systematic analysis of the information derived from newspaper articles, in an attempt to replicate the perceived creditworthiness of emerging markets in the eyes of contemporary international investors. For each emerging market, we classify every article in the *London Times* for the historical period and the *Financial Times* for the modern period into one of several broad categories (such as wars and instability, investor-friendly reforms, good economic news, and so forth). We then examine the impact of articles within each category on the cost of capital of countries. Chapter 4 focuses on "sharp changes" (defined in a number of ways) in spreads and the news associated with them. Chapter 5 is based on multivariate regression analysis, whereby the effect on spreads of the number of different types of news is measured controlling for macroeconomic developments. We find that the relationship between spreads and fundamental determinants (macroeconomic variables and news indicators) is stronger in historical times than modern times. And in both periods we find that wars and instability are more closely associated with variation in the cost of capital than are other events, such as institutional changes.

Our investigation of the determinants of the cost of capital for emerging markets yields somewhat different conclusions from previous attempts to address this issue. Our results suggest that the main determinant of low borrowing costs is the absence of violence. Alternative factors emphasized by previous studies, such as links to the British Empire (Ferguson and Schularik, 2004), the gold standard as a commitment mechanism to a stable macroeconomic environment (Bordo and Rockoff, 1996; Obstfeld and Taylor, 2003b), or institutions and the protection of property rights (North and Weingast, 1989) would clearly not suffice in the presence of violent conflict or political instability.

The second feature of historical and contemporary markets for sovereign debt we address in this book is co-movement, that is, the extent to which bond spreads of different countries tend to move together, and on the extent to which crises tend to coincide. This is the focus of Chapter 6. The 1990s were characterized by an unprecedented degree of co-movement in spreads, far greater than would be expected on the basis of the co-movement of macroeconomic fundamentals. By contrast, in the previous era of globalization country-specific shocks seemed to play a much bigger role and spreads of different borrowing countries followed different paths. The experience of the period following Argentina's recent default—which did not lead to a more generalized crisis for emerging markets—points to the possibility that the

1990s might have been an unusual period, and that co-movement in the most recent years (2001–2004) may represent a return to the behavior observed during the pre-First World War period. What could explain the high co-movement of spreads in the 1990s? Potential hypotheses include differences in the technology of trade in the markets; the characteristics of market participants, predominantly individuals then (Morgan and Thomas, 1969; Michie, 1986) and large investment funds now; and today's higher degree of co-movement of fundamentals, consistent with the increased similarity in the economic structure of emerging markets today, compared with the more specialized borrowing countries of 100 years ago. Our sense is that greater co-movement of fundamentals today is likely to be only a relatively small part of the explanation. It may still be too early to tell whether the future international environment is going to resemble the pre-First World War period, or the 1990s. Nevertheless, our impression at this time is that international co-movement of asset prices beyond what can be attributed to country-specific "fundamentals" is a phenomenon that is likely to reoccur and remain topical for many years.

The third feature that we examine for bond markets in the two periods relates to the mechanisms whereby sovereign debt defaults were handled. Chapter 7 focuses on the role of a fascinating institution, the "Corporation of Foreign Bondholders" (CFB), in seeking to reduce the cost of defaults and to facilitate workouts in the pre-First World War era. The CFB, an association of British investors holding bonds of foreign countries, organized creditors for joint action vis-à-vis borrowing countries. Debt resolution issues are currently topical; it is therefore of great interest to examine the way the Corporation functioned and to ask whether similar institutions might help coordinate bondholders' actions in the present international financial environment.[6]

Using archival data drawn the Annual Reports of the CFB, we characterize the methods used by investors to cope with defaulting sovereign borrowers, mechanisms of coordination among British bondholders,

---

[6] While a few previous studies, discussed in Chapter 7, have considered the CFB, our objective is to provide a more thorough description of the CFB's workings, and a more detailed analysis of its potential relevance in the context of the present-day policy debate. Indeed, relatively little is known about the history and operation of the CFB. Feis (1930) provides an early (and fascinating) treatment of this issue. A series of seminal related studies by Eichengreen and Portes (1986, 1988, 1989a,b, 2000) analyze sovereign debt, defaults and workouts in the interwar period (with some reference to earlier cases and to the 1980s).

and their cooperation with counterpart creditor associations on the Continent. The main conclusion that emerges from this chapter is that while the CFB helped coordinate creditors and resolve defaults, its success record was mixed and, even so, the achievements of this organization should probably be viewed as an upper limit to what coordination among investors could hope to attain today.

The concluding chapter of the book (Chapter 8) provides a concise summary of the empirical results, and offers some tentative conclusions and policy recommendations for today's international financial architecture. Even more generally, one of our objectives is to help show that a better understanding of today's international financial environment can be gained by studying both the similarities and the differences between the two eras of globalization and bond finance. We thus hope that, going beyond the results we obtain in this book, the information and data sets we provide will be of help to future researchers examining various aspects of globalization "then and now."

2

The London Market for Sovereign Debt, 1870–1913 versus Today's Markets

2.1 Introduction

This chapter describes the pre-First-World War London market for sovereign bonds issued by emerging countries, and compares it with the corresponding market today. We show that the London market was large, active, and liquid; indeed far larger than the corresponding market of today. Moreover, investors were able to rely on timely and comprehensive information regarding borrowing countries. Other financial centers such as Amsterdam, Berlin, and Paris also saw considerable activity with respect to emerging countries' bonds, but none matched the London market's size and liquidity. Having made the case that the comparison between the London market before the First World War and today's market is relevant, we then turn to a detailed discussion of the construction of the data sets used in this study, and to a broad analysis of the behavior of bond spreads in the historical and modern samples.

2.2 Emerging Market Countries in the Historical Sample

Before proceeding, it may be useful to define the term *emerging market countries*. We apply a similar definition to that adopted by Bordo and Eichengreen (2000). They classify countries as emerging markets—following modern parlance—on the basis of whether they were far from the industrial core of Europe, had relatively low per capita incomes, were net recipients of capital inflows, and had relatively underdeveloped domestic financial markets. For example, we include Canada and Australia, despite their relatively high incomes, because they remained recipients of capital and their domestic financial markets did not develop as much as in other advanced countries. In contrast, we exclude the United States from the sample because by the turn of the century, the United States was no longer a net recipient of capital flows, had a fairly developed domestic financial market, and was as economically advanced as the European core. To be included in the sample, we also require borrowing in pounds sterling; some European countries—notably Spain—are excluded from the sample because they borrowed extensively in their own currencies (Flandreau and Sussman, 2004). Of course, we recognize that there is no single definition or classification of emerging market countries, and therefore we strive in our estimation and interpretation to ensure that our key results are robust to changes in the sample of countries.

Our sample consists of the following eighteen emerging market countries: Argentina, Brazil, Canada, Chile, China, Colombia, Costa Rica, Egypt, Greece, Hungary, Japan, Mexico, Portugal, Queensland,[1] Russia, Sweden, Turkey, and Uruguay.[2] This includes all the largest borrowers of the time, and represents a diverse group of countries, varying substantially with respect to geography, trade structure, macroeconomic policies, political, institutional, and economic regimes. The sample includes three major less-developed European borrowers— Hungary, Russia, and Turkey—as well as the stable but as yet underdeveloped Sweden, a smaller borrower; the European peripheral countries of Greece and Portugal, the latter a declining colonial power; all the major borrowers in Latin America (Argentina, Brazil, Chile, Mexico, and Uruguay) and the two major Asian powers (China and Japan); the two largest countries with close ties to Britain, namely, Canada and Australia (proxied by Queensland), as well as Egypt, though only before it became closely tied to Britain in the 1880s.

2.3 The London Market for Sovereign Bonds, 1870–1913

The total market value of government bonds traded in London was £3.0 billion in 1875 and £4.1 billion in 1905. To put these figures in

---

[1] Queensland was a British colony starting in 1859 and became one of the states forming the federation of Australia upon independence in 1901.

[2] This is the sample used in Mauro, Sussman, and Yafeh (2002), augmented by two small Latin American borrowers—Colombia and Costa Rica.

perspective, Britain's gross domestic product (GDP) amounted to £1.4 billion in 1875 and £2.2 billion in 1905, according to Mitchell's *Historical Statistics*. Bonds issued by the emerging market countries in our sample accounted for £0.5 billion in 1875 and £1.0 billion in 1905 (or 46 percent, and 64 percent, respectively, as a share of Britain's GDP). Table 2.1, which is compiled from *The Economist's Investor's Monthly Manual (IMM)*, reports the total market value (the market capitalization) of the outstanding stock of bonds circulating in London, by issuing country. The London market was clearly both large and geographically diversified. This is also confirmed by the sheer number of bonds reported by the *IMM* on a regular basis. In 1870, the beginning of our study, almost 220 government bonds, issued by an impressive range of sovereign nations and British colonies and dominions, were already covered by the *IMM*. By 1905, as many as 300 bonds were listed in the *IMM*, offering an unprecedented variety of government bonds.

An alternative perspective on the depth and liquidity of the London stock market can be obtained by observing capital flows (rather than stocks of outstanding debt). Figures based on Stone (1999) for selected countries in our sample for the period 1865–1914, are presented in Table 2.2.[3] On the whole, it is clear that the London Stock Exchange was the most liquid capital market of its time, serving both for new issues and as a secondary market for a large number of bonds, including several bonds issued in other European financial centers.

The aggregate borrowing figures over the entire period mask substantial within-period variation: for example, the largest borrower in 1905–9 was the Japanese government, following Japan's impressive victory over Russia (see Sussman and Yafeh, 2000 and Chapter 3). As pointed out by Stone (1999), the relative popularity of investment destinations also varied by the type of investment: for example, while investments in raw materials were directed primarily to South Africa and the United States, these countries were relatively unimportant with respect to investment in foreign government securities. Railway-related investment was concentrated primarily in the United States, Argentina, Canada, and India. Stone (1999) reports also that the bulk of British capital exports in 1865–1914 took the form of investments in foreign government securities (36 percent) and in foreign railway securities (32 percent).

---

[3] Suzuki (1994) is another source of information on government-issued bonds during this period.

Table 2.1. Market Value of All Government Bonds Traded in London, 1875 and 1905

	Total volume of debt (in millions of pounds)		In percent of total		In percent of total excluding Britain	
	1875	1905	1875	1905	1875	1905
*Argentina	16.07	70.33	0.53	1.73	0.69	2.18
*Australia[a]	43.46	227.06	1.43	5.59	1.86	7.04
Austria	199.45	134.28	6.54	3.30	8.43	4.16
Belgium	27.27	n.a.	0.89	n.a.	1.17	n.a.
*Brazil	19.80	70.61	0.65	1.74	0.85	2.19
Britain	709.71	839.50	23.28	20.65	n.a.	n.a.
Bulgaria	n.a.	9.34	n.a.	0.23	n.a.	0.29
*Canada	21.63	50.27	0.71	1.24	0.92	1.56
Cape of Good Hope	0.93	38.74	0.03	0.95	0.04	1.20
*Chile	7.99	17.42	0.26	0.43	0.34	0.54
*China	0.50	38.71	0.02	0.95	0.02	1.20
Cuba	0.28	7.20	0.01	0.18	0.01	0.22
Denmark	1.82	7.26	0.06	0.18	0.08	0.23
Ecuador	1.82	n.a.	0.06	n.a.	0.08	n.a.
*Egypt	56.06	86.93	1.84	2.14	2.40	2.70
France	756.74	734.96	24.83	18.08	32.36	22.79
Germany	n.a.	86.47	n.a.	2.13	n.a.	2.68
*Greece	4.75	23.51	0.16	0.58	0.20	0.73
*Hungary	23.14	65.23	0.76	1.60	0.99	2.02
India	84.48	145.57	2.77	3.58	3.61	4.51
Italy	35.93	322.78	1.18	7.94	1.54	10.01
*Japan	3.05	62.38	0.10	1.53	0.13	1.93
*Mexico	27.47	46.95	0.90	1.16	1.17	1.46
Natal	0.31	19.12	0.01	0.47	0.01	0.59
Netherlands	79.79	98.02	2.62	2.41	3.41	3.04
Norway	n.a.	6.91	n.a.	0.17	n.a.	0.21
Peru	11.58	n.a.	0.38	n.a.	0.50	n.a.
*Portugal	66.15	20.79	2.17	0.51	2.83	0.64
Prussia	n.a.	246.94	n.a.	6.07	n.a.	7.66
*Russia	151.37	376.74	4.97	9.27	6.47	11.68
Spain	167.64	31.76	5.50	0.78	7.17	0.98
*Sweden	1.96	9.28	0.06	0.23	0.08	0.29
Switzerland	n.a.	13.80	n.a.	0.34	n.a.	0.43
*Turkey	147.24	57.24	4.83	1.41	6.30	1.77
United States	347.79	48.74	11.41	1.20	14.87	1.51
*Uruguay	3.21	20.56	0.11	0.51	0.14	0.64
Venezuela	6.69	6.11	0.22	0.15	0.29	0.19
Other[b]	22.23	23.48	0.73	0.58	0.95	0.73
Total emerging markets in our sample	505.66	1020.07	16.59	25.09	21.62	31.63
Total	3048.30	4065.00	100.00	100.00	n.a.	n.a.
Total excluding Britain	2338.59	3225.50	76.72	79.35	100.00	100.00

Notes: * Asterisks denote countries included in our sample of "emerging markets" for 1870–1913.
[a] Owing to data limitations, market capitalization refers to Australia, whereas later chapters use spreads for Queensland.
[b] "Other" includes Antigua, Barbados, Bolivia, British Columbia, British Guyana, Ceylon, Colombia, Costa Rica, Danubian Principalities, Gold Coast, Grenada, Guatemala, Honduras, Hong Kong, Jamaica, Liberia, Mauritius, Moorish territories, Nicaragua, Paraguay, San Damingo, Sardinia, Serbia, Siam, Sierra Leone, and St. Lucia and Trinidad

Source: Investor's Monthly Manual.

Table 2.2. Emerging Market Countries' Bond Issues in London, 1870–1913, Net Proceeds from Bond Issues by Large Borrowers

Country	In millions of pounds	Total Proceeds in percent of total net issues on the London market by all countries (excluding Britain)
Canada	116.22	8.75
Argentina	73.24	5.50
Brazil	72.81	5.48
Japan	72.62	5.47
Russia	55.60	4.19
China	47.56	3.60
Chile	26.07	1.96
Turkey	24.07	1.80
Greece	15.65	1.18
Mexico	15.19	1.14
Egypt	14.16	1.06
Uruguay	8.88	0.67
Total	542.07	40.80

Source: Stone (1999).

2.4 Market Information and its Availability, 1870–1913

For markets to function effectively, information needs to be timely, frequent, and available to a broad audience of investors. Investors in 1870–1913 had access to highly detailed information on financial variables as well as macroeconomic, political, and institutional developments in borrowing countries. Information on financial variables, including the yields on bonds issued by the emerging market countries of the day, was reported daily in the main newspapers, such as the *London Times*. It was also made available on a monthly basis by publications such as the *IMM*, one of the main data sources for this book. The following page, reproduced from the July 1891 issue of the *IMM*, reports a list of bonds quoted on the London Stock Exchange Note, for example, the number of Argentine bonds in default at that time—in the midst of the Baring crisis. (Bonds in default—not paying the coupon— are denoted by a special symbol, "‡.") The *IMM* provided readers with detailed information on the available bonds, their issue price, the original amount issued, the details of the sinking fund (for bond redemption), the amount of the loan unredeemed, several quotes for the price (latest, and high and low during the month) and yield (current, and high and low during the year), coupon payments dates, and bond underwriter. For example, the 5 percent bond issued by Argentina in

July 31, 1891.] THE INVESTOR'S MONTHLY MANUAL. 361

BRITISH, COLONIAL, AND FOREIGN STOCKS.

(The securities quoted below do not include the entire debts of the State or Nation referred to.)

STOCK.	Issue Price.	Original Issue.	Sinking Fund. Original Annual.	Sinking Fund. When Applied.	Sinking Fund. Final Redemption.	Amount of Loan Unredeem'd	Par.	Prices of the Month. Openg	Prices of the Month. Hghst.	Prices of the Month. Lowst.	Prices of the Month. Latest	Last Business Done.	Yield to Investor at Latest Price. Redemp. Included	Prices of 1891. Hghst	Prices of 1891. Lowst.	Dividends. Payable.	Dividends. Where Payable
ARG'NT'NE	%	£				£	£						£ s d				
6 % Railway, '81	91	2,450,000	1 %	May, Nov.	1915	485,040	100	55x	55	40	40	41	‡	90	38	1 June, 1 Dec.	C. de Murrieta
5 %, 1884.........	84½	1,683,100	1 %	Mr.J.Sp.D.	1921	1,533,400	100	42½	42½	29	30½	30	‡	68	29	Jn.Ap.Jy.Oc.	Baring Bros.
5 %, 1886	80&8	5½] 8290100	1 %	June., Dec.	1919†	7,810,200	100	67	67	52½	53	52½	9 8 9	79	53	1 Jan., 1 Jly	Baring Bros., & J.S.Morgan&Co
5 % N. Central Rly. Ext. Gvt. Mort. Bonds	91½	3,968,200	1 %	...	1921†	3,883,800	100	47	47	31½	32½	31½	‡	68	27½	1 Jan., 1 July	Murrieta.
5% Treasury Con	...	624,000	1 %	...	1924†	600,500	100	42½	42½	27½	27½	28¼	‡	67	26½	1 April, 1 Oct	
4½ % Internal Gold Loan ...	...	3,933,580	...	...	...	3,861,800	100	36	36	26½	26½	27	‡	59	26½	1 Mar., 1 Sep.	Barings.
4½ % Stg. Bonds	90	5,263,560	1	Mar., Sept.	1926	5,151,660	100	36½	36½	26½	26½	28½	‡	60	27¼	1 Apl., 1 Oct.	Baring Bros. and Murrieta
3½ % Extn., '89..	...	2,659,500	1	Mar., Sept.	...	2,600,440	100	30	30	22½	22½	22½	‡	47	22½	1JyAplJyOc.	Stern Bros.
7% do National, Cedulas	...	$15,000,000	...	...	...	$13,810,300	...	18½	18½	16¾	17	16¾	Depends ongld pm	31	14	1 Jan., 1 July	Ditto.
Do 6 % Funding Loan	...	14,880,000	...	...	...	800,000	...	58	58	48	49	49¾	...	67½	48	...	...
Buenos Ayres, 6%, 1824...	85	1,000,000	½ %	Pur.&dwgs	...	292,700*	100	...	...	...	...	...	‡	...	...	12Jan.,12Jly.	Baring Bros.
Do 6%, 1882-6	88½&	91]3982800	1 %	January.	1916	3,660,100	100	40	40	28	30	28	...	70½	28	1 Jn.ApJyOc.	Baring Bros.
Do 6 %, 1883	94	2,254,100	1 %	Septembr.1	1916	2,064,900	100	42	42	30¾	32	30¾	...	81	30¾	1 April, 1 Oct.	Morton, Rose.
Cordova 6 % ...	89	595,200	1 %	October 1	1919	569,100	100	24½	24½	22½	22½	24½	‖	42	22½	1 May 1 Nov.	Morton, Rose.
6 % do	91	1,190,400	1 %	June.	...	1,152,600	100	22½	25	20	22½	20	‖	40	20	1 Jan., 1 Jly.	Morton, Rose.
Ent. Rios 6 %, '86	91½	800,000	1 %	Jne & Dec.	1919	764,500	100	34½	34½	20	20½	20	‖	62½	20	1 Jan., 1 July	C. de Murrieta
Do 6 %, '88 ...	97	1,200,000	1	Incrsble by	Govt.	1,175,000	100	34½	34½	20½	20½	21	‖	62½	20½	1 Jan., 1 July	C. de Murrieta
Do Cent. Rly. 6% Mort. Bds	91½ & 94	1,530,800	1 %	Jne. & Dec.	1919	1,463,500	100	46½	46½	30	35	30¼	‖	82	30	1 Jan., 1 July	Ditto.
Do Exten. 6%, Mort. Bds.	95½ &99½	1,745,600	1 %	Feb.& Aug.	...	1,745,600	100	36½	36½	30	32½	35	‖	80	30	1 Mar., 1 Sep	R. Plate Trst Loan& Agncy
Santa Fé, 6 %, 1883-4......	86½ & 90	1,434,426	1 %	Pur.or dgs.	1914	1,303,300	100	32½	32½	20	22½	20	‖	60	20	1 May, 1 Nov	Morton Rose
5 % do	92½	2,000,000	1 %	H'lf-yearly	1923	1,946,100	100	27½	27½	18	20	18	‖	45	18	15 Apl. 15 Oc.	Ditto
Do 5% W. Centl. Col. Rys.......	84½	929,400	1 %	Mar.&Sept.	1916	905,000	100	55	55	30	50	30	‖	87	30	1 April,1 Oct.	C. de Murrieta.
Santa Fé and Reconq. Rly. 5% Mort Bnds.	86	1,261,700	1 %	Jne.&Dec.*	1925	1,255,400	100	50½	53	48	50½	49	‖	70	48	1 Jan., 1 July	Ditto.
Tucuman 6%, '88	92	600,000	1 %	Incrsble by	Govt.	587,700	100	32½	32½	27½	27½	34	...	52½	27½	1 Jan., 1 July	L. Cohen & Sons
AUSTRIAN.																	
5% Silver Rnts*	...	...	...	None	Irred.	100,200,000	100	81	81	78	78	79¼	5 8 6	81	78	1 Jan., 1 July.	Vienna in silver.
5% Paper do.*	...	...	...	None	Irred.	144,970,000	100	79	80	78	79	79½	5 8 6	82⅛	77	1 May, 1 Nov.	Vienna in paper.
4% Gold Rentes	...	...	...	None	Irred.	34,085,020	100	95	96	94	95	96	4 5 6	99	93	1 April, 1 Oct.	Vienna in gold.
[* The income	tax o	n dividend	s of	Austrian S	ilver a	nd Paper R	ente	s eq	uals	16 %	ded	ucted	from cou	pons	.]		
AUSTRALASI	A.																
N.S. Wales, 5 %	...	8,038,000	...	...	'88-94	5429600	100	101½	103	100	101½	100½	4 9 0	103	100	1 Jan., 1 July.	Bank of New South Wales.
Do 5 %	...		...	[1895	-1902		100	107½	112½	103	106x	105½	4 14 3	112½	102	1 Jan., 1 July.	
Do 5 %, 1868	98½	1,000,000	2 %	...	1898	389,300	100	105	105	103	103x	103½	4 10 0	106	102	1 Jan., 1 July.	
Do 4 % Bonds	90-2	7,201,000	...	... [19	03-10	7,201,000	100	104½	104½	102¼	104x	104½	3 14 3	108	101¾	1 Jan., 1 July.	
Do 4 % of 1882	102	813,700	...	...	1910	813,700	100	105	105½	104	105x	105¾	3 15 3	108	102	1 Jan., 1 July	
Do 4 %, Ins.'85	103½	7,186,300	...	...	1933	7,186,300	100	109x	110	108	109	109¼	3 11 9	115	108	1 Jan., 1 July	Bank of England.
Do 3½%, Ins.'85	95⅝	16,500,000	...	...	1924	16,500,000	100	101	102½	100½	101½	101¼	3 10 0	104	98	1 April, 1 Oct	
Do 3½% Ins.'88	103⅝	7,289,000	...	...	1918	7,289,000	100	101	102	100⅞	101	100⅞	3 10 9	103	98½	1 Mar., 1 Sept	
N. Zeal., 6 %, '61	...	150,000	...	...	1891	74,100	100	102	...	...	...	...	...	102	100	1 Jan., 1 July.	Crown Agents for the Colonies.
Do 5 %, 1864	81½	1,000,000	1 %	...	1914	378,800	100	113½	115	110¾	111x	111¼	4 5 0	115⅝	109	15 Jn., 15 Jly.	
Do 5% Consol. 1868-72 ..	99⅝	3,069,000	1 %	March 13.	1908	1,159,500	100	105	105	104	104x	103	4 13 3	107½	103	Jn. Ap. Jy. Oc.	
Do 6%, '66-67	99¾	1,000,000	2 %	...	1891	69,400	100	101	102	100	101	101½	6 1 0	103	100	15 Jne., 15 Dec	
Do Auck., 6 %	95	200,000	...	...	1896	19,800	100	105½	107	104	105½	106	5 3 6	109	104	April, Oct.	Bank of N.S.W.
Do 5% Con. Bds	vars	4,214,100	(se	e note belo	w)	4,214,100	100	110	112	110	111	110¾	...	113	103½	Quarterly	Bnk of England.
Do 4 % Inscr.	vars	24,564,255	...	...	1929	24,564,255	100	104	105½	104	105	104⅞	3 16 0	107½	100¼	1 May, 1 Nov.	Bnk of England.
Do 3½ % Ins.	...	3,200,181	...	...	1940	3,200,181	100	94x	94½	93⅝	94	94	3 15 9	98	92	1 Jan., 1 July.	...
Queensl., 6%, '86	91	1,936,550	...	...	1891	1,373,550	100	105½	108½	105½	107½	108	...	111	100	1 Jan., 1 July.	Queensland National Bnk.
Do 6 %, 1871	106⅛		...	...	1896		100	105½	108½	105½	107½	108	4 1 3	111	100	1 Jan., 1 July	
Do 4 %, Bonds	vars	10,267,399	...	... [1	913-15	9,805,200	100	103	104	102	102½	x102½	3 16 9	106	101	1 Jan., 1 July	Bank of England.
Do 4 % Inscr	vars	10,866,900	...	... [1	915-24	10,866,900	100	104x	106	104	106	105¼	3 13 9	110	102	1 Jan., 1 July.	
Do 3½ % Inscr.	...	4,764,734	...	...	1924	4,764,734	100	92½x	93½	91⅝	92	92⅛	3 18 9	93½	90½	1 Jan., 1 July.	
S. Australia 6%	107½	468,800	...	... ['91	-1900	463,800	100	108½	108½	106	108x	103	4 18 0	117	100	1 Jan., 1 July.	National Bank of Australasia.
Do 6 %	...	604,700	...	... [19	01-18	604,700	100	119½	124½	118	118x	118	4 10 0	130	109	1 Jan., 1 July.	
Do 5%, 1871-3	102½	-5½]278,500	...	... [19	11-20	240,000	100	110½	110½	109½	109½	x105¾	4 5 3	118	103	1 Jan., 1 July	
Do 4%, '74-5-6 7-8-80...[93	to 7½	7,766,700	...	... [18	94-191	6]7,766,700	100	103	103	100¼	102x	100¾	3 17 6	106	100	1 Jan., 1 July	
Do 4 %	93⅛	200,000	...	...	1929	200,000	100	104	104	101¼	104x	101¼	3 16 0	103	101¼	1 Jan., 1 July	
Do 4 % Bonds	103	1,365,300	...	...	1916	1,365,300	100	103	104	102	103	103	3 17 6	108	101½	1 April, 1 Oct.	
Do 4 % Bonds	vars	532,500	...	... [1	917-24	531,600	100	104	105	104	105	103⅞	3 15 0	109	103	1 April, 1 Oct	
Do 4 % Insc.	vars	7,620,800	...	... [1	916-35	7,620,800	100	105	106½	105	106	106½	3 16 6	109¼	102¾	1 April, 1 Oct	
Do 3½% Ins, '89	vars	1,317,800	...	...	1939	1,317,800	100	95½	97	95½	97	97	3 15 0	100	95½	1 Jan., 1 July	Glyn, Mills&Co.
Tasman. 6%, '66	...	102,500	...	...	1895	102,500	100	106½	106½	105¼	105½	x105¼	4 9 3	109	104½	1 Jan., 1 July	Consolidated Bank.
Do 6 %, 1868	102½	-5¾]700,000	...	...	1893-1	901]552,800	100	110½	110½	105	109½	x105	4 16 0	119	102	1 Jan., 1 July	
Do 4 %, 1881-3	98½-	9½] 1946650	...	...	1913-2	0] 1,900,000	100	102	102⅝	101	102x	102⅝	3 17 9	105	100½	1 Jan., 1 July.	
Do 4 %, 1886	99⅞	1,000,000	...	...	1911	1,000,000	100	102	102¼	101	102	102¼	3 17 0	105	99⅛	1 Jan, 1 July.	
Do 3½% Ins. '89	vars	2,106,500	St e	optaft 1920	1940	2,106,500	100	95x	96½	94⅞	95	93¼	3 14 6	98¾	94⅝	1 Jan., 1 July	Lon.& West. Bk
Victoria 5%, 1869	101	2,107,000	...	...	1894	2,107,000	100	105	105	102¼	103x	102¼	3 18 6	105⅝	102¾	1 Jan., 1 July.	Lon. & West. & Lndn. Jnt. Stock Bank
Do 4%, 1874-6	91⅝-	6½4,500,000	...	[1899	-1901	4,500,000	100	103	104	102	103x	102¾	3 12 9	105¾	101	1 Jan., 1 July.	
Do 4½ %, 1879	99	5,000,000	...	...	1904	5,000,000	100	107	108	106	107x	107¾	3 16 6	110	106	1 Jan., 1 July.	
Do 4% Rly, '81	...	764,900	...	..	1907	728,900	100	105	106	103	106x	105½	3 10 3	108	103	1 Jan, 1 July	...
Do 4 % '82-83	...	802,400	...	..	1908-1	3] 765,000	100	104½	106	104	105	105¼	3 14 6	109	103	1 Apl., 1 Oct.	...

New Zealand 5 % Debentures—Convertible in 1892 into 4 % Stock at rate of £100=£107. * Purchased below par or by drawings. † Or earlier. ‡ These are the Securities included in the Argentine Funding Agreement. ‖ Last coupon unpaid.

1886 is not in default and is traded at 50 percent of its original value with a yield of *9l 8s 9d* (9 pounds, 8 shillings, and 9 pence), relative to a face value of 100 pounds, that is, at a yield equivalent to about 9.4 percent.[4] Information on macroeconomic variables in emerging market countries was certainly harder to collect prior to First World War than it is today. In fact, some key modern macroeconomic concepts such as GDP were not even used in the historical period, and corresponding data did not exist at the time. Nevertheless, investors had sufficient information to form a well-reasoned view on the macroeconomic fundamentals that ultimately play a key role in determining whether countries' can meet their external obligations. Available macroeconomic indicators typically included external (and occasionally domestic) debt, imports and exports, fiscal revenues and expenditures, and population. Railway miles were also reported as an indication of the extent to which foreign capital was used for productive investment. Such data for all emerging market countries were widely available to British investors in easy-to-consult format in publications such as the *IMM*, though often the data were not updated and thus referred to previous years. The following page, taken from the December 1899 issue of the *IMM*, illustrates a sample of such information. Taking Queensland as an example, data were reported on population, area, debt, government revenues and expenditures, imports and exports, railway miles, profit margins of railway companies, and even information about livestock, an important staple export of the province.

The *Annual Reports* of the Corporation of Foreign Bondholders (an organization of British investors' holding foreign bonds, described in detail in Chapter 7) provided even more detailed information on certain aspects of economic development in some borrowing countries— for example, external trade by product and partner country, or a detailed decomposition of fiscal revenues. The *Reports* were focused, however, on countries with payment difficulties, and their coverage was somewhat haphazard.[5]

---

[4] Argentina was in default on other bonds at this time, such as the 4½ percent sterling bonds, trading at 28½; pounds per 100 pounds of face value. Interestingly, these prices are not too far from those observed in the aftermath of Argentina's 2001 default. The single bond that continued to pay interest regularly was jointly underwritten by well-known banks in London (Baring) and New York (Morgan)—which may explain why Argentina chose not to default in this case.

[5] Outside Britain, Flandreau (2003a) reports that the *Credit Lyonnais*—a leading French bank and a major investor in emerging market bonds—devoted substantial staff resources to gathering and analyzing macroeconomic data and information on political developments in a number of emerging markets, in an attempt to estimate the likelihood of default and therefore the appropriate levels of bond yields. These data are one of the main sources for the empirical analysis conducted by Flandreau and Zumer (2004).

BRITISH AND INDIAN GOVERNMENT STOCKS.

STOCK.	Market Prices in— 1895. Hghst.	Lowst.	1896. Hghst.	Lowst.	1897. Hghst.	Lowst.	1898. Hghst.	Lowst.	Closing Price Dec., 1898.
BRITISH.									
2¾ % Consols until 1903, then 2½% Conv. Stk., Red. 1923	108⅜	103⅜	113⅞	105⅛	113⅞	110	113⅛	106¾	110⅝x
New 2¾ %'s	106¾	103	108⅜	103	107½	104⅞	106⅝	102	104x
New 2½ %'s	106⅞	101⅝	108⅜	102	107	104	106⅜	101	104x
Local Loans 3 %	112⅛	107½	114⅞	109	115	111½	103¾	108	110x
Guar. Land Stock (Ireland) 2¾ %	...	...	...	...	114⅛	111¼	112⅞	110⅛	110⅛
Ans. 1908 (Rd. Sea Tel.)	11¼	10½	11	9¼	9 5/16	8½	9¼	8	8
Can. Intercolnial., 4 % guar. by Gt. Britain	112	108½	114½	106¼	111½	108¼	109½	103½	106
	115	112	117½	113	115	112	114⅛	109	109
4 %, 1878 (g. by G.Bt.)	119	105	120	112	119	111	117	111	111
Do	122	117	122½	111¼	123¾	116½	121¼	112½	114
Egyptian guar 3 %	107⅞	105½	110¾	104¼	110	107½	108¾	104¼	106
Greek Guar. 2½% Loan of 1898, Eng. Scrip	...	...	...	...	...	...	...	...	100
Isle of Man 3½% debs.	104	59	106⅜	103	106	103	107	104	104
Do 3 % deb. stock	100	60	103	98	106	101	105	102	102
Mauritius 3% guar.	118	109	120	115	118	115	115	106	111x
Turkish 4%, g. by England & France	117	113	117	106	113⅛	106½	111¾	102½	106
Bank of England Stock	335½	324½	345	322	351½	326	367	341	354½
Bank of Ireland Stock	361¼	336	376½	354	392½	366	402½	383	396
INDIAN.									
India 3½ % Stock	118⅝	112⅝	122½	114½	119⅛	116⅛	117⅛	111	116x
Do 3 % Stock	110	102⅞	115¾	105	112½	107½	109¼	103½	106x
Do 2½% Inscribed	...	...	103	95¾	99½	94	96⅝	84⅜	90x
Rupee Paper, 3½ %	61½	53	65	58¼	63¾	59	63⅛	60	61
Do 3½ %, 1854-5	62¾	60⅞	66⅛	59¼	64⅛	60½	64⅞	61⅛	62
Do 3 %, 1896-7	...	...	...	...	...	...	57⅛	53½	55

MEMORANDA.

—Pop. est. middle '99, 40,560,000, showing increase of fully 4 millions in ten years. Area, 121,607 sq. miles. In the following table the debt includes estimated "capital" of annuity liabilities. Debt per head in 1898, 15*l.* 16s, and annual charge per head, including sinking fund, &c., 12s.

Year.	Gross. Revenue.	Gross Expenditure.	National Debt. Capital.	Charge.	Foreign Trade. ‡Imports.	‡Exports.
	£	£	£	£	£	£
1888-9§	88,472,812	86,673,000	698,430,571	26,224,594	387,636,000	298,578,000
1889-90	89,304,000	86,083,000	689,944,000	25,227,000	427,638,000	315,693,000
1890-1†§	89,489,000	87,733,000	684,071,000	25,207,000	420,692,000	328,252,000
1891-2§	90,995,000	89,928,000	677,680,000	25,200,000	435,441,000	309,114,000
1892-3§	90,395,000	90,375,000	671,043,000	25,200,000	423,794,000	291,640,000
1893-4	91,133,000	91,303,000	666,154,000	25,200,000	405,063,000	277,432,000
1894-5	94,684,000	93,918,000	660,160,000	25,200,000	408,345,000	273,786,000
1895-6	101,974,000	97,764,000	652,540,000	25,200,000	416,688,000	285,832,000
1896-7	103,950,000	101,477,000	644,910,000	25,200,000	441,807,000	296,389,000
1897-8	106,614,000	107,936,000	638,266,000	25,200,000	451,238,700	294,153,700
1898-9	108,336,000	108,150,000	635,041,000	25,000,000	470,379,000	294,014,000

† Revenue and expenditure exclusive of receipts and payments on account of Army and Navy extra receipts, and contribution by India for military charges.
‡ The figures in these columns refer to the calendar and not the fiscal year.
§ After deduction of amounts payable to Local Taxation Accounts.

Railways, 1898, 21,669 miles; capital, 1,134,468,000*l*, of which 183,513,000*l* represents nominal additions.

—Pop., 287,223,000, and area, 1,560,160 sq. m, inclusive of feudatory States, 595,000 sq. miles and 66,050,000 pop. Revenue, 1897-8, Rx.96,442,000; Exp. Rx.101,801,200. Revised estimates for 1898-9: revenue, Rx.101,531,600; expenditure, Rx.97,510,100. Imports of merchandise in 1898-9, Rx.68,420,100; exports, Rx.109,351,700. 21,887 miles of rail. open at end of 1898; capital outlay, Rx.268,094,000.

COLONIAL GOVERNMENT STOCKS.

STOCK.	1895. Hghst.	Lowst.	1896. Hghst.	Lowst.	1897. Hghst.	Lowst.	1898. Hghst.	Lowst.	Closing Price Dec., 1898.
ANTIGUA.									
4% Inscribed Stock	113¾	110	118	110	116½	110	111½	108½	111
AUSTRALASIA.									
New South Wales 5 %	116	100¾	111	99⅛	109⅞	100¼	107½	101½	103
Do 4 % Bonds	108⅝	103	111¾	102	110¼	101½	108¼	101	105½
Do 4 %, Insc., 1885	114¼	107¼	123½	118	123¾	117	122½	112½	118
Do 3½ %, Insc., 1885	109½	00	112½	103⅝	111½	107¼	110½	102	105
Do 3½ %, Insc., 1888	108⅛	95½	110¼	102⅝	110½	106⅞	108⅛	102	105
Do 3 % Inscribed	97¾	95½	104	91⅜	104	100½	103½	95¼	99½
N. Zealand 5%, 1864	118	114¾	124¾	117¾	121¼	118	120	115⅛	116
Do 5% Consol., '68-72	111¾	106	111⅞	107	109	104	105	101¼	102
Do 4 %, Inscribed	113½	105¾	118¼	106½	117	112	110½	103	114
Do 3½ %, Inscribed	107⅛	100¾	110⅜	101½	111	104¾	109½	107	108
Do 3 % Inscribed	95	92½	103½	90	102	99½	101	96½	99
Queensland, 4% bonds	109⅛	101⅜	112½	104	110½	105½	108½	103½	107
Do 4 %, Inscribed	115	105¼	117⅜	105	116	111	114¼	104½	109½
Do 3½ %, Inscribed	107⅝	97	111½	101	108½	104⅜	106¾	101½	105
Do 3½ %, Inscribed	...	...	...	...	111	108½	109½	104¼	107
Do 3 % Inscribed	...	...	...	...	101¾	97½	100¼	95¼	97½
South Australia, 6 %	112	101	112	101⅞	[illegible]	101⅛	106	103½	103½
Do 6 %	122½	105½	124½	109½	125½	106	126	103¾	118
Do 5 %, 1871-3	115	107	120	111½	120	111	115½	113⅝	113½
Do 4%, 74-5-6-7-8-80	108½	100¼	111½	101¼	111	100¾	111	100	104
Do 4 %	110	102⅝	114	107	112	109½	111¼	104	109½
Do 4 %, Bonds	109¾	102	113½	103½	112¾	106½	111	104½	106
Do 4 %, Bonds	114	106	116	109	114	110	114	107¼	109
Do 4 %, Inscribed	113½	106	116½	107	114½	111½	114	106	109
Do 3½ % Insc., 1889	109⅝	100	112½	104⅝	113¼	109	110½	105⅛	107
Do 3 % Inscribed	...	...	99½	97½	102	97	102	98	98
Tasmania 6 %, 1868	110	102	114	101¾	111	101¾	106	101⅝	104
Do 4 %, 1881-3	110	102	111¾	101	110	105	110	103⅝	108
Do 3½ % Ins., 1889	108½	98½	112	102¾	111⅛	105	110¾	104¾	105
Do 4%, Inscribed	115⅝	105	118	107¾	117	113	116¾	112½	113
Victoria, 4 %, 1874-6	104	98	105¾	100¼	104	100½	103½	100	101½
Do 4½ %, 1879	110	102	111	103½	110	105¾	107	101¼	106
Do 4 % Rly., 1881	109	99	110¼	105	104	105	107	103⅜	107
Do 4 %, 1882-3	109	99½	112½	105½	111¼	106	110¼	103½	106
Do 4 %, Insc., 1881	108¼	101	111	103	107¾	105	107	102½	105
Do 4 % Ins., 1882-4	108¾	100¾	114¾	104	115½	105¼	113½	103	107½
Do 4 %, 1885	111⅛	99⅞	116⅞	106	115	111	113¾	109¼	111
Do 3½ Insc., 1889	106⅝	93½	109¼	99⅝	110	104	107⅝	101¼	105
Do 4 % Inscribed	109½	101	113⅞	104¼	112	107½	110¼	106½	108
W. Australian 4½ % 79	114½	109½	114	111	112	108	109	106½	107
Do 4 %, 1881	118½	106¾	110	103½	109	105	108	104	104
Do 4 % Inscribed	123	110½	128	120	123¾	120	120¾	114½	115
Do 4 % Inscribed	115½	107	118	111¼	113¾	109	113½	106	107
Do 3½ % Inscribed	...	...	113	103¾	111½	105½	107½	103½	104
Do 3 % Inscribed	...	...	102½	98¼	100	95	99⅜	91¾	94
Do 3 % Inscribed	...	...	...	...	100	95⅛	99¼	93	95
Do 3 % Inscribed	...	...	...	...	...	...	98¾	94	94
BARBADOS.									
3½ % Inscribed	107¾	104	112	107	111⅞	107¼	109½	104½	105
BRITISH GUIANA.									
4 % Inscribed	114¾	107¾	122	109¾	122¼	120	120½	113	113½
3 % Inscribed	...	...	...	...	...	...	...	...	98

MEMORANDA.

—Revenue, 1898, 39,700*l*; expenditure, 55,600*l*.

—Est. pop. end of Dec. '98, 1,346,200. Area, 309,000 sq. miles. Debt at end of 1898-9, 63,761,700*l*. At end of 1898-9, 2,791 miles of railway were in operation, yielding 3·83 % net. Revenue in 1898-9, 9,754,200*l*. Expend., 9,734,400*l*. Exports in '98, 27,648,100*l*. Imports, 24,453,600*l*. Horses in '98, 491,533; cattle, 2,029,500; sheep, 41,241,000. Wheat produced in '98-9, 9,286,100 bushels; maize, 6,064,000 bushels.

—Pop. end Dec., '98, 743,500, Maoris (42,000) excluded. Area, 104,471 sq. miles. Public debt in '72, 9,985,386*l*, including absorbed debts of provincial governments; ditto end of 1898-9, 46,938,000. As in other Australasian colonies, debts mostly raised for reproductive purposes. Ordinary rev. in 1898-9, 5,258,200*l*; expend., 4,658,500*l*. Imp. in '98, 8,230,600*l*. Exports, 10,518,000*l*. 2,257 miles of railway in operation in '98-9, yielding 3·29 per cent. Sheep, in '98, 19,673,700; cattle, 1,203,000. Yield of wheat in '98-9, 13,073,400 bshls.

—Pop. in '98, 498,500. Area, 668,224 sq. mls. Debt end of 1898-9, 33,598,400*l*. Revenue in 1898-9, 4,174,100*l*. Expenditure, 4,024,200*l*. Imports in 1898, 6,007,300*l*; exports, 10,856,100*l*. Miles of railway in 1898-9, 2,475, yielding 3·15 per cent. In '98, 5,571,300 cattle; 19,673,700 sheep; 480,500 horses.

—Population end of 1898, 367,800. Area, 380,070 square miles; ditto with North Australia, 903,485 sq. miles. Debt at end of 1898-9, 24,916,300*l*. Revenue in 1898-9, 2,731,200*l*. Expenditure, 2,777,600*l*. Imports in 1898, 6,298,800*l*; exports, 6,978,400*l*. 1,889 miles of railway open in 1898-9, yielding 3·42 per cent. Sheep in 1898, 5,076,100. Cattle, 613,900. Horses, 177,200. Wheat in 1898-9, 1,768,800 bushels.

—Pop. in '98, 177,300. Area, 26,375 sq. mls. Debt, end of 1898-9, 8,412,900*l*. Rev., 1898-9, 908,200*l*. Expend., 830,200*l*. Imports in '98, 1,650,000*l*; exps., 1,803,400*l*. Sheep in '98, 1,493,600. Cattle, 148,600. Horses, 29,800. Miles of railway in '98-9, 508, yielding 1·03 per cent.

—Pop. end of 1898, 1,175,500. Area, 87,884 square miles. Debt, end of 1898-9, 50,379,300*l*. Revenue in 1898-9, 7,378,800*l*. Expend., 7,027,400*l*. Imports in 1898, 16,768,900*l*; exp., 15,872,200*l*. 3,143 miles of railway open in 1898-9, yielding 2·96 per cent. Gross produce of wheat in 1898-9, 13,581,300 bushels; oats, 5,523,400 bushels. No returns of live stock collected since 1894.

—Pop. end of '98, 168,100. Area, 975,920 sq. m. Debt end of '98-9, 10,488,400*l*. Rev. in '98-9, 2,678,800*l*. Expenditure, 2,539,400*l*. Imps. in '98, 5,242,000*l*. Exps, 4,960,000*l*. Rails., 1,850 miles, yielding in 1898-9, 4·55 per cent. Sheep, in '98, 2,244,900; cattle, 245,900.

—Area, 166 sq. miles. Pop. in '95, 187,000. Debt in '96, 405,100*l*. Rev. in '98, 182,700*l*; expend., 185,800*l*. Imports, 1897-8, 1,058,900*l*; exports, 769,200*l*.

—Area, 109,000 square miles. Population in 1896, 285,000. Debt in 1898, 975,700*l*. Revenue in 1898-9, 525,800*l*; expenditure, 525,400*l*. In 1898-9, imports, 1,371,400*l*; exports, 1,775,700*l*.

Finally, investors in the nineteenth century were well informed regarding not only economic, but also political and institutional events for the emerging market countries of the day. In fact, these events were meticulously reported in the British press, and information reached investors in the advanced countries in a timely manner: international telegraph links to the emerging market countries in our sample were introduced in the 1870s. Our impression is that the press provided such detailed information on political events partly in response to considerable demand for the same on the part of investors, for whom this was a key input in investment decisions. One of the main contributions of this book is indeed to exhibit the extent of coverage of foreign borrowers' economic and political developments and to analyze the impact they had on bond prices.

2.5 Today's Markets

How do the figures on international capital flows to developing countries in the pre-First World War period compare with the 1990s? In modern times, there was no significant active secondary market for emerging country bonds prior to the introduction of the Brady bonds in the early 1990s. International financial flows to emerging market countries were essentially dormant until the early 1970s, and as late as the 1980s they still took primarily the form of bank loans. Following the wave of defaults of the 1980s by a number of emerging market countries, bank loans were eventually repackaged in the early 1990s as Brady bonds, setting the stage for secondary market trading to begin on a large scale. When they reentered international capital markets after the Brady deals, emerging countries relied on new bond issues for a substantial portion of their financing needs.[6] The change in the composition of modern emerging market sovereign debt, from bank loans to bonds, is described in Figure 2.1, where the upper panel refers to outstanding stocks, and the middle panel refers to new issues. The prevalence of bond finance in recent years is not unique to emerging market countries, and it applies to advanced countries as well (Figure 2.1, lower panel).

Despite a substantial increase since the first Brady deals, and a gradual shift away from bank loans and toward bonds, total market capitalization for bonds issued by emerging countries remains far

[6] Most sovereign bonds that have been issued internationally since the early 1990s carry fixed interest rates, in contrast with the floating rates (typically linked to the London Interbank Offered Rate—LIBOR) that usually characterized bank loans in the 1970s and 1980s (IMF, 2004). In this respect, too, the present environment resembles the features of the environment that prevailed in the 1870–1913 era. Further information on today's sovereign debt structures is provided in Borensztein et al. (2004).

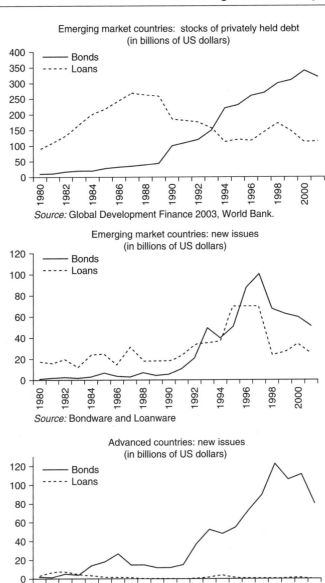

Figure 2.1. Structure of external public debt: bonds versus loans

Table 2.3. Emerging Market Countries: Outstanding Public Bonds December 2001, Billions of US dollars

Country	Public and publicly issued	General government	Central government	Brady bonds	Total bonds	Total bonds as a percent of GDP
Argentina	54.07	53.69	49.90	6.24	60.31	22.44
Brazil	32.78	25.18	25.18	17.47	50.25	9.87
Bulgaria	0.85	0.85	0.79	4.76	5.61	41.26
Colombia	11.25	10.83	10.73		11.25	13.77
Ecuador	0.50	0.50	0.50		0.50	2.38
Egypt	1.50	1.50	1.50		1.50	1.57
Korea	26.62	4.50	4.00		26.62	5.52
Malaysia	14.38	5.47	5.47		14.38	16.35
Mexico	39.58	30.33	30.33	7.41	47.00	7.53
Morocco	0.44	0.44	0.44		0.44	1.30
Nigeria	0.00	0.00	0.00	2.05	2.05	4.30
Panama	3.55	3.55	3.55	1.51	5.06	41.98
Peru	0.00	0.00	0.00	3.73	3.73	6.95
Philippines	10.73	8.83	8.83	1.29	12.02	16.92
Poland	21.59	21.47	21.44	4.17	25.76	13.86
Qatar	2.40	2.40	2.40		2.40	14.01
Russia	16.31	15.96	14.85		16.31	5.32
South Africa	11.32	5.30	5.30		11.32	9.91
Turkey	23.05	22.05	22.05		23.05	15.01
Ukraine	1.13	1.13	1.13		1.13	2.97
Venezuela	7.64	7.44	7.44	8.69	16.33	12.94
Total	279.69	221.39	215.82	57.32	337.01	10.08

Note: Data refer to all bonds issued on the international market. Public and publicly issued aggregates all bonds issued by the general government and all public enterprises. Total bonds is the sum of public and publicly issued bonds and Brady bonds. The countries listed are those included in J. P. Morgan's EMBI+ index.

Sources: Bondware, DealLogic. Data on Brady bonds is from Global Development Finance, 2003, World Bank.

lower today than it was before the First World War, as a share of the GDP (or the total bond market capitalization) of the core countries (Table 2.3). Total market capitalization for the countries included in J. P. Morgan's Emerging Markets Bond Index (EMBI+) index amounted to US$337 billion at end of 2001; by comparison, nominal GDP amounted to US$10.0 trillion for the United States and US$1.4 trillion for the United Kingdom in 2001. Total market capitalization for US Treasury bonds exceeded US$3 trillion in 2002, or about 100 times the market capitalization of emerging countries' bonds.

Trading is of course active, as shown in Tables 2.4 and 2.5.[7] Interestingly, Brady bonds were by far the most widespread and

---

[7] Trading volumes are shown individually for the countries in the sample that will be used in the empirical analysis in later chapters. The sample consists of the eight countries for which EMBI data are available starting in 1994. In 2003, secondary market trading activity was substantial for the instruments of several other countries—notably, Russia (US$288 billion), South Africa (US$158 billion), Turkey (US$142 billion), and Poland (US$135 billion).

Table 2.4. Secondary Market Transactions, Emerging Market Countries[a], 1993–2003

	1993	1994	1995	1996	1997	1998	1999	2000	2001	2002	2003
					(In billions of US dollars)						
All instruments	1,979	2,766	2,739	5,297	5,916	4,174	2,185	2,847	3,484	3,068	3,973
Brady bonds	1,021	1,684	1,580	2,690	2,403	1,541	771	712	573	459	456
Total Non-Brady bonds	177	165	211	568	1,335	1,021	626	936	1,255	1,063	1,485
Sovereign bonds	88	77	112	327	924	740	431	744	1,062	854	1,216
Corporate and unspecified bonds	89	88	99	241	411	281	196	192	193	209	269
Total local markets instruments	362	462	593	1,274	1,506	1,176	599	993	1,517	1,411	1,837
Local currency-denominated	207	371	461	851	977	869	460	845	1,393	1,361	1,806
US dollar-denominated	155	92	74	423	529	308	138	148	124	50	31
Loans	274	244	175	249	305	213	69	99	37	42	58
Options and warrants	57	142	179	471	365	223	119	106	102	93	138
Unspecified instruments	n.a.	12	n.a.	45	3	—	—	—	—	—	—

Source: Emerging Markets Traders Association.
[a] All emerging markets surveyed by the Emerging Markets Traders Association.

Table 2.5. Secondary Market Transactions in Debt Instruments, Emerging Markets, 1993–2003

	1993	1994	1995	1996	1997	1998	1999	2000	2001	2002	2003
					(In billions of US dollars)						
All EMTA countries[a]											
Total	1,979	2,766	2,739	5,297	5,916	4,174	2,185	2,847	3,484	3,068	3,973
Brady-bonds	1,021	1,684	1,580	2,690	2,403	1,541	771	712	573	459	456
Non-Brady sovereign bonds	88	77	112	327	924	740	431	744	1,062	854	1,216
Other instruments[b]	870	1,005	1,047	2,280	2,590	1,893	983	1,391	1,849	1,755	2,301
Argentina											
Total	544	590	610	1,292	1,236	612	319	366	384	38	54
Brady bonds	366	361	411	647	533	252	138	120	148	8	4
Non-Brady sovereign bonds	8	14	49	115	304	178	95	136	173	23	29
Other instruments[b]	170	216	149	531	399	182	85	110	63	7	21
Brazil											
Total	259	597	877	1,441	1,796	1,269	802	769	721	707	909
Brady bonds	141	440	583	1,020	1,102	869	420	394	308	360	363
Non-Brady sovereign bonds	14	n.a.	15	28	130	80	49	140	212	185	311
Other instruments[b]	104	157	279	394	564	320	333	235	201	162	235
Bulgaria											
Total	n.a.	n.a.	59	106	109	37	20	18	20	21	12

Mexico Total	465	601	510	946	980	640	313	662	1,111	949	1,304
Brady bonds	205	282	192	353	184	96	52	70	31	14	4
Non-Brady sovereign bonds	46	25	36	118	145	131	66	126	154	159	196
Other instruments[b]	214	295	282	476	650	414	195	466	926	776	1,104
Nigeria Total	35	54	33	23	15	8	4	3	3	2	3
Philippines Total	16	22	14	26	23	24	23	19	22	32	38
Poland Total	n.a.	n.a.	96	81	70	95	25	49	90	103	135
Venezuela Total	288	2	194	397	347	180	95	82	92	97	141

Source: Emerging Markets Traders Association.

[a] All emerging markets surveyed by the Emerging Markets Traders Association. Detail is provided for those countries in the main sample used for regression analysis in later chapters.

[b] Including loans, options and warrants, corporate and unspecified bonds, and local market instruments in both domestic and foreign currencies.

actively traded form of emerging market countries' sovereign bonds in the 1990s. Although their relative importance has been declining in recent years, they accounted for more than half of sovereign debt transactions in the emerging market countries surveyed by the Emerging Market Traders Association until 2000. They also accounted for a large portion of the sovereign debt issued by each of the countries considered in our sample.

2.6 Bond Characteristics, 1870–1913 versus Today

While the premise of this book is that the two periods considered share a number of similarities, the composition of emerging market countries' external liabilities in 1870–1913 differs from that of today in a number of respects:

• Sovereign bonds in the past were often of very long maturity: by 1870 very few bonds were issued with maturity of less than 20 years and practically none was of maturity below 10 years; a few bonds (notably some issued by Russia) were issued with maturity of up to 80 years. By the early 1900s, several sovereigns, especially the more advanced countries, routinely issued non-redeemable Consols (perpetuities). In contrast, the maturity of most of the emerging market bonds in the modern period has been 5 to 10 years, and the share of bonds with maturity of over 20 years has been relatively small (Borensztein et al., 2004). Consols are essentially nonexistent today, though a few advanced countries have recently issued 50-year bonds.

• In the period 1870–1913, many bonds included a "lottery" clause, providing for the possibility of early redemption (principal repayment at par) of a prespecified amount of outstanding bonds, to be selected through a lottery. This feature, which is discussed in more detail below, effectively shortens the duration of the bond.

• Although then as now almost all of the sovereign debt was denominated in foreign currency (pounds sterling in the past and US dollars today), in the historical period a few bonds were issued in domestic currency, by countries such as China, Hungary, Japan, and Russia. Nevertheless, such bonds usually included exchange rate clauses, which enabled investors to be paid in foreign currency at a predetermined exchange rate (see Flandreau and Sussman, 2004).

- Finally, country assets, specific export revenues, and tax revenues were used as collateral far more frequently during the previous era of globalization than they are today. This became crucial in times of default, an issue which we discuss in detail in Chapter 7. In a few cases, emerging market countries issued bonds guaranteed by the British government.[8]

Some of these features are illustrated in the next page (from the *London Times*). The picture describes a Chinese 7 percent 20-year bond issued in 1894 with lottery redemption starting in 1904. Note that

The SUBSCRIPTION LIST will be OPENED on Tuesday, 6th November, and CLOSED on or before Wednesday, 7th November, 1894.

Issued in LONDON, HAMBURG, AMSTERDAM, HONGKONG & SHANGHAI.

Chinese Imperial Government 7% Silver Loan of 1894.

For 10,900,000 TAELS (Shanghai Currency),

At exchange of 3/- per Tael = £1,635,000.

Authorised by Imperial Edict.

In Bonds of **500** Taels each, equal at the exchange of 3/- per Tael to **£75** nominal per Bond,

Bearing Interest from 1st November, 1894, at **7** per cent. per annum, payable half-yearly on 1st May and 1st November.

The Loan is for 20 years, redeemable by ten equal annual drawings commencing 1st November, 1904. The whole to be redeemed by 1st November, 1914.

A Full Half-yearly Coupon will accrue from 1st November, 1894.

PRINCIPAL AND INTEREST PAYABLE IN SHANGHAI IN TAELS, OR IN LONDON OR HAMBURG, AT THE OFFICES OF THE HONGKONG AND SHANGHAI BANKING CORPORATION, AT THE CURRENT RATE OF EXCHANGE OF THE DAY.

Principal and Interest secured by charges on the Imperial Maritime Customs Revenue of the Treaty Ports of China.

SUBSCRIPTION PRICE **98** PER CENT., or £73 10s. per Bond of **500** Taels, at which price, at present rate of exchange, the Bond will return **7%** to the Investor.

THE HONGKONG & SHANGHAI BANKING CORPORATION, 31, Lombard Street, London, invite Subscriptions for 10,900,000

---

[8] We exclude these cases from our sample, to avoid low spreads that would be easily explained by such guarantees.

even though the bond is denominated in *taels* it has a fixed exchange rate clause of 3 shillings per *tael*. In addition, the collateral for this bond is the customs revenues from the Treaty Ports of China.

We now turn to the construction of the data set we use to compare the two eras of bond finance.

2.7 Construction of the Data Set

Our focus is on the determinants and behavior of emerging market bonds. We therefore collect data on bond characteristics and prices, and on variables that may capture investors' perceptions of borrowing developing countries and their creditworthiness. We are interested in "country risk," defined as the interest premium a country has to offer investors in excess of the risk-free rate of return. More specifically, the analysis which follows is based on the assumption that differences in the default risk (measured in various ways) account for differences in the cost of capital of different borrowing countries.

Historical Spreads

In the historical sample, the risk premium is therefore the yield differential between the yield on emerging market bonds and British Consol yields. The data on spreads were collected by hand, carefully noting the characteristics of the bonds that affected the yields, such as varying coupons, and instances in which the coupons were changed or not paid.

For the eighteen emerging market countries in our sample, we collect end-of-month bond yields. (Details on the bonds used for each of these countries appear in Appendix 1.) In addition, our data set includes an average index of historical government bond yields for all emerging markets in the sample. Whereas previous studies used unweighted or GDP-weighted indexes of yields, this index is, for the first time, market-capitalization-weighted and thus similar in concept to the modern EMBI index. Specifically, we compute the index using 5-year variable weights based on the market capitalization reported in the *IMM*. Countries in default (where yields cannot be reliably computed) are excluded from the index during the default period.

In computing bond yields for the historical sample, we seek to stick as much as possible to the methods used by contemporaries, and to avoid the pitfalls often encountered in modern-day estimates of historical yields. In particular, as mentioned above, we note all bond details and covenants, as well as information on actual coupon values and payments, as reported in the *IMM*. This helps us generate the most accurate bond yield data currently available for 1870–1913. A thorough explanation of the methods we use in estimating yields, as well as a number of interesting methodological issues and changes that have occurred in this respect over the past 100 years or so, are provided in Annex 2.1.

Modern Spreads

The modern data used in this book are based on J. P. Morgan's EMBI. This is a standard and widely available source that reports secondary market spreads for emerging market bonds and also computes a weighted index of all the emerging market bonds covered by J. P. Morgan. Since the issue of sovereign bonds is a phenomenon of the 1990s, our sample is restricted to the years 1994–2004, and to eight countries: Argentina, Brazil, Bulgaria, Mexico, Nigeria, the Philippines, Poland, and Venezuela. These countries are among the most important in terms of market capitalization (for another important borrower, Russia, available data begin only in 1998). The modern data are drawn from a single source and computed using up-to-date financial methods.[9]

Investors' Information Set—The Historical Sample

We compile a dataset consisting of macroeconomic variables and news reports in order to generate a picture of each borrowing country's stability, economic and institutional development, and perceived creditworthiness. This data set, which is based on information from contemporary newspapers' articles, is used in subsequent chapters to relate bond prices to news items.

Two news sources are used for the historical sample. The first source, the *London Times* (and *Palmer's Index* to find news related to the countries we analyze), provides daily news reports on borrowing countries. This is our main source for reconstructing the perception of an emerging economy that a contemporary investor would have had on the basis of daily news reports (see below). Notably, we rely on this source for the numerical indicators of news that underlie our main regressions in Chapter 5. Unfortunately, neither the *London Times* nor the *Palmer's Index* provides a practical way of identifying major news

---

[9] A technical explanation of the EMBI index is available at the J. P. Morgan website.

based on criteria such as the size and location of the articles. In fact, *London Times* editions of the late nineteenth century were not structured like modern newspapers, with a front page and headline news: the newspaper began with what today would be the classified section of the newspaper, rather than news items.

The second historical news source is *The Economist*'s *IMM*, which provided biannual summaries (in June and December) of the key news items that "moved the markets" (referring to the London financial markets as a whole). In other words, this source identifies major news with hindsight, on the basis of the financial markets' observed behavior. Despite this drawback, we use this source, notably in a few exercises in Chapter 4, to relate events with sharp changes in the spread series, and, more importantly, to identify *the type* of news that affects the markets.

Some of the news items found in one of the biannual summaries of the *IMM* (from the December 1891 issue) are displayed on the next page. Many of the events are related to the Baring crisis. Examples include the following: news on debt negotiations with the Rothschild Committee, and news from the provinces of Cordova and Entre Rios in Argentina (first week of January); news about a civil war in Chile (second week of January); statement by the Bank of England regarding the progress of the liquidation of Baring's Bank (second week of June); and so on.

Table 2.6 compares the ranking of the countries in our sample according to the share of their debt in total market value in London in 1890 with the ranking based on their share of news articles collected from the *London Times* for the historical sample.[10] On the whole, the share of news tends to be higher for larger borrowers. Not surprisingly, however, the relationship is far from exact: the *London Times* was not a financial newspaper, and newspaper coverage was primarily determined by the countries' size and political importance. Thus, for example, news regarding Imperial China occupied a much larger share in total news than implied by China's share in market capitalization. Conversely, heavy borrowers from the periphery, such as Brazil or Argentina, received relatively little newspaper coverage.

[10] We provide separate estimates for 1870–90 and 1906–10, because of a difference in the construction of Palmer's Index starting in 1906, when the number of articles indexed increased by an order of magnitude. In this table, we do not use data for 1891–1905 and 1911–13 because news articles for Turkey were not collected for these years. Egypt is excluded because of British debt guarantees after the mid-1880s. In the calculation of the weighted average index of historical government bond yields for all emerging markets in the sample, the weight of Queensland's bonds is calculated on the basis of the entire Australian debt, a figure higher than the one in table.

Dec. 31, 1891.] THE INVESTOR'S MONTHLY MANUAL. 623

MARKET FOR THE 1ST HALF-YEAR, 1891.

Dates of Returns.	BANK OF GERM'NY. Bullion. and Specie.	Rate of Discount. Bk. Rate	Mkt Rte	UNITED STATES. Bullion and Specie in N.Y.Ass'cted Banks.	"Call Money" in New York.	INCIDENTS TENDING TO AFFECT THE MONEY MARKET, &c.
1890.	£	%	%	£	%	
Dec.31	39,075,000	5½	4¾	15,560,000	3	Dr. Plaza intimates the willingness of his Government to accept the proposals of the Rothschild Committee subject to minor modifications. Cordova and Entre Rios announce that interest payments on their coupons are "postponed pending negotiations." Newly formed Western Traffic Association watched with interest in connection with American Railroad securities.
1891.						
Jan. 7	37,934,000	6	3½	15,740,000	3	Bank rate reduced from 5 to 4 per cent. Scotch railway strike continues. Negotiations for settlement of Ecuador debt fall through. Encouraging American railroad dividend declarations (Denver and Louisville).
14	38,507,000	4	3⅛	16,220,000	3	Revolt of Chilian navy and outbreak of civil war. Free Coinage of Silver Bill rushed through the United States Senate. The Governor of the Bank of England expresses opinion that Baring liquidation is proceeding satisfactorily, and that no call will be made on guarantors. English railway dividend declarations generally equal to anticipations, although poor. French loan subscribed more than fifteen times over.
21	39,496,000	do	2⅞	17,160,000	2	Bank rate reduced from 4 to 3½ per cent. Nervousness arises in market owing to further heavy sales of Consols. Ministerial crisis in Brazil in connection with country's finances. Negotiations between Germany and Austria-Hungary as to a commercial treaty.
28	40,863,000	do	2¾	18,040,000	2½	Mr. Goschen delivers his Leeds speech on one-pound notes, and the insufficiency of our cash reserves. Scotch railway strike brought to a conclusion. The American Free Silver Coinage Bill shelved.
Feb. 4	41,386,000	do	2⅞	18,060,000	2	Fall of the Crispi Ministry in Italy. Failure of the South Australian loan. Uncertainty as to the course of affairs in Chili, communication being impeded. Pig-iron warrant gambling attracts Parliamentary attention, a Bill declaring it illegal being introduced.
11	41,982,000	2	2⅝	17,760,000	3	Repayment by the Bank of England of the £3,000,000 borrowed from the Bank of France during the November crisis. Board of Trade returns show a decrease in our foreign commerce. Allsopp's dividend passed.
18	42,499,000	3	2½	17,680,000	2½	Issue of new German 3 per cent. loan for £22,500,000. The Trust companies appoint a committee for the protection of their interests in the Argentine negotiations. Debenture Corporation puts a receiver into Hansard Union.
25	43,521,000	do	2⅝	16,780,000	2½	Sir Richard Moon, in the speech on his retirement, expresses a somewhat gloomy view of the railway situation. Telegram received from Chili that Iquique and Pisagua fallen into the hands of the Congress party. Tranquil termination of the Presidental elections in Brazil. The German Empress Frederick insulted in Paris.
Mar. 4	43,661,000	do	2¾	16,260,000	3	Long delayed settlement of the Argentine Funding Scheme at last arrived at. Gloomy rumours disseminated as to the position of leading financial houses. Scotch railway dividends prove disappointing.
11	43,896,000	do	2¾	15,720,000	2½	Financial crisis in Paris. Issue of new national Argentine loan in Buenos Ayres practically a failure. Desperate fighting in Chili.
18	43,964 000	do	2½	15,540,000	3	Conversion of the firm of Murrieta into a joint-stock company. "Other Securities" in Bank return continue to show effects of the Bank's action in the Baring liquidation. The Government purchases Consols publicly. Leading railway companies determine to drop new capital clauses of their Parliamentary Bills in retaliation against the results of the Board of Trade rate revision.
25	43,840,000	do	2¾	15,540,000	3	More Argentine provinces postpone interest payments on their coupons. Gold leaving United States in large quantities. Negotiations as to an amalgamation of the leading London omnibus companies.
Apl. 1	43,840,000	do	2⅝	15,540,000	2½	Death of Mr. Thomas Charles Baring. Dispute between Italy and United States over the Mafia incident. Successful conversion of the Ottoman Defence Loan. Continued restriction of the output of nitrate owing to the Chilian civil war.
8	41 822,000	do	2¾	15,420,000	3	Argentine State Banks defer payment. Railway Committee to consider the extension of the Sheffield line to London commences its deliberations. Rumours as to weakness in the Paris market.
15	42,673,000	do	2¾	15,340,000	2½ to 3	Advance of the Bank rate from 3 to 3½ per cent. Failure of the Victorian loan. Government interference with the Indian opium trade talked of. Further Argentine Provincial defaults announced. Sir Henry Tyler answers Sir Charles Tupper's attack on the Grand Trunk management.
22	43,653,000	do	2½	14,820,000	2½ to 3	The Council of Foreign Bondholders appoint an Argentine Committee. Gold shipments from New York continue.
29	44,455,000	do	2⅝	14,640,000	6 to 6½	Failure of the Portugese Tobacco Loan in Paris. Harvest prospects in the United States, unlike those of Europe, reported excellent.
May 6	43,971,000	do'	2¾	14,360,000	4 to 4½	Bank rate advanced from 3½ to 4 per cent. Sudden postponement of the Russian loan issue. Railway bridge accident on the Brighton line.
13	44,155,000	do	3⅛	13,640,000	2½ to 3	Bank rate advanced from 4 to 5 per cent. Decree issued by Portuguese Government suspending payments for 60 days. Determined efforts to spread false and alarming rumours throughout the Stock Exchange.
20	44,625,000	4	3⅛	12,880,000	2½ to 3	Heavy influx of gold to the Bank of England continued, the Bank raising its buying price for the metal. Light Whitsun holiday railway traffic owing to wet weather.
27	45,606,000	do	2¾	12,380,000	2½ to 3	The larger joint-stock banks combine to maintain rates. Failure of the Queensland loan. Decree closing Argentine State banks extended indefinitely. Cedula Bondholders' Committee call in unpaid April coupons, contemplating the institution of legal proceedings.
June 3	45,623,000	do	2⅝	12,200,000	2½ to 3	Panic in Buenos Ayres, premium on gold rising to 323. New issue of India stock successful. Renewed attempts to manipulate the copper market. London omnibus strike commences.
10	45,791,000	do	3⅛	11,960,000	3 to 3½	Shipments of gold to Russia. Bank of England publishes statement as to the progress of the Baring liquidation. London omnibus strike ends. Argentine Government proposes a six months' moratorium, the period being afterwards reduced to three months.
17	46,183,000	do	3½	12,100,000	1½ to 2	Bank rate reduced from 4 to 3 per cent. Adoption of gold standard by Austria-Hungary a prominent question. Further speculative manipulation in the silver market. Censure of the Board of Trade on the Brighton Company in connection with the bridge accident. Doubling of note issue by Bank of Spain, in return for advance to Government, proposed.
24	46,[illegible]05,000	do	3⅝	13,080,000	2 to 2½	Rumours as to the position of Messrs. Murrieta. House of Commons Committee assents to the Kirkcaldy Bill of the Caledonian Railway Company. Outbreak of revolt in Argentine provinces.

Table 2.6. Share of Newspaper Coverage and Share in Total Market Value of Debt

Country	Share of news in 1870–90	Share in market value 1890	Country	Share of news in 1906–10	Share in market value 1910
Russia	22.3	20.8	Russia	29.3	35.5
Turkey	43.5	16.5	Japan	4.4	9.6
Argentina	1.3	8.6	Brazil	2.3	7.4
Portugal	2.7	6.6	Argentina	2.5	6.6
Canada	8.1	6.4	Hungary	1.9	5.5
Brazil	3.2	5.0	Turkey	22.1	5.3
Queensland	0.9	3.5	Mexico	1.3	3.7
Greece	6.5	2.9	Canada	18.2	3.6
Mexico	1.3	2.7	China	3.9	3.4
Uruguay	0.4	2.1	Queensland	0.8	3.1
Chile	0.8	1.3	Chile	1.3	2.6
Sweden	0.7	1.2	Uruguay	0.8	2.1
China	5.8	0.5	Greece	4.0	2.0
Hungary	2.0	0.2	Portugal	5.0	1.7
Japan	0.5	0.1	Sweden	2.1	1.0

Sources: News items from the Palmer's Index to the London Times and bond market capitalization from The Economist's Investor's Monthly Manual.

For each country in our sample, we classified all news articles reported in the Palmer's Index to the *London Times* into the following categories:

(i) Wars and instability: including events such as coups, assassinations, riots, and strikes; but also suppressions of rebellions (relatively good news following a period of turbulence);

(ii) Bad economic news: natural disasters, poor crops, and other adverse economic developments including those reflected in statistical data releases on macroeconomic variables such as fiscal or trade deficits; excludes adverse changes in asset prices, especially bond spreads (the variables we seek to explain);

(iii) Good/neutral economic news: includes economic news that seem either positive or neutral from the viewpoint of foreign investors, such as good harvests and increased tax revenues;

(iv) Investor-friendly reforms and institutional changes, including tax reforms, adoption of the gold standard or currency boards, tariff reductions, and changes in the constitution, the legal system, the franchise, or the school system;

(v) Domestic politics: news on elections and political parties. (It would not have been possible to classify such news into good, neutral, or bad news, as perceived by contemporaries);

(vi) Foreign relations: exchange of ambassadors, diplomatic visits, peace treaties, trade agreements, and so forth;

(vii) Miscellaneous other articles.

Investors' Information Set: The Modern Sample

For 1994–2002, the news items are drawn from the *Financial Times* (*FT*), through a systematic (electronic) search of all the news items that contained the name of the country in the title or electronic subject line. Many news items were discarded as not relevant for the purpose of this research (e.g. the numerous items related to sports events such as the soccer world cup matches). We then allocated the news items among the same categories as for the historical sample, as listed above. The electronic search makes it possible to distinguish between articles that appear on the front page and articles that appear in other pages; and between articles that only appear in brief summary form on the front page and articles that appear also in other pages.

Macroeconomic Data

To complete our information set on emerging markets we compile essential macroeconomic variables that are usually associated with country risk. For the historical period, we collected annual data on government finance, exports, and population from Mitchell's *International Historical Statistics* and a host of other country-specific sources, as described in detail in Appendix 2 (the notion of GDP did not exist at the time). We supplemented a few of the missing series by using the data collected by Obstfeld and Taylor (2003b), kindly provided by Alan Taylor (and, through him, several earlier vintages of scholars). Ideally we would have preferred to use data that contemporaries had. However, the data coverage by the *IMM* has some gaps which would have rendered the econometric tests infeasible. Therefore, we opted to use the *IMM* only as a complementary source, for the countries where data from other sources were not available or seemed less reliable.

For the modern period, annual data on GDP per capita, exports, government revenues and expenditures, and the exchange rate are drawn from the International Monetary Fund's *International Financial Statistics*; public debt data are from the World Bank's *Global Development Finance*. Quarterly data are drawn from the *International*

Financial Statistics and the International Monetary Fund's country desks.

Some of the data we work with are, of course, of uncertain quality, especially for the historical sample, and one has to recognize this in interpreting the results of our empirical analysis. As the title of a study by Platt (1989) suggests ("Mickey Mouse Numbers in World History"), one has to be careful not to base grand theories on historical data of dubious source and quality. At the same time, statistics—however imperfect—do convey useful information that allows for meaningful economic analysis. What is clear is that some of the data we use are more reliable than others. Financial variables, notably bond yields, are presumably not subject to error, although of course we are unable to take into consideration all of the detailed features of all of the bonds; in addition, there are challenges involved in computing yields appropriately in times of partial or complete default, or around changes in relevant bond features (all of these issues are discussed in Annex 2.1 at the end of this chapter). The news we rely on are drawn from the newspapers and of course there is judgment involved in classifying them in various categories. Nevertheless, generally speaking, and for our purposes, we do not think that the accuracy of the news indicators today is substantially different from that of a hundred years ago. The one type of data where we believe quality is a more serious issue, and to an even greater extent in historical times than modern times, relates to the macroeconomic variables. To some extent, this is because macroeconomic concepts were different in the pre-First World War period (see more discussion in Chapter 5); in addition, some of the variables were not systematically constructed or monitored.

2.8 Emerging Market Spreads: A First Look at the Historical and Modern Data

We begin by considering the broad patterns displayed by the emerging market spreads series in the period 1870–1913, and discussing individual country characteristics. The average (market-capitalization-weighted) spread declined from a high of 600 basis points in 1870 to a low of 75 basis points in 1913 (Figure 2.2) The decline was gradual, yet continuous, with the exception of the rise in average spreads in 1876 because of wars involving some of the largest borrowers, especially Turkey (whose weight in the average spread in that period is nearly a

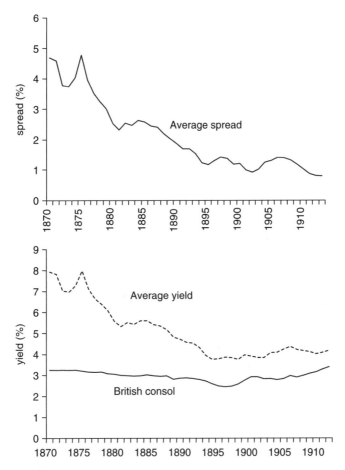

Figure 2.2. Market-capitalization-weighted average bond spreads, emerging market countries, 1870–1913 (excluding countries in default)

third). While several authors have offered possible explanations for this declining trend, there is no clear consensus on what caused it. Our preferred explanation is that the period 1906–13 was relatively tranquil for the countries in our sample, with fewer wars and episodes of violence reported in the press: the share of war news in total news in our sample roughly halved compared with that of 1870–1905.[11]

---

[11] Another, possible factor is a "supply effect," namely, the increase in the outflow of capital from the UK, which may have lowered the relative cost of borrowing for developing

The relatively smooth decline of the cross-country average spread, however, masks substantial variation in the individual country spreads, which all displayed remarkably idiosyncratic fluctuations, often caused by wars (Figure 2.3). Default periods are shaded, and events that moved the spreads in dramatic way, typically wars, are noted. Instances when bonds were redeemed by countries that introduced new bonds with significantly lower coupons are also marked.[12]

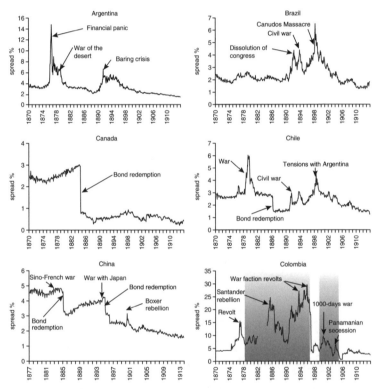

Figure 2.3. Bond spreads, emerging market countries, 1870–1913

Note: Default periods are shaded.

countries (for a discussion of this capital flight, see, for example, Clemens and Williamson, 2004). Flandreau and Zumer (2004) attribute this decline in spreads to economic growth in borrowing countries. While this may account for the decline in the average spread up to about 1900, much of the decline in the first decade of the twentieth century is due to increasing interest rates on British Consols.

[12] Note also that there are discontinuous jumps when bonds approach maturity, because the yield calculation assumes that the bonds are perpetuities.

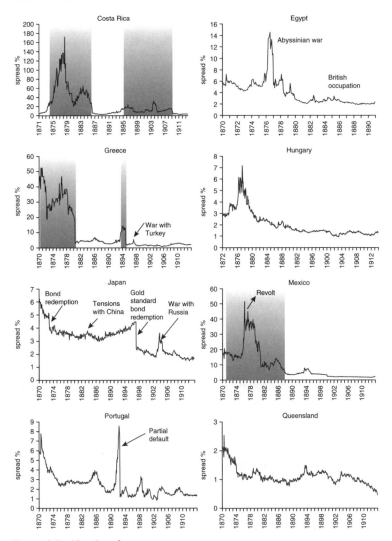

Figure 2.3. (*Continued*)

There were two major clusters of wars and revolts, one in the late 1870s and the other in the early 1890s. In the 1870s, several countries were involved in, or affected by, wars: Egypt, Greece, Hungary, Russia, and Turkey in Europe; and Argentina, Chile, Colombia, and Mexico in Latin America. The wars of the 1890s affected Brazil, Chile, and

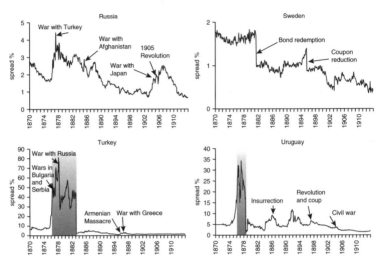

Figure 2.3. (*Continued*)

Colombia in Latin America, and China and Japan in Asia. The war between Russia and Japan in 1904–5 also had an important impact on those two countries.

In the modern sample, spreads are much higher than in the historical sample (Figure 2.4). Moreover, two major "spikes" in spreads are common to all countries in the sample, in late 1994 to early 1995 (the Mexican crisis) and August 1998 (the Russian crisis), and a smaller but similarly common spike in mid-1997 (the Asian crisis). Unlike in the past, there are fewer country-specific deviations prior to the crisis in Argentina that began in mid-2001. Differences in sharp changes and crises in the two periods are discussed in further detail in Chapter 4, and co-movement and common crises are analyzed in Chapter 6.

2.9 An Illustration of the Data on News Reports: Argentina, 1870–1913

British investors received news regarding foreign events with minimal delay (Japan, for example, was connected to a telegraph system in 1876) and ample detail. Thus, British investors were familiar with the benefits and drawbacks of the Japanese Meiji Constitution, adopted after 9 years of deliberations in 1889. They were also well aware of the

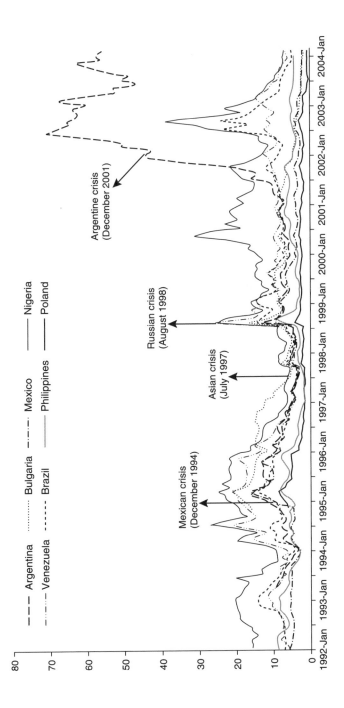

Figure 2.4. Emerging market countries' spreads, 1994–2004

Source: J. P. Morgan

Boxer Rebellion in China (1900), which was covered in dozens of news articles, the banking crisis in Portugal (early 1890s), the wars in the Balkans, and almost every other event of economic or political significance.

To illustrate the fact that British investors were well aware of events in the emerging markets of the day, Table 2.7 displays information available to investors regarding Argentina, based on news articles from the *London Times*.[13]

Figure 2.5 provides a first look at the kind of news that may have had an impact on the perception of Argentina by British investors. The figure portrays the spread on Argentine bonds (the interest rate differential between Argentina and Britain), together with the fraction of news reports related to wars and instability, and news reports classified as good economic news.

The impression conveyed by Figure 2.5 is that there is a relationship between Argentina's cost of capital and these two categories of news items. In the 1870s, news reports on wars and instability (the war with Paraguay in 1870, the Mitre rebellion in 1874, and Roca's War of the Desert in 1879–80) are prevalent and spreads are high. In the 1880s, when stability is restored, spreads decline. Instability, partially related to the economic crisis that led to the Baring crisis, reappears in the early 1890s, resulting in higher spreads. From 1895 onward, the share of good economic news increases dramatically, reaching 90 percent of all news and spreads decline to their lowest levels ever. Naturally, the figure provides only a rough impression. In the next chapters, we investigate the relationship between news and spreads more rigorously, through in-depth case studies and systematic statistical analysis, controlling for other factors.

Annex 2.1 Calculation of Historical Yields and Spreads

Participants in modern bond markets are accustomed to evaluate bonds on the basis of their yields, which are now conveniently reported in the financial press. However, this was not always the case.

---

[13] A detailed description of the rich information available to British investors about China and Japan is provided in Sussman and Yafeh (1999a; 2000).

Table 2.7. News Reports about Argentina in the *London Times*

Year	Wars and instability	Bad economic news	Good economic news	Reforms	Foreign relations	Politics	Misc.	Total
1870	1	0	4	1	3	0	6	15
1871	0	0	13	1	3	0	23	40
1872	5	0	1	0	7	0	6	19
1873	6	0	0	0	0	1	1	8
1874	26	3	2	4	1	6	2	43
1875	8	2	6	0	5	3	6	30
1876	4	4	5	0	3	1	5	22
1877	5	0	3	0	0	3	1	12
1878	2	1	1	0	5	2	1	12
1879	3	2	7	1	10	3	5	30
1880	18	3	13	3	5	19	9	67
1881	1	0	6	4	13	1	4	29
1882	0	0	5	0	11	4	2	22
1883	0	0	3	2	5	2	2	14
1884	0	1	2	0	3	1	4	11
1885	0	3	4	4	1	2	4	17
1886	0	0	0	0	0	3	1	4
1887	0	1	1	1	0	0	1	4
1888	0	0	5	1	0	0	3	9
1889	0	3	10	2	0	4	1	20
1890	17	18	24	13	2	12	6	84
1891	18	27	54	24	1	31	10	160
1892	21	3	24	5	5	33	5	90
1893	16	1	18	5	5	21	4	68
1894	2	18	16	8	1	3	3	50
1895	1	2	17	5	0	8	2	33
1896	0	1	15	1	0	3	1	21
1897	0	6	24	3	0	3	2	38
1898	0	0	8	1	4	4	0	17
1899	0	7	19	16	2	0	0	44
1900	4	11	25	0	9	2	7	56
1901	2	2	39	4	4	5	4	60
1902	5	14	27	3	13	1	9	72
1903	0	4	12	1	4	3	2	26
1904	0	0	8	0	0	5	0	13
1905	8	0	17	0	0	0	3	28
1906	0	14	60	7	3	6	3	93
1907	8	7	80	1	10	7	4	116
1908	3	6	102	3	1	4	8	127
1909	4	9	115	14	21	8	6	176
1910	5	11	112	0	25	14	24	185
1911	3	15	118	2	16	3	7	162
1912	1	29	132	14	10	4	8	196
1913	0	14	87	7	9	8	12	137

Note: Some news items are classified as belonging to more than one category. The sum of the first seven columns may therefore be in excess of the totals reported in the last column.

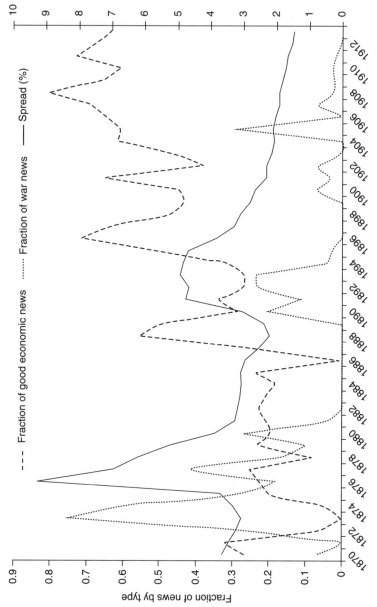

Figure 2.5. Spreads and the percentage of news reports on wars and instability and good economic news: Argentina, 1870–1913

The formulae for exact calculations of yields on bonds with various clauses were only developed in the middle of the twentieth century, and their application often requires the use of calculators and computers. Instead, investors in 1870–1913 relied on approximations, tending to regard bonds as perpetuities (with no redemption date), and focusing on bond prices. Yields were derived by dividing the value of the coupon by the market price of the bond. This approximation was reasonable, given that bonds were usually of very long maturity, and probably seemed natural to the large proportion of investors who were *rentiers* living off the fixed income provided by the bonds. Of course, over time, investors realized that more sophisticated formulae should be applied, and some business manuals provided tables that helped investors calculate more accurately the yield on the bonds they purchased. Nevertheless, for the most part, the contemporary financial and general press continued to report only bond prices, and not their yields.

With the development of the London bond market, and the entrance of new borrowers, new financial instruments were introduced. Some new borrowing countries and railway companies began issuing bonds with maturities of 10 to 25 years, and bonds with lottery clauses. Bonds with lottery clauses were redeemed periodically (usually in equal amounts each period) by holding a lottery and withdrawing at par the bonds whose numbers came up in the lottery. This innovation made it more difficult to compute the yields and to compare yields across bonds because of constantly varying durations (Box 2.1).

In our calculations we use the simplest yield calculation, the ratio of the coupon to the price, as if all bonds were perpetuities. (As mentioned above, we note, however, instances in which the coupons were changed or not paid.) In doing so, we attempt to emulate the way contemporary investors regarded the bonds they invested in, even if today's investors would apply a different formula for the valuation of these assets.[14] Figure 2.6 presents three alternative calculations for the yield of the 1873

---

[14] The lottery scheme acted as a price support to bonds trading below par, because there was always a positive probability of immediate redemption at par and an immediate capital gain, a probability that increased rapidly as the announced maturity date approached. Therefore, yields calculated according to the consol formula would understate the true yield (and spread) making the bonds appear less risky than they were. For bonds trading above par, the opposite was true. As a result, perceived differences between good and bad borrowers were seemingly compressed. This may have been one factor underlying the shift in the 1890s by creditworthy borrowers toward issuing perpetuities, which investors could correctly price to reflect their true value.

Box 2.1 NINETEENTH-CENTURY DIFFICULTIES IN CALCULATING YIELDS ON LOTTERY BONDS

Consider a bond with a maturity of 10 years with annual drawing of 10 percent of the original subscription that pays an annual fixed coupon. The holder of such a bond bought a stream of uncertain returns: a 1-year bond with probability of 0.1, a 2-year bond with probability 0.1, and so on (the expected maturity in this example is 5 years). Owing to the emergence of such bonds, the *IMM* started reporting yields in the late 1870s. However it warned its readers:

NOTICE TO CORRESPONDENTS.
With respect to the additional column—'Last two dividends yield to investor at the latest price'—introduced into this month's lists of stocks and shares, a few words of explanation are desirable. It is proposed to reproduce it from month to month, as a guide to investors; but it should be borne in mind that the yield to the buyer has been calculated without making any allowance for accrued dividend, which in the majority of instances will make the actual return rather in excess of the percentages printed, neither has any allowance been made for the value of redemption drawings, which form an additional item of prospective profit to investors in many foreign stocks, railway bonds (*IMM* June, 1876, p. 192.)

In November 1881, the *IMM* apparently responded to numerous queries by confused investors who were unable to calculate the yield of lottery bonds. In particular, the *IMM* cites cases of bonds trading above par that are therefore expected to suffer capital losses when redeemed. The following paragraph aimed to assist readers:

Lastly, there is the action of the haft-yearly or yearly drawings for redemption to be explained. In 1871, when the Argentine Public Works loan was brought out, its amount stood at 6,122,400*l*., and twenty one half-yearly drawings, at 2 per cent per annum accumulating, has reduced the amount outstanding to 3,928,000*l*. and this is to be paid off to the last bond by 1892, eleven years hence. The present price is 95 ex accrued dividend, so that a gain of 5*l*. may upon the doctrine of chances be expected to accrue in about seven years, by which date one-half the at present outstanding bonds will have been redeemed. But to calculate in this manner in respect to any loan is to assume that all future redemptions will take place in due course, an assumption by no means warranted in every case. Chili, for instance, has recently stopped all sinking funds, and various other governments are yet more seriously in default. (*IMM*, November, 1881 p. 491)

Thus, the *IMM* advised readers to calculate just the first term of future lottery, for which there is some certainty with respect to the amounts to be withdrawn. The *IMM* suggested the following method to calculate the value of a redeemable and callable loan (Ibid. p. 546.):

P—Probability of redemption as the amount redeemable divided by the amount outstanding
B—bond price ex dividend
I—coupon interest rate
Y—yield of the bond = I/B
R—Adjustment for redemption = P*(100 − B)
TY—Total yield = Y + R

This method, of course, does not correspond to what modern finance would advise; for example, it does not take into account the probability of early redemption in any year beyond the first. Despite providing this formula to its readers, the *IMM* thus continued to publish the unadjusted yields (coupon over price). Indeed, we follow this practice and use the unadjusted yields, though we checked that our main results hold when using yields corrected for the lottery feature based on modern-day methods.

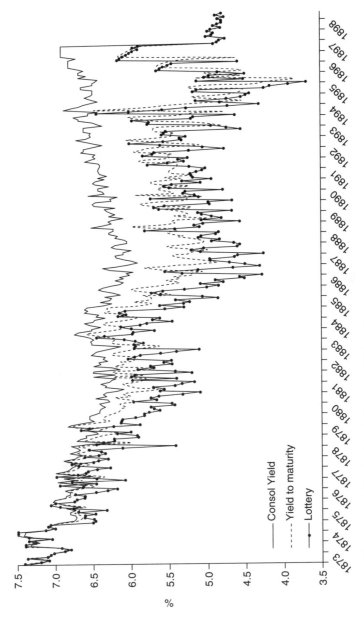

Figure 2.6. Alternative yield calculations, Japanese 7% bond

43

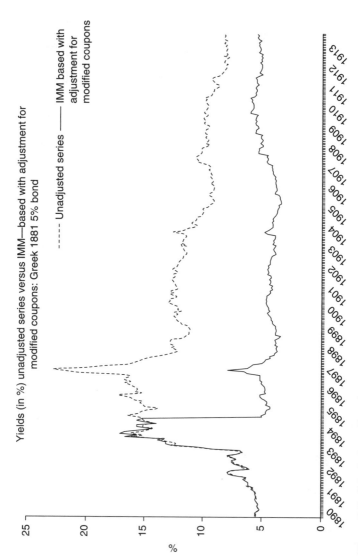

Yields (in %) unadjusted series versus IMM—based with adjustment for modified coupons: Greek 1881 5% bond

----- Unadjusted series ——— IMM based with adjustment for modified coupons

Figure 2.7. Calculation of bond yields when coupons are modified

Japanese 7 percent bond. The trends are similar, although the calculations diverge as the bond approaches maturity in 1897.

One shortcoming of the yields and bonds we calculate should be noted: none of them takes into account the nature of the securities provided by the borrowing country; pricing them was a difficult task (involving estimating their true value, the likelihood that investors will actually be able to possess them, and so on), and these features were therefore not (explicitly) incorporated in the bond price data in contemporary sources.

Avoiding Common Pitfalls in the Calculation of Historical Spreads

A common error by modern scholars seeking to calculate historical yields is the following. Most bonds had an announced coupon, usually referred to in the bond's name (e.g., "Argentina 6 percent," or "Mexico 5 percent"). When coupons are not paid out for some time (during partial defaults) yields calculated assuming regular coupon payments are often largely overstated. Furthermore, coupons were often changed following defaults, again rendering the simple official coupon divided by price calculation incorrect. Our hand-collected data procedure avoids this pitfall. The *IMM* provides all the details and covenants of the bond, as well as information on actual coupon values and payments. The calculation we use is thus based on all the available information and generates the most accurate bond yield data currently available. Figure 2.7 compares our own yield series for the 5 percent bond issued in 1881 by Greece with a series used by modern scholars that computes the yield as the original coupon price divided by the bond price, ignoring the change in coupon. Our series, based on the *IMM*, uses the actual coupon, which was reduced to 1.5 percent in December 1894 (following Greece's default in 1892) and subsequently increased annually in small increments to 3.2 percent in 1913.

3

The Determinants of the Cost of Capital: Case Study Evidence

3.1 Introduction

In this chapter and the following ones, Chapters 4 and 5, we examine the determinants of the cost of borrowing—a key factor in economic development—both over time and across countries. What makes it possible for some countries to borrow more cheaply than others do? A variety of factors might affect a country's perception in the eyes of (foreign) investors. In what follows, we focus on four main categories:

(1) Sound macroeconomic policies.

(2) Narrowly defined institutions embedding commitment to monetary discipline, such as the gold standard in the past (Bordo and Rockoff, 1996; Obstfeld and Taylor, 2003b), or currency boards today, may also affect the perceived creditworthiness of borrowing countries.

(3) Institutions protecting property rights constitute the third category of factors we examine. Following North (1990) and North and Weingast (1989), investor-friendly institutions protecting property rights, and reforms designed to establish such institutions are a possible explanation for variations in the cost of debt of borrowing countries. According to this school of thought, enforcement of property rights lowers the cost of capital (of both governments and private borrowers), can explain the development of financial markets in England and, more generally, the rise of the British Empire to supremacy

in Europe and the whole world. A large, more recent and influential literature in financial economics has followed this approach, and suggested that the protection of property rights is the most important determinant of financial market development and of the ability of firms to raise external finance around the world (see La Porta et al., 2000, for a survey of this literature.) Related studies by other authors, such as Levine and Zervos (1998), find a link between financial development and economic growth. Even institutions that do not affect the development of financial markets directly may have an impact on the cost of borrowing if they are expected to bring about growth or otherwise improve future economic performance.[1]

(4) Peace and stability in a country's domestic and international political environment is likely to affect the cost of borrowing as well. Riots and wars disrupt economic activity and discourage investment; government changes attained through violence may also result in reduced willingness to honor existing debt obligations.

The main conclusion that emerges from Chapters 3 through 5 is that strong macroeconomic fundamentals and, perhaps even more important, absence of violence (internally and vis-à-vis other countries) are crucial prerequisites for countries seeking to borrow at reasonable cost. By contrast, investor-friendly institutional changes rarely elicit an *immediate* response by investors and financial markets. Meiji Japan, for example, introduced a beautifully crafted constitution, yet this fundamental change in the country's polity apparently failed to impress investors. One interpretation of this finding is that *de facto* rather than *de jure* institutions matter: it takes time to establish the credibility of a new constitution and to verify that the lofty ideas embodied in it are indeed going to be implemented in practice.

---

[1] A recent wave of studies has empirically analyzed the relationship between indicators of institutional quality and a host of economic outcomes. See Knack and Keefer (1995), Mauro (1995), Kaufmann et al. (1999) Acemoglu, Johnson, and Robinson (2001), Acemoglu and Johnson (2005) and Acemoglu, Johnson, and Robinson (2005) on institutions, investment, economic development, and growth; Bénassy-Quéré, Coupet, and Mayer (2005) and Wei (2000) discuss institutions and foreign direct investment; Alfaro et al. (2004) focus on capital flows and Faria and Mauro (2004) and Wei and Wu (2002) on their composition; Mauro (1998) studies the relation between institutions and the composition of government expenditure; economic and political instability is discussed in Acemoglu and Johnson (2003); Acemoglu, Johnson, and Robinson (2004) and Johnson et al. (2000) relate institutions to the frequency and severity of crises.

Furthermore, even with the most elaborate property rights protection clauses, a constitution is unlikely to convince investors that their money is well protected, unless wars and other episodes of violence are credibly resolved. Another possible factor (which does not apply to the case of Japan) underlying the absence of an immediate market response to institutional changes is that these often lead to domestic instability, at least in the short run; in some cases this happens because vested interests are adversely affected.

In contrast with institutional reforms, international wars and episodes of domestic turmoil seem to have an immediate and substantial impact on the ability of countries to access international capital markets. Blood flowing in the streets has a far more immediate and substantial impact on a country's ability to borrow than institutional reforms. Of course, this could still be broadly interpreted as evidence that property rights and the macroeconomic environment are never secure in periods of violence and extreme instability.

Our analysis of these questions proceeds in three stages. This chapter is focused primarily on one historical case study: Japan in the Meiji Period (1868–1912), an era containing some of the most dramatic institutional and economic changes in modern history (see Sussman and Yafeh, 2000). Not only can this period be used to illustrate the response of investors and financial markets to the introduction of new, investor-friendly institutions; it also provides interesting historical evidence on the importance of the gold standard and of the impact of wars. When discussing the risk premium on Japanese debt, we make some brief comparisons with Russia, a country that adopted the gold standard in the same year as Japan (1897) and was its military rival in the most important war of the period.

After discussing the Japanese case study, toward the end of the chapter, we depart briefly from our focus on the nineteenth century and move back in history 200 years to England following the Glorious Revolution (1688). This digression is illuminating, because it follows the highly influential work by Nobel Laureate Douglass C. North and Barry Weingast (1989). They argue that England in the late seventeenth and early eighteenth century is a good example of investor-friendly institutional changes (upholding property rights) that were adequately rewarded by financial markets; we find that the evidence fails to support this argument.

The impressions from the historical episodes discussed in this chapter serve as a preamble for the more systematic analysis of the relative importance of macroeconomic factors, institutions, and political stability, which are presented in Chapters 4 and 5. The main conclusions that we draw in this chapter are reinforced in the more rigorous analysis of the following chapters.

3.2 Wars, Reforms, and Cost of Capital: Evidence from Meiji Japan

In this case study, we attempt to assess the impact of major reforms on the risk premium associated with Japanese Government debt traded in London. We find that most reforms, including the establishment of a central bank and the promulgation of a modern constitution, did little, at least in the short run, to affect the way Japan was perceived by British investors. The only institutional reform that clearly led to an immediate improvement in Japan's "credit rating" was the adoption of the gold standard, discussed below. In addition, Japan's war with Russia (1904–5) and its successful outcome had a far more visible impact on spreads than most institutional reforms.

Figure 3.1 reports the spread (yield difference relative to British Consols) on Japanese and Russian government debt (denominated in pounds sterling and traded in London) from 1870 to 1913. While yields on Japanese bonds fell in the 1870s, they increased moderately from the early 1880s until the mid-1890s, even though the 1880s witnessed the establishment of some of Japan's most important institutions, including the Bank of Japan, a modern system of government, and an elected parliament. The culmination of these institutional changes was the promulgation of the Meiji Constitution in 1889, which explicitly guaranteed the protection of property rights and the rule of law. Nevertheless, no effect is discernible on market perceptions of Japan's country risk.

Similarly, the volume of foreign borrowing and the composition of the Japanese government debt on the London market (described in further detail in Sussman and Yafeh, 2000) failed to react to Japan's institutional reforms. With the exception of two debt issues floated in London during the early 1870s, the period of institutional reform was characterized by net capital outflows, largely accounted for by payments to service and retire foreign debt. This outflow of capital is mirrored in the steady decline in the share of foreign debt in total debt until 1897. The trends of both the share of foreign debt and capital

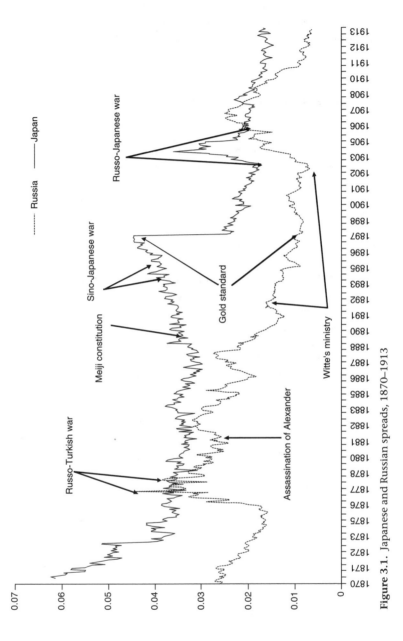

Figure 3.1. Japanese and Russian spreads, 1870–1913

flows were reversed following the adoption of the gold standard. In particular, Japan was able to raise large amounts of capital from abroad to finance the war with Russia; indeed, Japan's foreign debt reached a peak at this time (see below). Perhaps one should not be surprised that British investors were not impressed by the establishment of the Bank of Japan, because this followed several unsuccessful attempts to reform the banking system in the late 1870s. However, the lack of impact of the Meiji Constitution of February 1889 is more intriguing. A large number of articles in the *London Times* described the Meiji Constitution; thus, the absence of a strong market reaction to its promulgation could not have been because investors were unaware of the institutional changes taking place in Japan. The Constitution was described favorably, as a major step forward, granting Japanese citizens substantial liberties and, more importantly, establishing an independent judicial system, a feature that was highly regarded by the *Times*. Nevertheless, British commentators did not seem convinced that the Constitution would prove a major turning point, and investors did not modify their perception of the Japanese government following its promulgation.

In contrast with the Meiji Constitution and other reforms of the Meiji period, the adoption of the gold standard in 1897 had a dramatic effect on Japan's creditworthiness. In its aftermath, the yield differential between Japanese and British bonds declined from approximately 4 percentage points to a 2 percent premium. The observed decline coincided with the early and complete withdrawal of the 7 percent bonds (issued in 1873), and the issuance of new, 5 percent bonds.[2] An additional indication of improved confidence on the part of investors is that the newly issued bonds were of much longer maturity—over 50 years (with restrictions on early redemption), compared to 25 years on previous issues. The adoption of the gold standard was also accompanied by an increase in the volume of debt issued by the Japanese government in London. The share of Japanese foreign debt in total Japanese debt rose from the low single digits prior to the adoption of the gold standard to around 20 percent by the turn of the century. Unlike the establishment of a new state structure, the gold standard was apparently interpreted as evidence of a significant improvement in Japan's creditworthiness.

---

[2] It seems reasonable to argue that if the Japanese government had been able to reduce its borrowing costs by refinancing its debt earlier, it would have done so even prior to the adoption of the gold standard.

Judging by reports in the *Economist*, the Japanese government was well aware of the impact of the gold standard on its borrowing ability:

Japan is very much in earnest over the adoption of the gold standard. The principal motive for this change, however, is . . . because the (Japanese) government find(s) it necessary to borrow money abroad, and the opinion prevails that Japan as a gold standard country would command higher credit, and be able to borrow on more favourable terms in foreign countries than she would as a silver-standard country. There is also an idea that as Japan now considers that she has the right to be regarded as a first-class Power, she ought to adopt for her currency the same standard of value as other first-class Powers. (24 April, 1897, p. 603)

It is interesting to compare the impact of the gold standard on Japan with its impact on Russia.[3] Although neither country had defaulted prior to going on gold, Russia was a familiar and well-established European empire, whereas Japan was a new emerging Asian power. Conveniently for our purposes of comparison, both countries adopted the gold standard in the same year, 1897. As shown in Figure 3.1, the gold standard did not affect the two countries in the same way. Whereas 1897 represented a clear break from the past for Japan, this was not the case for Russia, where the gold standard was adopted at a time when spreads had already reached their historical lows. In fact, Russian spreads registered a continuous decline after the end of a period of instability (the war with the Ottoman Empire in 1877–8, the assassination of the Czar Alexander II in 1881 and the wars near the Asian borders and Afghanistan in 1885). Spreads continued falling while Sergei Witte, the finance minister, held the reins of the Russian economy, running a tight fiscal policy and promoting industrialization. This decline ceased, however, around the time of the adoption of the gold standard.[4]

The discussion of the gold standard in Japan and Russia is closely related to an ongoing debate in the literature about the impact of the gold standard on the ability of countries to raise foreign debt. Several scholars, notably Bordo and Rockoff (1996) and Obstfeld and Taylor (2003b), argue that the gold standard was important in determining countries' ability to borrow. Whereas a constitution may serve as a commitment mechanism to respect the rights of investors, the gold standard, they argue, served as a commitment to sound macroeconomic policies in the pre-1914 period. Flandreau and Zumer (2004)

[3] The case of Japan is analyzed in detail in Sussman and Yafeh (2000).
[4] Gregory (1979) suggests that the gold standard improved Russia's ability to borrow. However, data on debt volumes (drawn from the Investor's Monthly Manual) remain broadly stable until the early 1900s.

disagree, and view the adoption of the gold standard as the result, rather than the cause, of other economic changes. Ferguson and Schularik (2004) argue that the evidence supporting the importance of the gold standard is misleading; in fact, they view affiliation with the British Empire as the crucial factor, though it often coincided with the gold standard.

The evidence discussed here (and in the next chapter) on the impact of the gold standard is mixed. In some cases, the introduction of the gold standard or other institutions buttressing the monetary regime seems to have elicited an immediate response on the part of financial markets. The introduction, in 1897, of the gold standard in Japan, still a relatively untested borrower in the eyes of British investors resulted in a sizable and immediate decline in borrowing costs. (As shown in Chapter 4, the establishment, exactly 100 years later, of a currency board in Bulgaria, a transition economy, had similar effects.) Our interpretation is that investors immediately rewarded Japan and Bulgaria because they viewed the introduction of the gold standard and the currency board, respectively, as focal points of reform packages committing these relatively untested countries to a stable macroeconomic environment. In contrast, the adoption of the gold standard (also in 1897) failed to convey much new information to investors in the case of Russia, a more established borrower that investors were already familiar with.

Moving from monetary policy to military conflicts, the war between Japan and Russia in 1904–5 had a major impact on the spreads of both countries. Before the war, Japan was perceived as the underdog, and yields on Japanese government bonds rose dramatically, reaching the highest level of the decade in early 1904. Subsequent Japanese victories over Russia led to a decline in the perceived risk of Japanese bonds, and Japanese spreads returned to their prewar levels in 1905. Interestingly, at the beginning of the war, spreads did not rise as sharply in Russia as they did in Japan. However, Russia's spreads continued to rise through the war, as the prospect of a Japanese victory looked increasingly plausible. The Revolution of 1905 and the subsequent turmoil maintained Russian spreads high for another couple of years after the war; spreads declined gradually only as the internal situation stabilized.

The need to finance the war with Russia prompted Japan to increase massively its borrowing, especially its foreign borrowing. It is quite likely that Japan's adherence to the gold standard was an important factor making it possible for Japan to raise such borrowing abroad at reasonable rates. As a percent of government revenues, total debt increased from about 200 percent around 1900 to over 400 percent in 1905. Most of the new debt was issued abroad: foreign debt accounted for about half of the total outstanding Japanese debt after the end of the war with Russia, compared with one-fifth around 1900. Japan thus became one of the largest borrowers on the London market and was now able to issue in other foreign bond markets as well. Following Japan's victory, spreads continued declining, albeit slowly, until about 1910.

The fact that military victory over Russia improved Japan's credit rating is explicitly stated in many news articles. For example, starting in 1905 there was concern in Britain over the burden of Japan's war expenditures. The *Economist*, however, advised its readers not to worry because "*the sagacity with which the finances of Japan have been administered during a period of stress and anxiety is a good augury...*" (23 February 1905, p. 2072). A later *Economist* article, titled "*Japan as a Borrower*," explained the "*phenomenal success*" of Japan's loan operations as "*due about equally to the enhanced reputation of Japan by reason of her military and naval exploits, and the skillful manner in which her loan flotations ha[d] been conducted...*" (20 July 1907, p. 1212). It seems that the reputation acquired during the successful war with Russia made it possible in later years for Japan to withstand investors' concerns (expressed in many news articles) regarding its increasing fiscal deficit. The London market for sovereign debt was much more interested in, and impressed by, the outcome of the war against Russia than by the fundamental institutional reforms in the decades prior to the war.

3.3 Digression: Evidence from Britain after the Glorious Revolution

The case of Britain after the Glorious Revolution has famously been cited as evidence of a link between institutional changes and the cost of debt. In a seminal contribution, North and Weingast (1989) argue that the institutional changes of the late seventeenth century, following the Glorious Revolution of 1688, made the British government and Crown credibly committed to respect the property rights of the Kingdom's citizens. This set of institutional changes is purported to have resulted in a substantial fall in the cost of borrowing for the British government.

In Figure 3.2, we contrast this view of the world with three measures of the interest rate differential (or contemporary spread) between

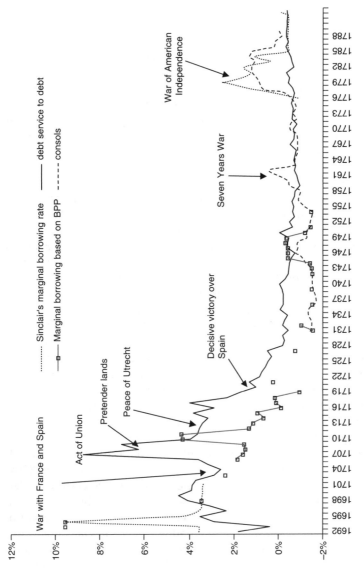

Figure 3.2. Interest rate differential: Britain versus the Province of Holland, 1692–1795

British government debt and debt issued by the Province of Holland, the world's main financial center in the seventeenth and early eighteenth centuries. One measure is based on the ratio of debt service to total debt, drawn from Mitchell's International Historical Statistics (Europe); another on Sinclair's (1803) marginal interest rate; the third is based on annuity prices between 1731 and 1753 and daily market Consol yields thereafter. The figure shows that interest rates remained relatively high in the decades following the Revolution, with considerable fluctuations in response to wars and instability. Indeed, interest rates in Britain were substantially higher than in Holland until approximately 1730, about four decades after the Glorious Revolution.

Much like what we observe for Meiji Japan, turning points in the UK–Holland interest differential series closely correspond to outbreaks and conclusions of major wars. For example, interest rates rose substantially during the War of the Spanish Succession (1701–13, against France and Spain, and ending with the peace of Utrecht). Spreads declined following the Act of Union between England and Scotland. A small increase occurred when the Pretender (claimant to the British throne) landed in Scotland. In 1715, Britain faced a Jacobite rebellion, and, for a short period, interest rates rose again. In 1717, Britain was again at war with Spain (the War of the Quadruple Alliance, 1717–20), and interest rates increased— a trend that was reversed following Britain's decisive victories in 1718, when the Spanish fleet was destroyed. A similar pattern is observed (using Sinclair's interest rate series and the Consol rates) for the second half of the eighteenth century. The interest rate differential between Britain and Holland increased during the Seven Years War, and even more sharply during the American War of Independence.

In sum, evidence from Britain in the seventeenth and eighteenth centuries (discussed in far more detail in Sussman and Yafeh, 2004) indicates that interest rates remained high and fluctuated considerably for a long period after the completion of the institutional changes of the seventeenth century. Only after the establishment of peace both domestically and internationally did rates fall durably to a lower level. We conclude that even some of the most dramatic institutional changes in history did not lead to an immediate response in financial markets. This theme will be corroborated in subsequent chapters.

3.4 Concluding Remarks

The main conclusion that emerges from the historical case studies presented in this chapter is that financial markets do not seem to reward countries for institutional reforms in the short run. This conclusion is illustrated in an 1877 caricature, deriding the Ottoman

ONE BUBBLE MORE!!

Source: John Tenniel, 6 January 1877. Reproduced with the permission of Punch, Ltd.

Empire's attempts to introduce constitutional reforms as yet another institutional "bubble," merely designed to attract investors. Clearly, investors would carefully observe whether the constitution would be respected over the following years, before gradually rewarding the country with lower spreads.

While there is little doubt that institutional reforms can be beneficial for long-run growth, the mechanism through which they make a difference does not seem to be an immediate reduction in the cost of capital. In a few cases, fundamental monetary reforms can become focal points of investors' attention, though these seem to constitute exceptions. In contrast, financial markets do respond immediately to major wars, which of course could still be interpreted as a fundamental threat to property rights and investor protection, or, in the case of Japan's victory over Russia, as credible evidence of the country's institutional and economic strength. In the following chapters, we support these conclusions with evidence that is more systematic.

4

News and Sharp Changes in Bond Spreads

4.1 Introduction: The Impact of Events on Bond Spreads

In this chapter, we seek to gauge the extent to which various types of political and economic news affect bond spreads in the historical and modern sample periods. We systematically relate bond spreads to news items, conducting several different types of exercises. Our analysis focuses on the relation between sharp changes (defined in a number of ways) in the spread series and news items belonging to various categories (as described in Chapter 2: instability and wars; economics—separating good/neutral from bad; domestic politics; foreign relations; and reforms and institutions).[1] In the first exercise, we identify the dates when the sharpest changes in the spreads took place, and then consider whether the news reported on those days were significant. In the second exercise, we identify the dates when major news were reported in the newspapers, and then test whether spread changes on those dates were larger (in absolute value) than spread changes during the other months in the sample period.

This approach is similar to that taken by a number of studies that have sought to relate asset price changes to news items, and is closest to the seminal work of Cutler, Poterba, and Summers (1989), who assessed the relationship between changes in the US stock market index and publicly available news bearing on fundamental values. The results of these studies are rather mixed, and typically find that news do not explain a large portion of asset price changes. Drawing on

[1] As mentioned in Chapter 2, the classification of news into categories requires some judgment, and we strive to be systematic and consistent.

weekly prices of British government Consols in 1900–20, Elmendorf, Hirschfeld, and Weil (1996) find that the variance of returns is higher for weeks with important news than for weeks without such news, and the probability of a very large (positive or negative) return is higher for weeks with news than for weeks without news. Nevertheless, the magnitude of these differences suggests that much of the variability in bond prices cannot be explained by news. In a study of daily stock price changes during the Asian crisis of 1997–8, Kaminsky and Schmukler (1999) find that market movements are often triggered by local and neighboring country news, especially news regarding agreements with international organizations and the views of credit rating agencies. However, several large movements seem unrelated to news, and appear instead to be driven by herd behavior. Using data on prices of closed-end country funds for 1985–94, Klibanoff, Lamont, and Witzman (1998) find that, in weeks with major news (relevant to the specific country) appearing on the front page of *The New York Times* prices react much more to fundamentals. One may interpret this finding to suggest that investors only pay attention to fundamentals when newspaper reports bring a particular country onto their "radar screens."

The mixed record of previous studies in identifying relationships between news and asset prices suggests that, in approaching our own empirical analysis, one's *ex ante* expectations should not be overly optimistic. Our main interest is in finding out—to the extent that news matter—whether country-specific news mattered more in the past than they do today, and what types of news seem to matter more.

Turning to our results, in the modern sample period we find the relationship between news and changes in bond spreads to be tenuous. Indeed, most relationships become statistically insignificant when Argentina is omitted from the sample. To the limited extent that news matter, items related to violence and unrest, and to lesser extent, bad economic news seem to play the largest role. For the historical sample, data constraints imply that while we can undertake an exercise going from large changes in spreads to news items, we cannot go from news—selected on an *ex ante* basis—to changes in spreads. This second exercise can in fact only be conducted drawing on a set of news that is known *ex post* to affect the markets. Bearing that strong caveat in mind, we find that the association between news and spread changes is more significant in the historical sample.

Perhaps less subject to caveats, the news that matter the most are related to "wars and instability," "bad economic events," and "foreign relations." Thus, overall, the conclusions from the case study evidence discussed in Chapter 3 seem to hold for the analysis in this chapter as well.

4.2 Historical Sample—From Large Spread Changes to News

We begin by identifying, for each country, the 10 months with the largest absolute change and absolute percentage change in spreads;[2] and reporting, for those country/months, the main news items and number of related articles (in brackets) in the *London Times* (Table 4.1).[3]

Table 4.1 suggests that our sample can be split into countries with large basis points changes in spreads—the Latin American countries and the European lesser developed countries (with the exception of Russia)—and countries with small basis point changes in spreads—Canada and Australia, the Asian emerging markets of Japan and China, and Sweden. Generally, the large spread changes in the first group of countries are associated with wars and instability, as well as with bad economic news. There is a clustering of sharp changes around military conflicts involving the Ottoman Empire (the war in the Balkans in the late 1870s), which affect Turkey, Russia, Greece, and Hungary. Other armed conflicts such as a crisis in Egypt (late 1870s), the Chilean wars in Latin America (1879), the war between Greece and Turkey over Crete (1897), the Boxer Rebellion in China (1900) and the Japan–Russia war (1904–5) are all associated with sharp changes. In contrast with the "contagious" spread of the crises of the 1990s (see below), the major financial crisis of the 1890s (emanating from the Baring Crisis in Argentina) does not seem to have caused sharp changes elsewhere.

Table 4.1 also suggests that the immediate effect of institutional reforms on spreads appears to be very small. For most countries, we cannot identify any sharp change with an institutional change. The only

---

[2] We treat separately periods of default when spread calculations are problematic. Moreover, in order to focus squarely on events exogenous to the debt market, all observations involving bond exchanges are excluded.

[3] Colombia and Costa Rica are excluded from the analysis because of very limited news coverage.

Table 4.1. Sharp Changes in Spreads, 1870–1913, and News Reports

	Change in spread (b. points)	Change in spread (percent)	Salient news
Argentina			
Mar 1876	295	50.1	Revolution and political Unrest (11); ministerial crisis (1); financial crisis and panic in Bourse
Jul 1890	117	45.2	(numerous); tensions with Chile (1); Pan American Confederation (1).
Nov 1876	465	38.8	End of panic (1); forced currency (1); commercial news (1).
Jul 1891	199	38.6	Revolt (3); financial panic (1); budget (1); tariff bill (1).
Jan 1912	33	27.4	Railway workers strike and riots (22); tensions with Paraguay (4); new railways (4); meat exports (4); crops output (3).
Jul 1901	55	26.3	New small change coinage (1).
Feb 1877	171	25.5	Stamp on bills of exchange (1).
May 1876	222	24.1	Argentina and Paraguay confederation (1).
Feb 1876	84	23.9	First Census (1); international exhibition (1).
Jul 1870	80	23.8	
Brazil			
Apr 1898	155	31.2	Taxation; rubber export duty (1); further reduction proposed (1); railways (7); trade statistics
Oct 1913	31	21.2	(1); companies' dividends (2).
Oct 1896	63	20.6	Finance problems (4); stable financial situation (official contradiction to former article) (1); trade restrictions (1); loans and rates (1).
May 1898	-127	-19.4	Government revenues (1).
Apr 1913	24	17.8	Engineering contracts abroad (1); finance: expenditure (2); loans: new issue announced (2); railway (10).
Jan 1891	37	17.6	Commercial frauds (1).
Mar 1898	74	17.5	Growing budget deficit (1); general election (3).
Oct 1912	22	17.3	Brigandry (1); coffee exports (6); damaged coffee, freeze (5); finance: Federal Authorization Bill (1); railways (5); trade (3); presidential election (1).
Apr 1891	44	16.9	Financial situation (2); financial difficulties and fall in Brazilian securities and bonds following the fall of Argentinian and Chilean securities (1).
Oct 1891	45	16.9	Riots in Rio (2); budget surplus (1); new steamers for Brazilian trade (2); restriction on issue of paper money (2); reduction of public debt (1).

Canada

Nov 1912	14	65.3	Labor strike (3); economic situation (15); railways (20); shipping, trade (7); Canada and the United States (3); elections (9); labor regulations (4); naval policy (7); parliament (9).
Apr 1903	23	60.8	Budget (2); customs policy (6); immigration into Canada (1); trade (2); charge against the Ontario govt. (1); parliamentary visit to newfoundland (4). Commercial news (2).
Jan 1889	16	38.7	Canada and commercial union (2); Canada and Great Britain (1); Canada and the United States (3); commercial news (3); legislative news (3).
Mar 1888	−15	−34.8	Labor strike (5); economy (5); railway (6); trade and shipping (7); marriage and shipping (7); marriage and divorce bill (1); companies law (1); governor general (4).
Feb 1913	10	34.2	Increase in paper money (1); railways (22); trade (16); economic news (19); elections (19); navy bill (9); parliamentary news (10).
Nov 1911	8	32.2	Legislative news (3); trade and tariffs (8); Canada and the United States (4).
Jan 1890	12	30.4	Crop failure (1); railways (14); fiscal policies (3); trade and tariffs (3); economic news (31); various parliamentary bills (13).
May 1910	10	27.0	US–Canada fishing dispute (2); railway crisis (1).
Jan 1888	8	24.7	Prohibition (1); finances (1); speculation (1).
May 1902	11	23.8	

Chile

Sep 1891	−72	−26.0	Disorders (2); finance (5).
Oct 1878	461	22.1	
Jul 1876	64	22.1	
Jul 1893	55	21.9	
Jul 1878	60	21.0	
Oct 1879	463	20.4	War news (1).
Jan 1879	−94	−20.3	
Apr 1879	91	17.8	War with Peru and Bolivia(14).
Apr 1891	37	16.0	Revolutionary movement (2); dynamite at president's house (1); elections (4).
Jul 1897	45	16.6	Chilean finance (1).

Table 4.1. (Continued)

	Change in spread (b. points)	Change in spread (percent)	Salient news
China			
July 1900	54	20.9	Military situation (3); new loans (2).
Aug 1900	−44	−14.1	Chinese crisis and its settlement (2); reform (1).
Apr 1903	22	10.9	Anti-foreign appointments (1); famine in Kwangs (1); affray between foreign soldiers in Peking (1).
Apr 1913	16	10.4	Bomb in Fuchau (1); Indian border: Chinese troops attack British police (2); danger internal and external (2); loans (18); Comm. treaty—Russia (2).
Oct 1911	16	9.9	Revolutionary movement (215); railways (4); economic news (12); financial reform (2); political reform (2); ministerial appointments (6); military reorganization
Aug 1891	36	9.9	Floods (1); crisis (2).
Feb 1904	22	9.9	Foreign troops in China (2); burst of dam (1).
Mar 1904	−23	−9.6	Anti-foreign riots (3)
Feb 1883	42	9.6	
Oct 1907	17	9.5	Weights and measures reforms (1); railways (4); economics (6).
Egypt			
Apr 1976	525	64.4	Egypt and Abyssinia (1); Egyptian loan finance (17); unification of bonds (2); postponement of payment on bonds (1).
Apr 1879	167	42.1	Famine (1); Egyptian finances and loan (8); new government (2); proposition on reducing the rate on the debt (1); reorganizing the debt (1).
Jul 1870	203	39.1	Fight at Ashab Bay (1); Suez canal returns (1).
Jun 1882	92	35.5	War in Egypt–Cairo, Sudan, and Alexandria (114).
Apr 1877	155	32.1	Egypt and the War (1); financial problems (5); new arrangements for setting claims against Egypt (1).
May 1878	−184	−29.2	Neutral army movement (2); good news about finance, unified debt (18).
Oct 1875	157	27.1	Egypt and Abyssinia (1); financial difficulties (1); new codes of Consular Jurisdiction (3).
Apr 1875	63	22.9	War news (37); money order on Khedive stopped (9); financial prospects (1); progress of railways (1); steamboats on the Nile (1).
Jun 1879	−111	−22.3	Finances: the debt and budget (9).
Jan 1874	110	21.7	Suez canal (5).

Greece (excluding default period)			
Feb 1897	110	40.5	War against Turkey–Crete (4).
Apr 1897	137	33.8	War against Turkey–Crete (16).
May 1892	−151	−32.1	General Elections (6).
Jan 1892	110	31.9	Affairs of Greece (2).
May 1897	−161	−29.7	War in Crete (19).
Apr 1903	28	27.1	Greco-Turkish commercial relations (3).
Jul 1907	32	25.3	Floods (1); trade statistics (3).
Jul 1880	68	24.6	Foreign relations (2).
Aug 1897	−77	−23.1	Peace negotiations with Turkey (22).
Dec 1905	16	21.3	Political reform (1).
Hungary			
Apr 1877	233	48.3	National debt (3).
Oct 1876	138	29.0	Financial crisis (1); corn market crisis (1); elections (10).
Oct 1878	78	20.8	Wine industry (1).
Oct 1873	53	18.4	Hungarian taxation (3); new loan (2); parliamentary news (2).
Oct 1874	55	17.2	Hungary and the Austrain budget (1).
Jun 1877	−112	−16.7	
Apr 1876	78	16.4	Hungary and the Austrian loan (1).
Jun 1878	−69	−15.5	
Aug 1987	−84	−14.7	Deputation to the President on confidence in his cabinet (1).
Jan 1878	−73	−14.5	

Table 4.1 (*Continued*)

	Change in spread (b. points)	Change in spread (percent)	Salient news
Japan			
Feb 1904	54	19.0	Japanese army mobilization (1).
Dec 1899	33	16.7	Tension between Russia and Japan (3); taxation (1).
Dec 1903	40	16.3	
Jan 1889	52	16.2	
Jan 1879	49	16.0	Miscellaneous (2).
Apr 1903	23	13.3	Economic relationship with Korea (1); politics (3).
Jan 1905	−36	−12.4	
Sep 1913	20	12.4	Banking (1); loans (1).
Feb 1905	−31	−12.3	Budget (1); railways (1).
Jul 1894	45	12.2	Korea (1).
Mexico (excluding default period)			
Jun 1893	124	23.8	Indian war (1).
Jul 1893	139	21.5	
Nov 1893	−100	−14.3	Foreign loans (2).
Dec 1913	27	13.7	Military coup (93); railways (17); bank crisis, devalution, and default on wage payments (13); banking reforms (4).
Sep 1893	−105	−13.6	Instability (3).
Jul 1891	51	13.2	Finance (1).
May 1893	61	13.1	
Apr 1903	24	13.0	
May 1895	−62	−12.7	Finance (4).
Feb 1895	−67	−12.2	Foreign trade (1).

Mexico (default period)			
Jul 1870	655	46.2	Mexican bond holders' meeting (1); trade (1).
Jan 1882	367	43.1	Economic progress (1); new silver mines (1).
Jan 1881	−618	−43.0	
Apr 1876	1130	39.8	Revolutionary movement (5).
Jan 1876	769	38.7	
May 1876	1173	29.5	Revolutionary movement (5).
Apr 1880	548	29.3	
Apr 1877	570	21.6	
Jan 1880	−484	−20.5	
Portugal			
May 1891	113	40.3	Explosion of a bomb at the Ministry of the interior (1); financial crisis (11); suspension of payments (2); ministerial crisis (7).
Jul 1891	138	37.7	Commercial treaties (6); monetary crisis (10); financial crisis (2).
Jul 1870	211	37.3	
Oct 1895	36	32.0	Trouble in India (3).
Sep 1898	−75	−31.4	
Feb 1899	−46	−26.7	
Apr 1898	65	24.3	Debt (1).
Aug 1898	−73	−23.2	
Jan 1892	126	20.5	Speech of the king (2).
Nov 1891	90	17.5	Attacks on settlements (1).
Queensland			
Jul 1870	77	43.3	Gold and revenue increase (2).
Jan 1889	21	26.9	Mineral wealth of Queensland and South Australia.
Aug 1870	−56	−22.2	Meat freezing works in Queensland (1); change of ministry (1).
Jan 1882	19	20.5	
Jul 1873	27	18.0	Tin in Queensland (1).
Jul 1872	26	17.6	Revenue returns—increase of revenue (1).
Jan 1881	15	15.6	Fearful account of the floods in Queensland (2).
Apr 1893	17	14.0	
Jul 1874	14	13.4	Gold in Queensland (1).
Nov 1878	−17	−12.3	

Table 4.1. (*Continued*)

	Change in spread (b. points)	Change in spread (percent)	Salient news
Russia			
Apr 1877	158	55.7	Russo-Turkish war (4); suspend payment (1); commercial treaty with Spain (1); custom receipts (2); finance of Russia (1); new loan (2).
Jun 1876	74	34.4	Russo-Turkish war (4); exports of oats and cattle prohibited (1); loans (4); trade in Russia (1);
Oct 1876	67	26.6	paper money (1).
Nov 1905	39	23.8	Internal violence (57); general strike (1); political crisis (20); the Tsar's manifesto (6); peasant conference in Moscow (10).
Jan 1878	−73	−20.3	Russian victories and restoration of calm (7); budget (1); finances (3); loan (1); plentiful harvest (1).
May 1877	−89	−20.2	Warships (1); new loan (6); politics (5).
Mar 1878	57	17.5	Dutch loan and finance (4).
Apr 1875	42	16.8	Preparations for war and outbreak of war in Afghanistan (9); finance (5); import duties (1).
May 1878	−58	−15.2	Purchases of ships (10); trial jury to be abolished for political offenses (1).
May 1875	−37	−12.7	Frontier claimed by Russia in Afghanistan (1); riots against Jews (1); opening of St Petersburg sea canal (2).
Sweden			
Oct 1913	10	26.3	State Bank of Sweden rate changed (1); iron ore output (1); shipping company trade (1);
Oct 1910	14	25.9	Swedish Norwegian Australian Shipping Co. formed (1).

Apr 1913	8	21.7	Iron ore: electric smelting: process adopted (1).
Oct 1912	−7	−20.3	State Bank of Sweden: rate changed (1).
Apr 1904	10	18.8	
May 1888	13	18.5	
Jan 1889	16	17.9	
Apr 1889	15	15.4	Representation in Sweden of all public sectors (in the election to the 2nd Chamber) (1).
Oct 1902	7	15.4	
Apr 1905	11	15.3	Swedish navy—reform (1).
Uruguay			
Aug 1878	91	74.5	Economic conditions (1); tariff bill (1); redemption of paper money (1).
Jan 1891	319	41.8	Political situation (1).
Oct 1890	122	32.2	
May 1890	167	32.1	
Sep 1882	−132	−31.9	Insurrectionary movement (1); treaty of peace with Spain (1).
Mar 1887	−153	−25.9	
May 1876	325	21.7	The budget (1).
Jul 1879	−140	−21.3	
Nov 1874	120	21.2	
Jul 1887	−147	−19.7	

Note: Months shown are those with the top 10 changes in spreads (in percent, in absolute value), for each country, ranked by the change in spreads. Numbers in brackets refer to the number of news articles on the topic indicated.

Source: News reports from the *London Times*. Bond Spreads from the *Investor's Monthly Manual*.

exceptions are the British-sponsored reform in Egypt in the late 1870s, and reforms in China following the Boxer Rebellion of 1900, both of which involved political dimensions beyond the actual institutional changes.

Bad economic news figure prominently as a cause for sharp changes in the table. Sharp changes in spreads associated with bad weather are found in the resource- and agriculture-dependent economies of Brazil, Canada, and China. Fiscal and financial difficulties are also associated with sharp changes in many of the countries (e.g. Argentina, Brazil, Chile, Egypt, Hungary, Mexico, and Portugal). Labor unrest may have affected Canadian spreads in 1912.

To shed more light on the relationship between sharp changes in spreads and news coverage, we compare whether months with sharp changes had, on average, more news items than the average news coverage of that country by the *London Times*. Table 4.2 reports the results

Table 4.2. Sharp Changes in spreads and number of News Articles, 1870–1913 (Average number of news reports per month in the *London Times*)

	Instability and wars	Bad economic news	Institutions and reforms	Total
Argentina				
Months with sharp changes, 1870–1905	2.0	0.8	0.0	6.6
Months with sharp changes, 1906–13	1.0	22.0	0.0	49.0
All months, 1870–1905	0.4	0.3	0.3	3.0
All months, 1906–1913	0.3	1.1	0.5	12.4
Brazil				
Months with sharp changes, 1870–1905	0.3	0.9	0.0	3.7
Months with sharp changes, 1906–13	0.3	1.7	0.0	16.7
All months, 1870–1905	0.6	0.3	0.2	4.4
All months, 1906–13	0.3	0.5	0.0	12.1
Canada				
Months with sharp changes, 1870–1905	0.0	0.2	0.0	17.3
Months with sharp changes, 1906–13	0.0	0.8	0.3	81.3
All months, 1870–1905	0.9	0.4	0.1	13.2
All months, 1906–13	0.2	1.7	0.2	97.7
Chile				
Months with sharp changes, 1870–1905	2.0	0.1	0.0	4.3
All months, 1870–1905	0.4	0.1	0.1	2.0
China				
Months with sharp changes, 1870–1905	1.6	0.1	0.1	13.0
Months with sharp changes, 1906–13	113.5	8.5	2.0	156.5
All months, 1870–1905	2.2	0.5	0.2	10.5
All months, 1906–13	15.4	0.7	1.7	41.3

Table 4.2. (*Continued*)

	Instability and wars	Bad economic news	Institutions and reforms	Total
Egypt				
Months with sharp changes, 1870–85	16.3	4.2	0.6	46.7
All months, 1870–85	11.1	2.2	1.0	37.2
Greece				
Months with sharp changes, 1881–92; 1895–1905	4.4	1.0	0.1	15.1
Months with sharp changes, 1906–13	0.0	1.0	0.0	7.0
All months, 1881–92; 1895–1905	0.2	0.3	0.1	5.6
All months, 1906–13	1.9	0.5	0.5	24.3
Hungary				
Months with sharp changes, 1870–1905	0.2	0.7	0.0	3.8
All months, 1870–1905	0.6	0.2	0.0	1.9
Japan				
Months with sharp changes, 1870–1905	0.6	0.1	0.0	4.7
Months with sharp changes, 1906–13	0.0	0.0	0.0	12.0
All months, 1870–1905	0.5	0.2	0.1	1.2
All months, 1906–13	0.0	0.9	0.0	16.5
Mexico				
Months with sharp changes, 1870–87	1.2	0.0	0.0	2.6
Months with sharp changes, 1888–1905	0.4	0.0	0.0	1.7
Months with sharp changes, 1906–13	93.0	19.0	7.0	158.0
All months, 1870–87	0.6	0.0	0.0	1.8
All months, 1888–1905	0.2	0.0	0.0	1.1
All months, 1906–13	3.8	0.6	0.1	11.1
Portugal				
Months with sharp changes, 1888–1905	1.2	2.6	0.0	8.0
All months, 1888–1905	0.3	0.3	0.1	4.7
Queensland				
Months with sharp changes, 1870–1905	0.0	0.2	0.0	1.1
All months, 1870–1905	0.0	0.1	0.1	1.4
Russia				
Months with sharp changes, 1870–1905	8.7	0.3	0.0	34.7
All months, 1870–1905	4.7	0.7	0.2	26.3
Sweden				
Months with sharp changes, 1870–1905	0.0	0.0	0.3	1.7
Months with sharp changes, 1906–13	0.0	0.0	0.0	4.8
All months, 1870–1905	0.1	0.0	0.1	1.1
All months, 1905–13	0.1	0.6	0.2	8.7
Uruguay				
Months with sharp changes, 1870–1905, excl. 1875–7	0.1	0.2	0.0	0.8
All months, 1870–1905, excl. 1875–7	0.3	0.1	0.0	1.1

Note: Pre- and post-1906 are separate because of the change in Palmer's Index. Other subsamples are chosen to treat default periods separately. Periods without sharp changes are omitted.

both for total news and for the salient categories, namely wars and instability, bad economic news, and reforms.[4] For most of the countries studied, we find a larger frequency of news items reported in times of sharp changes than otherwise (the exceptions are Canada, Queensland, and China).

In sum, readers of the *London Times* were well informed about major events in emerging market countries, and reacted to them. Indeed, most of the sharp changes in the 1870–1913 can be attributed to country-specific events, suggesting that "contagion" was rare during the previous era of financial globalization. As we show below, this stands in sharp contrast with the 1990s, when crises often affected several emerging markets at the same time.

An alternative approach to the identification of sharp changes is a search for "structural breaks" in the spread series. The methodology of the search for structural breaks, which we apply in order to identify sharp and long-lasting changes in time series, is based on Perron (1989), and is discussed in detail in Sussman and Yafeh (2000).[5]

Applying this procedure to the historical sample, and in line with the previous results on the determinants of sharp changes, we find no break in the cost of capital of any country that is the result of institutional reforms, or improved protection of property rights. By contrast, most of the historical breaks (listed in Mauro, Sussman, and Yafeh, 2002) correspond to country-specific events that are directly related to a country's ability to repay its external debt. Beginnings or ends of wars and rebellions feature prominently. For example, domestic revolts are associated with breaks in the Argentine and Brazilian spread series; wars in the Balkans generate breaks in the spreads of

---

[4] Because of the change in Palmer's Index to the *London Times* in 1906, we make the comparison separately for the years up to 1905 and from 1906 onward.

[5] Essentially, this is a statistical technique designed to find the most significant long-lasting "jump" or change in a time series. It is based on the following equation: $\log(Y_t) = \beta_0 + \beta_1 \log(Y_{t-1}) + \beta_2 \Delta \log(Y_{t-1}) + \beta_3 EVENT_t$, where Y_t represents the variable of interest (e.g. the spread on a country's bonds); *EVENT* is a dummy variable that takes the value zero at all times prior to the proposed break and the value one from the time of the break onwards. Assuming the series is not unit root, if an event had a long-term impact on yields, then the coefficient on the *EVENT* dummy variable will be different from zero. The search for breaks involves repeated estimation of this equation while moving the break date and the corresponding *EVENT* dummy variable one observation at a time and recording their statistical significance. The break date is the point where the statistical significance of the *EVENT* dummy is highest (the process can then be repeated within each half of the sample to detect additional break points in subperiods). It is also possible to use a variant of this methodology to capture short-term "blips," that is, events that affect the series for a limited time only.

countries involved in them, and political instability in Egypt causes a break in the late 1870s. Some breaks are related to (bad) economic news: for example, a banking crisis in Australia in 1891 affected Queensland's spreads. In several cases, changes in monetary regime were also associated with breaks in the spread series. For example, a break in the spread series was observed in Portugal at the time when that country abandoned the gold standard.

4.3 Historical Sample—From Major News to Spread Changes

To analyze the potential impact of news on spreads, we list, for each country in our sample, major events as reported by the *Investor's Monthly Manual* (*IMM*) and the corresponding dates.[6] Ideally, we would have preferred to select major news events using *London Times* articles, but there was no practical and objective criterion for doing so.

For the pooled sample of all emerging market countries, we find that country/months with events reported in the *IMM* are associated with spread changes that are twice as large as in other country/ months, and the difference is statistically significant. This result is robust to dropping any one of the countries from the sample. The difference is significant at the 5 percent level (using at least one definition of spread changes, and with the expected sign) for five out of twelve countries in the sample, and the countries where it is not significant tend to be those with the smallest number of news items. Table 4.3 reports (for the period when the country in question is not experiencing payment difficulties) the results for the eight countries where there are at least fifteen events.[7]

---

[6] For the purposes of this exercise, we exclude the following countries from our sample: Egypt, because of its status as a near-British colony for a large share of the sample period; Hungary, to avoid difficult choices on whether events affecting Austria should be considered relevant; Russia and Turkey, because both countries were involved in border conflicts that were reported in the news but did not have a bearing on repayment prospects; and Queensland, to avoid difficult choices on whether one should consider news related to other parts of Australia. Moreover, collecting events data on Russia and Turkey would have been a daunting task in light of the vast number of peripheral incidents and border skirmishes they were involved in at the time.

[7] Only four countries in the sample experienced payment difficulties under the somewhat restrictive *IMM* definition: Colombia, Greece, Mexico, and Uruguay. For each of these countries, we exclude the years when the country experienced payment difficulties. This does not make a substantive difference to the results, except in Greece where the significance of the relationship becomes visibly stronger.

Table 4.3. IMM News and Sharp Changes in Spreads by Country, 1870–1913

		Observations	Avg. |Δ Spread|	Avg. |% Δ Spread|
All countries	Months with events	232	0.0038	10.1395
	All other	5326	0.0019	6.5543
			(0.0000)*	(0.0000)*
Argentina	Months with events	44	0.0056	10.3694
	All other	483	0.0032	6.7533
			(0.0167)*	(0.0023)*
Brazil	Months with events	24	0.0028	8.4272
	All other	503	0.0013	5.3991
			(0.0000)*	(0.003)*
Canada	Months with events	18	0.0011	8.3600
	All other	509	0.0009	9.4452
			(0.6971)	(0.7735)
Chile	Months with events	25	0.0027	9.1572
	All other	502	0.0014	5.2648
			(0.0020)*	(0.0025)*
China	Months with events	29	0.0043	15.5789
	All other	410	0.0030	13.1497
			(0.0603)	(0.5434)
Greece	Months with events	35	0.0056	11.0273
	All other	350	0.0027	4.5063
			(0.0550)	(0.0000)*
Japan	Months with events	16	0.0026	11.4043
	All other	501	0.0020	7.9577
			(0.2953)	(0.2507)
Portugal	Months with events	17	0.0030	10.3100
	All other	510	0.0014	5.7657
			(0.0367)*	(0.013)*

Note: Non-debt related news. *p*-values reported in parentheses refer to the null hypothesis that the average change in spreads for country/months with events of type mentioned is the same as for country/months with no events. Asterisks denote significance at the 5% level.

In interpreting the results, it is of course necessary to bear in mind that *IMM* news are selected with the benefit of hindsight as those that "affect the money markets." On a more positive note, however, the mere fact that a well-established publication such as the *IMM* would publish a detailed exercise of this kind twice a year suggests that market participants then, as now, thought that a relationship between asset prices and events did indeed hold.

In view of the *ex post* way in which the events were selected by the *IMM*, our main interest is to ask which types of events are associated

Table 4.4. IMM News by Category and Sharp Changes in Spreads 1870–1913, pooling all country/months

Type of events	Number of events	Average |Δ Spread|	Average |% Δ Spread|
All types	232	0.0038 (0.0000)*	10.1395 (0.0000)*
Good economic	21	0.0025 (0.5369)	5.6485 (0.7136)
Bad economic	42	0.0050 (0.0000)*	11.6508 (0.0037)*
Political	35	0.0036 (0.0276)*	8.5251 (0.3038)
Reforms	13	0.0035 (0.2067)	8.4119 (0.5537)
Instability and wars	86	0.0037 (0.0005)*	10.2337 (0.0028)*
Foreign relations	51	0.0037 (0.0074)*	12.1791 (0.0004)*
Debt-related	128	0.0032 (0.0027)*	7.6018 (0.3655)
No events	5326	0.0019	6.5543

Note: Non-debt related news. *p*-values reported in parentheses refer to the null hypothesis that the average change in spreads for country/months with events of type mentioned is the same as for country/months with no events. There are 5,326 country/months with no events. Asterisks denote significance at the 5% level.

with a higher average change in spreads (Table 4.4). Country/ months with "bad economic news" and news about "instability and wars" and "foreign relations" are significantly associated with larger spread changes than other country/months, using both definitions of spread changes. Country/months with "political" news and, not surprisingly, "debt-related" news are also significantly associated with larger spread changes, though only under one definition of spread changes. Finally, neither "good/neutral" economic news nor "reform" news are significantly related to spread changes.

4.4 Modern Sample—From Large Spread Changes to News

As in the historical sample, we begin by identifying the months with the ten largest spread changes (in absolute value) for each country, and show in Table 4.5 whether major news were reported in those

Table 4.5. Sharp Changes in Spreads, 1994-2002, and News Reports

	Change in spread (b. points)	Change in spread (percent)	Salient news
Argentina			
Nov 2001	1210	56.0	Negative economic news items (11) about failing debt restructuring attempts (9) and dealings with IMF (2); political bad news (1).
Jun 2002	1095	18.5	Riots (3); Central Bank President resigns (1).
Dec 2001	1000	29.7	Riots/strikes (7); President/cabinet changes (5); controls (3); talk of debt default (7).
May 2002	975	19.5	More negotiations with IMF to take place (4).
Aug 1998	824	181.5	No news (Russian crisis).
Mar 2002	18		Negotiations with IMF stalling (6); foreign exchange controls tightened (1).
Aug 2002	−578	−8.2	O'Neill's visit initially lifts hopes (1) but then fails to secure IMF agreement (1).
Jul 2001	549	52.3	Spending cuts (3); protest/strikes (2); Washington signals no extra cash (1).
Oct 2001	547	33.9	Debt swap to take place (2); US loses confidence in Argentina's creditworthiness (4); neutral political news (2).
Feb 1995	397	33.6	May sign accord with IMF (2).
Brazil			
Aug 1998	813	133.7	Labor reform (1); relaxation of short-term capital controls (1). (Time of Russian crisis.)
Jul 2002	793	51.2	IMF negotiations not going well (2); US seeks to soothe Brazil after remarks by O'Neill (2).
Sep 2002	765	46.9	Elections: Serra stages comeback; Lula rides on wave of disillusion over reforms (6).
Aug 2002	−711	−30.4	Back from the brink on prospects of IMF deal (4); doubt about IMF deal (1); O'Neill heals rift with Brazil (1); Bank of Brazil to aid troubled companies.
Oct 2002	−653	−27.3	Lula decries market fears of default (1); Lula pulls ahead, poised to win, transition team planned, victory (9).
Jun 2002	567	57.8	Taking over liabilities of pension funds (2); IMF line of credit (2); relaxing inflation targets (2).
Mar 1994	471	90.1	Debt restructuring (5); plans for real currency (1); cut in import duties (1); IMF slow to act on Brazil loan (1).
Mar 1999	−335	−24.3	Real stability plan (2); IMF deal reached (3); $4 billion in aid for Brazilian companies (2); Cardoso wins tax boost from Congress, budgetary discipline.
Oct 1997	319	89.6	Coffee bumper crop (2).
Jan 1999	276	22.4	Brazil blocks payments as states default (2); IMF negotiations (2); floating of the real (4); Cardoso pledges to keep inflation down (2).

Bulgaria			
Aug 1998	153.6	1000	Approves budget (1); becomes hub for Russian gas transit (2). (Russian crisis.)
Sep 1998	−31.1	−513	No news.
Apr 1995	−17.9	−385	No news.
Feb 1997	−26.2	−339	Bulgaria "steps back from abyss": socialists give way (3); petrol increased (1); IMF talks (1).
Oct 1997	68.0	315	Agreement with Russia on gas deal (1).
Feb 1996	23.7	265	No news.
Oct 1998	−23.1	−263	No news.
Jan 1995	15.0	254	No news.
Nov 1996	−15.4	−234	Reformist leads in polls (3); cash run on Bulgaria bank (1).
Jan 1996	−16.9	−228	No news.
Mexico			
Aug 1998	104.1	480	Political poll results (2). (Russian crisis.)
Dec 1994	106.4	434	Peso devaluation (5); Chiapas rebellion (2); Mexico seeks to shape international support package (1).
Apr 1995	−24.3	−386	Rescue plan for Mexican banks (1); provincial government debts (1); financial aid to Mexico to continue (1).
Feb 1995	37.7	376	Rebellion (2); financial aid package (8); Mexico's ruling party in trouble (1).
Jun 1995	−20.6	−247	Riots and assassination (2); loans to Mexico (3).
Oct 1995	22.2	226	High-level defection from Mexico's ruling party (2).
Mar 1995	15.7	216	Peso slide (1); tough economic package (2); protests (1); rescue plan for Mexican banks (1).
Jan 1996	−17.3	−174	Mexico to bail out indebted companies (2).
Oct 1997	59.7	172	Zedillo faces the budget blues (1).
Apr 1996	−20.2	−164	Reforms to foreign ownership rules threatens privatization process (1); pension reform (1).

Table 4.5. (*Continued*)

	Change in spread (b. points)	Change in spread (percent)	Salient news
Nigeria			
Aug 1998	1628	186.1	Attempts to curb corruption (1); prospects for civilian rule to last (1).
Oct 2002	-1261	-32.1	US plan for regional military base (1); court ruling on Nigeria–Cameroon dispute (2).
Jul 2002	1106	67.2	US pushes for fair poll (1); World Bank cuts lending to Nigeria (1).
May 2000	998	46.1	Attacks on foreign executives (1); clashes (1); budget approved (1).
Jul 2000	-945	-33.7	Doubts about President's ability to reach deal with IMF (1).
Sep 2002	846	27.4	Attempts to curb corruption (1); effort to register voters (2); political battle intensifies (1).
Nov 2002	-814	-30.5	US warns Nigeria on dirty money (2); riots (2); fears grow over Nigeria's poll security (1).
Oct 1998	-786	-34.3	Pipeline disaster with hundreds dead (1).
Jul 1994	785	43.3	Oil workers' stride (3); protests (1).
Mar 1994	715	61.4	Currency shortage (2); clash with Cameroon on oil-rich area (1); big cocoa crop (1).
Philippines			
Aug 1998	423	93.4	Severe fiscal crunch in context of economic crisis (1) (Russian crisis.)
Oct 1998	-247	-24.7	No news.
Nov 1998	-246	-32.6	No news.
Feb 1994	155	39.4	No news.
Jan 1996	-151	-23.3	No news.
Oct 2000	131	24.0	Hostages/rebels (3); motion to impeach President (3).
Sep 1998	125	14.3	Philippine Airlines look likely to close (5).
May 1994	-124	-18.7	Opening up to foreign banks (1); securities scandal (1).
Nov 2001	-188	-17.4	No news.
Oct 1997	115	34.4	No news.

Poland			
Aug 1998	226	120.2	Plan for large privatization (1). (Russian crisis.)
Jan 1996	−207	−38.8	Political crisis (3); spying row (1).
Apr 1995	−175	−20.2	Poland presses case for EU entry (1).
Jun 1995	−130	−20.0	No news.
Oct 1997	94	56.3	Poland lines up finance minister, unveils cabinet (2).
Jan 1995	92	14.3	Early election, budget veto (1); Poland, Russia write off debt (1).
Feb 1995	83	11.3	Doubt over reforms (1); Prime Ministerial uncertainty, political changes (5); Polish changes (5); Polish-Russian pipeline deal (1).
Oct 2002	−75	−24.8	No news.
Oct 1998	−65	−18.3	No news.
Sep 1998	−59	−14.3	Coal sector restructuring (1).
Venezuela			
Aug 1998	1746	210.6	No news. (Russian crisis.)
Sep 1998	−1017	−39.5	Backing for reforms (1); US and Venezuela close to tax treaty (1).
Aug 1994	−514	−24.4	Good economic policy news (1).
Jun 1994	498	41.1	Right of economic freedom restored (1); bank bailout payments raise fears (1); controls imposed (1).
Dec 1995	−465	−23.4	Opposition advances (1); overvalued exchange rate complicates policy (1).
Mar 1994	458	45.1	No news.
Jul 1994	396	23.1	Uncertainties on economic policy (2).
Apr 1999	−332	−29.6	Political uncertainty, possible state of emergency (3); Chavez pledges to abide by constitution (1).
Dec 1998	−329	−20.4	Elections, Chavez win (7).
Feb 1994	318	45.6	Bank bailouts (3).

Note: Months shown are those with the top 10 changes in spreads (in percent, in absolute value), for each country, ranked by the change in spreads. Numbers in brackets refer to the number of news articles on the topic indicated.

Source: News reports from the *Financial Times*. EMBI bond spreads from J. P. Morgan.

months in the *Financial Times (FT)*. For most countries in the sample, the biggest change in spreads takes place in August 1998, at the time of the Russian Long-Term Capital Management (LTCM) crisis—an event unrelated to events occurring in the other countries considered in the sample. We present the tables with the results using spread changes in terms of basis points. The results are similar using spread changes in percent. We also ask whether the frequency of front-page news is the same for months with large spread changes and all other months (these results are summarized in the text but not reported in tables, for the sake of brevity).

There are only two countries (Argentina and Brazil) where the frequency of news is noticeably higher in months with the largest spread changes than in the remainder of the sample period. The same is true for the frequency of *front-page* news. Both statements hold regardless of whether the months with "sharp changes" are defined in terms of changes in basis points or percentage changes in spreads. (In Bulgaria, a country with relatively few news reported in the *FT*, defining sharp changes on the basis of changes in basis points leads to an especially high frequency of news in February 1997—a month associated with a large change in spreads.)[8]

For Argentina, the largest changes are associated with bad economic news during the crisis of November–December 2001 and news about the ensuing riots in December 2001. For Brazil, the largest changes seem to be associated with news regarding the likelihood of presidential election victory on the part of Mr Luiz Inácio Lula da Silva (commonly known as Lula) during the course of 2002. Interestingly, in the early stages of the campaign, an increasing likelihood of a victory by Lula was interpreted as negative news by foreign investors, leading to sharp increases in spreads; in contrast, nearer election day, markets seemed to interpret an ever-increasing probability of a Lula victory as good news for Brazil's willingness and ability to meet its external obligations. For the other countries in the sample, however, there is no clear pattern between news and spreads, and the results for the cases of Argentina and Brazil are very much driven by the specific sets of episodes highlighted above.

---

[8] Bulgaria experienced a severe economic and political crisis in late 1996 and early 1997. In February 1997, early elections were won by a reformist government. In 1997, Bulgaria undertook a program supported by the international financial institutions, including the introduction of a currency board in July of that year.

Could it be the case that we fail to identify a strong relationship between news and changes in spreads because the news during this period are just not sufficiently important to move the markets? Our impression is that this is unlikely. Although none of the countries in our sample experienced a major war during the modern period we consider, many important events did take place, including coups, assassinations of leading political figures, violent uprisings, suspensions of existing constitutions, the adoption of new constitutions, major changes in the party in power, changes in the domestic currency, and the establishment of common trade areas. A necessarily incomplete list of major events that failed to be reflected in large spread changes includes the following examples. In Nigeria, the sudden death of General Abacha (June 1998) and the subsequent return to democracy following years of dictatorship. In Mexico, the election of President Fox (June 2000) following 70 years of PRI government. In the Philippines, the impeachment of President Estrada (November/December 2000), the transition to the government of President Macapagal (January 2001), and the peaceful passage of elections in May 2001 following a period of domestic tensions. In Poland, ratification by voters of entry into NATO (March 1999); and public backing (February 1998) by French President Chirac and German President Kohl of Poland's bid to join the European Union. In Argentina, consideration of plans to adopt the US dollar (announced by President Menem in January 1999 and later dropped). On the whole, these can hardly be described as uneventful times.

4.5 Modern Sample—From Major News to Changes in Spreads

In the modern sample, we identify forty-five country/months with news items related to the emerging market countries in our sample that appear in a long article on the front page of the *FT*. These instances of "really big" news seem to have had a significant impact on spreads: country/months with front-page news and a long article display significantly larger changes in spreads than other country/months (Table 4.6). (With eight countries and 108 months, there are 864 country/months in the sample—reduced to 836 owing to missing observations in the spread series for some countries.) On average, the absolute value of the change in spreads amounted to 199 basis points

Table 4.6. Front-Page News and Spread Changes, 1994–2002

Country		Observations	Average |Δ Spread|	Average |% Δ Spread|
All countries	All front page and long article	45	199.422	17.207
	No front page and long article	791	111.858	12.885
			(0.002)*	(0.122)
All countries	All front page	310	135.571	13.214
	No front page	526	105.375	13.061
			(0.022)*	(0.907)
Argentina	Months with front page news	43	237.047	14.226
	All other	64	107.313	16.029
			(0.004)*	(0.676)
Brazil	Months with front page news	50	168.260	16.370
	All other	57	93.684	13.396
			(0.019)*	(0.27)
Bulgaria	Months with front page news	10	172.400	22.763
	All other	87	91.736	10.571
			(0.057)	(0.031)*
Mexico	Months with front page news	57	75.123	13.919
	All other	50	70.560	13.066
			(0.786)	(0.783)
Nigeria	Months with front page news	47	225.340	13.066
	All other	60	246.617	16.666
			(0.708)	(0.481)
Poland	Months with front page news	34	25.206	10.110
	All other	63	32.857	11.178
			(0.348)	(0.720)
Philippines	Months with front page news	34	33.882	6.567
	All other	73	53.904	10.541
			(0.105)	(0.093)
Venezuela	Months with front page news	35	137.571	12.437
	All other	72	151.500	15.153
			(0.749)	(0.553)

Note: p-values reported in parentheses refer to the null hypothesis that the average change in spreads for country/months with events of type mentioned is the same as for country/months with no front-page events. Asterisks denote significance at the 5 % level.

in country/months with front-page news and long articles, and 112 basis points in the remaining country/months. Defining spread changes in percent terms, the absolute value of the change in spreads amounted to 17.2 percent in country/months with front-page news and long articles, and 12.9 percent in the remaining country/months. The p-value of the null hypothesis that changes in spreads are the same regardless of whether they occur in country/months with front page and long article news, or in other months, is 0.002 for spread changes in basis points and 0.122 for spread changes in percent. (This finding is robust to excluding Argentina—a country that has a large influence on the results of other exercises reported below.)

Using a less stringent concept of major news, namely, the 310 country/ months with front-page news (including those in brief summary form, in the so-called briefing or shorts section of the *Financial Times (FT)*, but not necessarily a long article), the significance of the results is somewhat diminished and no longer robust to small changes in the sample of countries. Months with front-page news see significantly larger changes in spreads than other months, though only when spread changes are measured in basis points (See Table 4.7). Moreover, the results for the overall sample are driven, to a large extent, by Argentina: excluding Argentina, country/months with front-page news are no longer significantly associated with larger spread changes.

Drawing on the 310 country/months with front-page news, it is possible to analyze the potential relationship between news and spread changes for each country individually. Defining spread changes in terms of basis points, the association between news and spread changes is significant at the 5 percent level for Argentina and Brazil, and at the 10 percent level for Bulgaria (though only 10 months had news for this country) and the Philippines; it is not significant in Mexico, Nigeria, Poland, and Venezuela.

Are certain types of news more likely to be associated with large spread changes? Considering the 310 country/months with front-page news for the emerging markets in the sample, bad economic news, good/neutral economic news, and "instability and war" news are all significantly associated with larger spread changes, whereas political news, foreign relation news, and "reform and institutional" news are not (though the p-value is 0.076 for "reform and institutional" news). Again, these relationships are only significant when spread changes are measured in basis points. Excluding Argentina, only good/neutral economic news are significantly associated with larger spread changes.

Before concluding this section, we repeat the search for structural breaks procedure for the sample of emerging markets in the 1990s. For eight emerging markets during 1994–2000, there is only one major break—in August 1998, at the time of the Russian crisis—affecting all countries. Using this procedure, the Mexican crisis of late 1994 also had a discernible impact on Mexico and Venezuela. Although there

Table 4.7. Front Page News by Category and Spread Changes, 1994–2002, pooling all country/months

Type of events	Observations	Avg. |Δ Spread|	Avg. |Δ % Spread|
All Front Page	310	135.571	13.214
No Front Page	526	105.375	13.061
		(0.022)*	(0.907)
Good	128	144.531	14.461
		(0.027)*	(0.467)
Bad	134	156.246	13.657
		(0.004)*	(0.737)
Neutral/unsure	132	134.871	12.991
		(0.083)	(0.968)
Good/neutral economic	121	164.901	15.153
		(0.001)*	(0.278)
Bad economic	70	200.171	15.068
		(0.000)*	(0.41)
Political	104	115.769	11.201
		(0.572)	(0.337)
Foreign relations	76	100.395	15.220
		(0.809)	(0.361)
Reforms	57	149.561	12.811
		(0.076)	(0.926)
Instability and wars	58	170.828	11.264
		(0.01)*	(0.486)

Note: p-values reported in parentheses refer to the null hypothesis that the average change in spreads for country/months with events of type mentioned is the same as for country/months with no front page events. There are 526 country/months with no front page events. Asterisks denote significance at the 5% level.

are a number of cases of suspension of existing constitutions, the adoption of new constitutions, major changes in the party in power, changes in the domestic currency, and the establishment of common trade areas during the period, none elicited an immediate response from financial markets. The only exception is the Bulgarian currency board of 1997.

The exercises on news and spread changes reported in this chapter suggest that the relationship between news and spread changes was stronger in the historical period than it is in the modern period. Of course one needs to be cautious in interpreting this result, because there are far more data points in the historical sample than in the modern sample, and the news to spreads exercise for the historical sample is based upon events that were selected with the benefit of hindsight. Beyond this technical explanation, there may well be a fundamental reason behind this result—in the modern sample country-specific news about emerging markets did not seem to matter much to investors, who treated these countries as a group. This feature may be closely related to the high co-movement between emerging market bond spreads in the 1990s, as well as to the contagious spreads of crises, in sharp contrast with the historical sample. We discuss this issue in more detail in Chapter 6 (see also Mauro, Sussman, and Yafeh, 2002).

Despite the differences in the impact of news on spreads in the two periods, an important conclusion that emerges from the analysis in this chapter is that the kinds of news that seem to be more closely associated with large spread changes are consistent in the historical and modern samples. "Instability and war" news seem to matter the most, together with economic news. The results are therefore consistent with one of the main themes of this book, namely those events associated with blood flowing in the streets tend to explain a greater share of variation in spreads, at least in the short run, than do events associated with reforms of political or economic institutions. In the next chapter, we continue the analysis of these issues using multivariate regressions, which take into account, in addition to news reports, macroeconomic and other country-specific characteristics.

5

Spreads, News, and Macroeconomics: A Multivariate Regression Analysis

5.1 Introduction

While previous chapters focused on a few case studies (Chapter 3) or sharp changes in spreads (Chapter 4), in this chapter we systematically consider all variation in spreads for our entire sample of emerging markets, in an attempt to identify the determinants of bond spreads more generally. Using multivariate regression analysis, we simultaneously relate emerging market bond spreads to macroeconomic variables and the number of news items regarding various types of events. This allows us to measure the extent to which fundamentals—including both macroeconomic variables and the information available to investors from news on political, economic, and institutional events—explain variation in spreads on bonds issued by emerging markets, for 1870–1913 and the modern period.

Existing studies suggest that, as for other asset prices, it has not been easy to relate bond spreads to fundamentals. Studies on modern period data usually find that macroeconomic fundamentals explain, if anything, a small portion of the variation in spreads.[1] Moreover, different studies identify different variables as relevant. Indeed, the only variable that seems to be consistently significant across several empirical studies is a country's credit rating. Rating agencies, however, are likely to pay close attention not only to macroeconomic variables and other fundamentals, but also to spreads and market participant

[1] Examples include: Cline and Barnes (1997); Dell'Ariccia, Schnabel, and Zettelmeyer (2002); Eichengreen and Mody (1998); Kamin and von Kleist (1999); Min (1998); Sy (2002); and International Monetary Fund (2004, pp. 60–70).

views in providing ratings; thus, we do not use credit ratings in our estimates below.

This is not to say that fundamentals do not matter or have no predictive value. On the contrary, some private analysts (notably in investment banks) provide model-based views to their clients on whether countries' current market spreads are justified by fundamentals. All in all, however, the predictive power of existing models seems to be rather limited.

A few recent studies have analyzed the determinants of spreads for the historical period. Bordo and Rockoff (1996) found that adherence to gold standard rules acted as a "seal of approval" that was reflected in significantly lower spreads on sovereign bonds; in contrast, the role of fiscal policy and monetary policy indicators was significant in only few of Bordo and Rockoff's specifications. Obstfeld and Taylor (2003a, 2003b) confirm the importance of gold standard adherence for the period 1870–1913, but argue that public debt and membership in the British Empire were significantly related with spreads in 1925–31 (though not before the First World War). Ferguson and Schularik (2004, 2005) challenge the empirical validity of the gold standard as a determinant of spreads and instead highlight the importance of the British Empire as a determinant of spreads. Flandreau and Zumer (2004) find a significant association between bond spreads and macroeconomic variables (emphasizing especially the roles of the ratio of interest payments to revenues, and economic growth).[2]

The analysis in the present chapter is the first to provide a systematic comparison of the determinants of spreads in the 1870–1913 period and today, using the same methodology for both sample periods. Moreover, this is the first study of the determinants of emerging market bond spreads to incorporate systematic summary measures of events reflected in news, and to assess the importance of various categories of news.

Our main finding is that fundamentals matter in determining bond spreads in the historical sample. Both the country's political and economic climate as reflected in quantitative summaries of news items, and macroeconomic variables, such as exports and the fiscal balance, play a significant role. In contrast, country-specific fundamentals seem to matter to a lesser extent in the modern sample. At the same

---

[2] We do not consider interest payments as a determinant of interest rates, because of concerns about the direction of the causal relationship; such concerns would remain even using lagged values, owing to the autocorrelation of interest rates.

time, the same broad patterns regarding the types of variables that matter remain valid in both the historical and the modern sample. In particular, low spreads are associated with sound macroeconomic policies and absence of violence.

5.2 Data and Methodological Issues

In choosing the historical variables and data to be used in the analysis, we strive to stay as close as possible to the data that were available to investors active on the London market. We draw our news indicators from the *London Times* and many of our macroeconomic data from the *Investor's Monthly Manual*. As potential explanatory variables, we focus on the variables that were reported regularly and seemed to feature prominently in analyses published in the contemporary financial press. For example, we do not use data on gross domestic product (GDP), a concept not used at the time.[3] We collect all of our spread series directly from the *Investor's Monthly Manual*, correcting them on the basis of bond features as published in the same source. To ensure the quality of the spreads data, we exclude all observations where the *Investor's Monthly Manual* notes that the country is not paying coupons (see also Chapter 2).[4]

Given that one of our main findings is that news items, and especially war news, are associated with higher spreads, the reader might wonder whether our approach, based on the number of news, provides substantial value addition compared with an alternative approach that might be based upon simply noting when important wars were taking place. More generally, does the number of news really present major advantages compared with dummy variables that might be chosen to represent important events? In our opinion, an approach based upon the number of contemporary news reports has three related advantages. First, it leaves far less room for the researchers' judgment in influencing the results: although we do exercise a minimal degree of judgment in allocating news among the various categories,

---

[3] The quality of the GDP data constructed by modern scholars for the historical period might also be a source of concern.

[4] In addition, we exclude eight observations where the yield is above 10 percent (implausibly high given the standards of the time, and likely to reflect measurement errors). Our results are essentially unchanged if we include all such observations in the estimates.

we include all news reports related to a given country, and therefore have essentially no discretion in choosing which news items to include in our analysis. We would have far more discretion if we were to select events from history books or other sources (in that case, we would have to choose what constitutes an event with no objective criterion to guide us). Second, history books have the benefit of hindsight in highlighting major events. Thus, if we were to use dummies for "major wars," for example, drawing them from history books, we would be picking our events on the basis of more information than was available to contemporary investors at the time. Third, the number of news items is a reasonable proxy for the perceived degree of importance at the time. Minor wars were probably reflected in fewer news items than were major wars, as viewed by contemporaries.

Our regression estimation approach does not introduce technical innovations, as most of the techniques that we use have been adopted by at least one previous study on related topics. Nevertheless, as existing studies have used a variety of approaches, it is worth highlighting a number of features of the approach we take, as follows:

• We use secondary market spreads, rather than primary market spreads. An advantage of this approach is that secondary market spreads are available at all times, not just at times when bonds are being issued.

• We include country-specific dummies (fixed effects) in most of our estimates, though we also present estimates without such dummies, mainly for the sake of data description. Country dummies are necessary to take into account that both spread levels and many, possibly unobservable, country-specific characteristics tend to persist in time. Failure to include such dummies would be equivalent (informally speaking) to overestimating the number of observations that can be truly claimed to be independent.

Our main approach is to run panel regressions with the logarithm of spreads (expressed in basis points) as the dependent variable, and several independent variables, as follows.

News

Our "raw data" consist of the number of news of various categories for each country and each year. (Monthly data are here aggregated to yearly data to be consistent with the macroeconomic data). These data range from zero, very frequently, to—in a few rare cases—hundreds or even thousands of news items per country per year. To use these data in regression analysis, we adopt either of two transformations of the data. The first is the logarithm of one plus the number of news in each of the following categories: "good economic," "bad economic," "political," "reform," "war/violence," and "foreign relations." The second is the share of news in each of the categories listed above in total news for the country and the year in question.[5] (A final category, "other," or "none of the above," is omitted from the regressions, and therefore all estimated coefficients need to be interpreted with respect to it.) A disadvantage of the first approach is that it does not allow for an easy assessment of the importance of news of a given category as a share of total news. Moreover, Palmer's Index to the *London Times*, from which we draw our news, changed format and became far more detailed beginning with the news for 1906. This resulted in approximately a trebling of news items reported from 1906 onward.[6] To correct for this change, we divide by three the number of news for each country, category, and year, beginning in 1906. A disadvantage of the second approach is that instances in which a given country's news items are few but all refer to the same category take an even greater value than do instances in which news items are plentiful but do not all refer to the same category. Thus, for example, a minor incident of violence that generated a handful of news items in otherwise uneventful times may take a greater value than a major war in a country where news is usually plentiful.

Macroeconomic Variables and Other Controls

Exports: the logarithm of exports expressed in common currency (pounds sterling)—an indicator of economic performance, availability of foreign currency, and ability to repay the foreign debt.

Fiscal surplus: the difference between fiscal revenues and expenditures, divided by revenues, as an indicator of fiscal performance.

---

[5] For the few country/years with no news reports, we set all fractions to be zero. This is preferable to treating these cases as missing values, and is equivalent to adding one news item to the category "other news" when the total number of news would otherwise be zero.

[6] More precisely, the average number of news for all countries and all news categories in 1906–8 is 2.96 times the average number of items for all countries and all categories in 1903–5. (The increase does not seem to affect particular countries or categories more than proportionately.) This approximate "splicing" procedure assumes that the years 1903–5 were as "eventful" as 1906–8.

(We use revenues as a "scaling" variable—today we would use GDP instead.)

Debt per capita: as an indicator of debt sustainability. The *IMM* often provides data on debt in this form, and contemporary commentary often refers to debt per capita. We find this preferable to the debt/GDP ratio because GDP is a modern concept that was not used at the time, and the GDP series that have been constructed for the historical period may not be sufficiently reliable. We also prefer this indicator to the ratios of debt to exports or debt to revenues because, compared with data on population, data on exports or revenues have more missing observations and seem less reliable. We only use this variable in a limited number of specifications, because debt levels are likely to be endogenous to interest rate spreads.

Gold standard: dummy variable taking the value of 1 when countries were on the gold standard in a given year and 0 otherwise.

Default history: dummy variable taking the value of 0 when a country has never defaulted, and 1 in the year of default and all subsequent years.

Market-capitalization-weighted average of the spreads for all emerging markets: to control for developments that affected all emerging markets simultaneously. This is especially useful to capture the decline in spreads experienced by most emerging markets in the early twentieth century (see discussion in Chapter 2).

5.3 Results for the Historical Sample

Overall, the results in this section indicate that several macroeconomic variables and news-related indicators are significantly associated with spread levels with the expected signs, though for some variables the results are not robust to changes in sample and specification.

We begin with descriptive statistics and simple cross-sectional exercises. We report the 1870–1913 average of the spreads and all the potential explanatory variables for each emerging market individually and for the subgroups of countries that ever defaulted at some point in 1800–1913, and those that never did.[7] Few variables differ systematically

---

[7] We include Russia in the list of countries that defaulted, in light of its default in 1839 and imposition of a coupon tax in 1885 (Beim and Calomiris, 2001). The results are unaffected if we include Russia among the non-defaulters.

across the two subgroups, reflecting several instances where individual countries really stand out as having particularly high values of some of the variables (debt per capita in Queensland, for example), and such countries fall in both subsamples. These patterns suggest that the pure cross-sectional information in the data may not lead to strikingly significant results; moreover, the results are likely to be subject to "influential observations," that is, the results may change substantially if a particular country is removed from the sample. In what we present in the tables below, we check to the best of our ability that our main results are not substantially affected by such changes in the sample.

We now turn to regression analysis. To focus on the news data, which constitute one of the main contributions of this book, we provide the results of regressions using news indicators only (Table 5.2). This also allows us to explore the relationship between news and spreads for a larger sample of countries, because for some of the countries in our sample macroeconomic variables are not available (and were not available to investors at the time).

As a preliminary descriptive exercise, and to provide a sense of the results including not only the time series information, but also the cross-sectional information in the data, we report the results of pooled regressions without individual country fixed effects. The regressions include quantitative indicators of news and, in some specifications, the average (market-capitalization-weighted) spread for all emerging markets of a given type (using either logarithms or shares) of news. More precisely, in some regressions we use the logarithm of the number of news of each type (our preferred specification); in other regressions, we use the share of news of a given type in total news (i.e. for example, the share of war news in total news).

Recalling that our dependent variable is the logarithm of the spread, the size of the coefficients on quantitative indicators of news needs to be interpreted as follows. When using the logarithm of the number of news, the size of the coefficient is the estimated elasticity with respect to the number of news, that is, the percent increase in spreads resulting from a 1 percent increase in the number of news of a given category. When using fractions, the size of the coefficient indicates the percent increase in spreads resulting from a 1 percentage point increase in the share of news of a given category. The omitted category is "other" news (those that were not classified in any of the categories listed in the estimation), and the coefficients are to be interpreted with respect to that omitted category.

Table 5.1. Averages of Spreads and Potential Explanatory Variables, 1870–1913

Country	Spread (percentage points)	News Items per year							Govt. Balance	Exports (mill. Pounds)	Debt per capita (pounds)	Fractions (in percent of total news)					
		Wars	Econ. Good	Econ. Bad	Foreign	Reform	Political	Total				Wars	Econ. Good	Econ. Bad	Foreign	Reform	Political
Never defaulted																	
Sweden	1.0	1	5	1	8	1	4	29	-0.01	18.43	3.38	2.7	17.2	2.0	15.8	5.4	20.1
Queensland	1.1	0	11	2	0	2	3	23	0.00	7.41	63.00	1.8	49.6	6.9	1.3	7.9	10.6
Canada	1.2	9	173	8	26	2	62	343	-0.13	31.14	10.22	4.7	37.7	3.0	9.9	0.8	19.5
Hungary	2.0	9	7	1	3	2	11	42	-0.25	69.79	9.76	10.4	21.7	2.6	5.7	3.5	26.9
China	3.1	55	48	7	48	6	4	193	n.a.	25.08	0.12	18.2	27.4	5.3	32.2	2.8	1.2
Japan	3.2	4	27	3	36	1	7	56	0.13	19.18	2.11	24.1	54.5	8.7	41.1	6.9	9.6
Defaulted																	
Russia	1.8	92	69	16	153	5	100	515	-0.18	77.62	4.77	14.5	15.8	3.0	31.9	0.6	15.7
Brazil	2.2	7	34	4	7	2	10	74	-0.16	32.17	2.31	9.8	31.6	6.2	15.8	5.1	16.6
Portugal	2.4	16	14	7	26	5	19	102	-0.07	4.98	9.35	8.6	16.1	5.8	25.4	2.2	16.6
Chile	2.5	4	13	1	10	1	5	36	-0.10	12.88	4.86	13.0	23.6	3.5	28.6	3.7	17.3
Turkey	2.7	44	133	12	274	11	113	517	n.a.	14.48	3.79	6.1	23.5	3.2	48.4	1.7	20.2
Greece	3.0	8	24	6	67	2	26	148	-0.14	3.75	12.50	2.9	19.7	5.4	34.7	1.6	24.0
Mexico	3.0	16	23	2	9	1	2	50	0.05	18.31	1.83	15.1	54.4	1.3	7.6	3.0	4.3
Argentina	3.2	4	28	6	5	4	6	56	-0.36	29.07	12.82	10.5	38.8	8.4	11.5	6.8	12.5
Uruguay	4.2	4	13	1	1	0	5	25	0.01	5.90	22.71	9.7	37.0	9.7	6.9	1.9	21.1
Egypt	4.7	133	53	26	98	12	42	446	-0.14	12.12	15.92	11.4	25.4	5.4	25.6	5.3	9.2
Colombia	4.8	1	8	0	1	0	0	10	-0.06	3.35	1.00	15.7	30.8	0.8	4.7	0.6	2.2
Costa Rica	6.1	0	1	0	0	0	0	2	-0.01	1.26	9.85	8.8	31.6	15.8	3.5	5.3	0.0
Averages (unweighted)																	
Never defaulted	1.9	13	45	4	20	2	15	114	-0.05	28.51	14.76	10.3	34.7	4.8	17.7	4.6	4.6
Defaulted	3.4	27	34	7	54	4	27	165	-0.11	17.99	8.48	10.5	29.0	5.7	20.4	3.2	13.3

Notes: The list of countries that defaulted is based upon Beim and Calomiris (2001). Data sources and definitions are provided in the text. Within each category (defaulters and non-defaulters), countries are ranked by their average spread.

Table 5.2. Spreads and News, Panel Regressions, 1870–1913

	News In logarithms						News in fractions					
	No fixed effects			With fixed effects			No fixed effects			With fixed effects		
Wars	0.114 [0.021]*	0.109 [0.020]**	0.095 [0.018]**	0.052 [0.017]**	0.044 [0.014]**	0.044 [0.014]**	0.640 [0.115]*	0.540 [0.106]**	0.509 [0.096]**	0.359 [0.084]**	0.232 [0.065]**	0.234 [0.065]**
Good/Neutral economic	-0.165 [0.027]*	-0.098 [0.026]**	-0.049 [0.024]*	-0.147 [0.023]**	-0.033 [0.019]	-0.034 [0.020]	-0.302 [0.078]*	-0.108 [0.073]	-0.055 [0.067]	-0.314 [0.058]**	-0.088 [0.046]	-0.091 [0.047]
Bad economic	0.069 [0.032]*	0.066 [0.030]*	0.056 [0.027]*	0.041 [0.023]	0.052 [0.018]**	0.051 [0.018]**	0.834 [0.241]*	0.910 [0.221]**	0.783 [0.200]**	0.163 [0.175]	0.260 [0.136]	0.254 [0.137]
Reform	0.010 [0.034]	-0.006 [0.031]	0.020 [0.028]	-0.008 [0.026]	-0.017 [0.021]	-0.018 [0.021]	0.160 [0.293]	0.003 [0.269]	0.248 [0.245]	0.241 [0.211]	0.123 [0.164]	0.119 [0.165]
Political	-0.119 [0.023]*	-0.126 [0.021]**	-0.162 [0.019]**	-0.014 [0.023]	0.014 [0.018]	0.014 [0.018]	-0.346 [0.160]	-0.273 [0.147]	-0.280 [0.133]*	0.164 [0.124]	0.262 [0.097]**	0.261 [0.097]**
Foreign	0.071 [0.022]*	0.042 [0.021]*	0.019 [0.018]	0.007 [0.021]	-0.008 [0.017]	-0.007 [0.017]	0.360 [0.121]*	0.329 [0.111]**	0.249 [0.101]*	0.087 [0.108]	0.041 [0.084]	0.041 [0.085]
Default history			0.522 [0.041]**			0.027 [0.083]			0.488 [0.042]**			0.045 [0.082]
Portfolio spreads		0.453 [0.044]**	0.517 [0.040]**		0.561 [0.029]**	0.563 [0.030]**		0.498 [0.046]**	0.545 [0.042]**		0.555 [0.028]**	0.559 [0.029]**

Note: The sample consists of 627 country/year observations. Single asterisks indicate significance at the 5% level; double asterisks indicate significance at the 1% level. Standard errors are in brackets.

Table 5.2 indicates that news on wars and violence are significantly associated with higher spreads, in all specifications. The impact of war news on spreads seems to be substantial: on the basis of the log specification (first column), a doubling of the number of war news would result in an 11.4 percent increase in the spreads; on the basis of the shares specification (seventh column), a 10 percentage point increase in the share of war news at the expense of "other" news would result in a 6.4 percent increase in the spreads.

The estimated coefficients on both bad economic news and good/neutral economic news have the expected signs, though they are statistically significant only in a subset of specifications. In the shares specification, the coefficient on bad economic news is always significantly larger (more positive) than the coefficient on good/neutral economic news. This implies that a shift of news items from the category "other" to the category "bad economic news" tends to raise spreads more than a shift to the "good/neutral economic news" category. The coefficients on other types of news are not robust to changes in specification. Default history is significantly associated with higher spreads when individual country fixed effects are omitted. Controlling for country effects, default history has the expected sign but is no longer statistically significant (i.e. the default history variable is strongly correlated with the country fixed effects). The average (market-capitalization-weighted) spread for all emerging markets is significantly and robustly associated with the spreads in individual markets (with an elasticity of 0.45 to 0.55): co-movement of spreads across emerging markets was substantial in historical times, though—and this is one of the main themes of this book—not as high as in the 1990s.

Table 5.3 presents regression specifications with controls for various macroeconomic characteristics. In addition to default history and market-capitalization-weighted average spreads, we include gold standard adherence, exports, the government surplus, and debt per capita. In this table, we report the results obtained using not only fixed effects panels, but also two econometric techniques (Feasible Generalized Least Square and Arellano-Bond) aimed at taking into account the fact that spreads tend to be persistent in time.[8] The Annex to this chapter

---

[8] The first technique, feasible generalized least squares, lets the residuals (unexplained portion of the spreads) take an AR(1) form, with a country-specific autoregression coefficient. The second technique, developed by Arellano and Bond (1991), includes the lagged dependent variable in the list of regressors, and corrects the well-known bias that would result in a panel context by using further lags of the variables (in levels and changes) as

Table 5.3. Spreads, News, and Macroeconomic Variables, Panel Regressions, 1870–1913

	Fixed effects panel			Feasible generalized least squares			Arellano–Bond	
Wars	0.032 [0.016]*	0.045 [0.013]**	0.042 [0.015]**	0.024 [0.006]**	0.023 [0.007]**	0.027 [0.006]**	0.028 [0.008]*	0.034 [0.008]**
Good/Neutral Economic	−0.024 [0.023]	−0.032 [0.020]	−0.021 [0.023]	0.002 [0.009]	−0.004 [0.010]	0.008 [0.009]	0.012 [0.013]	−0.005 [0.013]
Bad economic	0.013 [0.022]	0.048 [0.018]**	0.030 [0.021]	0.011 [0.008]	0.013 [0.008]	0.012 [0.007]	0.029 [0.011]*	0.026 [0.011]*
Reform	−0.017 [0.024]	−0.021 [0.020]	−0.006 [0.023]	−0.006 [0.009]	−0.009 [0.010]	−0.006 [0.009]	−0.008 [0.013]	−0.007 [0.013]
Political	0.028 [0.021]	0.014 [0.018]	0.022 [0.020]	−0.007 [0.008]	−0.002 [0.009]	−0.009 [0.008]	0.008 [0.012]	−0.001 [0.011]
Foreign	0.041 [0.019]*	−0.001 [0.017]	0.019 [0.019]	−0.003 [0.007]	−0.004 [0.008]	−0.000 [0.007]	0.014 [0.011]	0.004 [0.010]
Gold standard	−0.052 [0.045]	−0.093 [0.038]*		−0.178 [0.037]**		−0.184 [0.034]**	−0.151 [0.045]**	−0.158 [0.041]**
Default history	0.213 [0.116]	0.057 [0.084]	0.229 [0.110]*	0.079 [0.068]		0.238 [0.060]**	0.518 [0.169]**	0.566 [0.118]**
Exports	−0.465 [0.042]**		−0.195 [0.057]**		−0.230 [0.026]**		−0.114 [0.060]	−0.088 [0.054]
Fiscal surplus	−0.143 [0.069]*		−0.053 [0.068]		−0.040 [0.032]		−0.018 [0.037]	−0.010 [0.035]
Debt per capita			0.014 [0.052]				0.077 [0.042]	0.077 [0.042]
Portfolio spreads	0.541 [0.031]**		0.411 [0.054]**			0.445 [0.042]**	0.264 [0.055]**	0.175 [0.046]**
Lagged spreads							0.425 [0.039]**	0.462 [0.033]**
Number of observations	531	627	522	627	531	627	482	477

Note: Single asterisks indicate significance at the 5% level; double asterisks indicate significance at the 1% level. Standard errors are in brackets. News indicators refer to the logarithm of the number of news for the category indicated.

reports the results obtained using alternative econometric techniques and equation specifications, showing that our key results are robust to such changes.

The importance of war and violence news is confirmed when controlling for other variables, including macroeconomic variables and adherence to the gold standard. As before, a shift from bad economic news to good economic news would typically tend to be associated with a decline in spreads. Controlling for the gold standard is of special interest, in view of the significant results obtained by Bordo and Rockoff (1996) and Obstfeld and Taylor (2003b). In our sample, and controlling for individual country effects, the gold standard is significantly associated with lower spreads in some, though not all specifications.[9] In a number of specifications, some macroeconomic variables are significant. In particular, higher exports and a higher fiscal surplus are negatively and significantly associated with spreads. Other macroeconomic variables, such as debt per capita and inflation, are typically not significant.[10]

While we prefer techniques that include individual country fixed effects, we are aware that the individual country fixed effects contain useful information and try to assess whether they are systematically related to time-invariant (or near time-invariant) country characteristics. The estimated individual country dummies seem to bear some relationship to characteristics such as adherence to the gold standard, geographic location, links to the British Empire, and a history of default. Table 5.4 ranks the countries in our sample according to the individual country dummies estimated in the fixed effects regression in the fifth column of Table 5.2, which includes news and the portfolio

instruments. In the Arellano-Bond specifications, we let debt per capita be an endogenous variable because, as discussed above, spreads contribute to determining the debt level.

[9] At the same time, countries with a perfect record of adherence to the gold standard clearly enjoyed lower spreads, an issue we discuss below.

[10] The coefficient on debt per capita is usually not significantly associated with spreads; moreover, the coefficient is not robust to changes in specification and sample (not reported for the sake of brevity), especially in regressions without individual country fixed effects. In particular, the results are highly sensitive to the inclusion of Queensland in the sample. This may partly reflect the endogeneity of debt with respect to bond spreads: countries that are able to borrow at relatively low interest rates will accumulate considerable amounts of debt. Queensland may be an example of this, as it had relatively low spreads and an unusually high debt to population ratio in our set of countries. In additional (unreported) specifications, inflation (which reduced the size of the sample considerably, owing to limited data availability) did not turn out to be significant. Perhaps this should not be too surprising, given that inflation was not one of the variables of interest in publications such as the *Investor's Monthly Manual*.

Table 5.4. Individual Country Effects and Country Characteristics, 1870–1913

Country	Individual country effect	Gold Standard	History of default	Links to British Empire	Europe
Costa Rica	0.90	~	+		
Colombia	0.68	~	+		
Uruguay	0.60	~	+		
Mexico	0.47	~	+		
China	0.32				
Japan	0.31	~			
Argentina	0.29	~	+		
Egypt	0.27	~	+		+
Greece	0.26		+		
Turkey	0.25	~	+		
Chile	0.10	~	+		
Portugal	−0.03	~	+		+
Brazil	−0.05	~	+		
Hungary	−0.17	~			+
Russia	−0.33	~			+
Queensland	−0.66	+		+	
Sweden	−0.80	+			+
Canada	−0.87	+		+	

Note: Individual country effects are the estimated dummies from the regression in the fifth column of Table 5.2. For the gold standard, a "plus" sign indicates adherence for essentially the entire period, and a 'tilde' indicates adherence for only part of the period.

spreads, but excludes the gold standard dummy and macroeconomic variables.[11] The dummies represent the (period average) portion of the spreads that is not explained by the independent variables in the regression for each country. Serial defaulters such as Costa Rica, Colombia, and Uruguay display the largest individual country dummies; more generally, countries with a history of default have larger individual country fixed effects than do countries with an impeccable repayment record. Countries located in Europe, countries that adhered to the gold standard for essentially the whole period (Queensland, Sweden, and Canada), and countries with close links to the British Empire (Canada and Queensland) also have relatively low individual country fixed effects. Given the substantial overlap of countries across categories, and the small sample, the reader will note how difficult it is to tell whether what matters is, for example, links to the Empire or adherence to the gold standard. Interestingly, China and Japan faced relatively high spreads (controlling for fundamentals), despite their

[11] Similar exercises based on alternative regression specifications yield broadly similar rankings.

unblemished repayment record, possibly because they were not well known to British investors: not only were these countries far from Britain in terms of geography and culture, but also they had accessed the London market for the first time relatively recently. Alternatively, Chinese bonds may have been issued with more collateral, whereas following its victory over Russia, Japan was able to borrow in London with limited guarentees for its debt (Suzuki, 1994; Sussman and Yafeh, 2000).

In Box 5.1. we show that French investors in Paris were roughly in agreement with their peers in London regarding the ranking of borrowing countries. All in all, regression analysis on the historical data

---

Box 5.1. INVESTMENT BANKS AND INFORMATION: LONDON VERSUS PARIS

While the London Stock Exchange was the largest in the world, Paris was in second place. Investor characteristics in the two bourses were, however, quite different. In London there were 250,000 individual investors in 1870 and approximately one million by 1913, each holding an average of 15 different securities (Michie, 1987, p. 120). By contrast, in Paris large banks played a major role. In Britain, investors had access to economic and political information which was used to assess the creditworthiness of sovereign borrowers. In France, the large bank Credit Lyonnais developed its own research department that specialized in assessing the creditworthiness of borrowing countries (Flandreau, 2003b). It turns out that both the Credit Lyonnais and British investors reached similar conclusions. As illustrated in the table below, the grading system of the Credit Lyonnais (on a scale from I to III, see Flandreau 2003b, p. 44) is very similar to the ranking of country spreads in London: countries with lower spreads in London tend to have a higher grade in Paris. We conclude that private investors (in London) and investment banks (in Paris) were in broad agreement regarding the quality of borrowing countries.

1898 Spreads and the Grading System of the Credit Lyonnais (c.1898)

Country	Average Spread in London	Credit Lyonnais Grade
Sweden	0.03	I
Russia	0.03	I
Hungary	0.04	II
Japan	0.05	II
Portugal	0.05	III
Greece	0.04	III
Argentina	0.06	III
Brazil	0.07	III

suggests that some types of news, notably "war and violence" news are significantly and fairly robustly associated with higher spreads; and that macroeconomic variables such as the fiscal deficit and exports are significantly associated with spreads, with the expected signs.

5.4 Results for the Modern Sample

For the modern period, we find substantially weaker results regarding the importance of news, and similar or slightly weaker results for the role of macroeconomic variables. We present estimates based on both annual and quarterly data. Our sample consists of the eight emerging markets for which spreads are available beginning in 1994. This yields about seventy annual observations with the requisite macroeconomic data and news indicators. Using quarterly data makes it possible to increase the number of observations to around 150 to 230 (depending on the specification), though this requires excluding Nigeria from the sample, owing to data limitations.[12]

Quantitative indicators of news are often significant, especially in the regressions without individual country fixed effects. News about wars and violence seem to play some role, but to a smaller extent than in the past. To the extent that news seem to matter, economic news bear the closest association with spreads (Table 5.5). Somewhat paradoxically, positive/neutral economic news seem to raise spreads even more than do negative economic news, though the difference is not statistically significant. Our interpretation is that the financial press tends to pay more attention to countries experiencing trouble, and will report economic news both positive and negative about countries experiencing a crisis or emerging from a crisis. In the modern sample there are also some signs that news regarding investor-friendly reforms are associated with lower spreads—an empirical association that we do not find in the historical period.

In some specifications, macroeconomic variables are significantly associated with spreads: the higher exports, real economic growth, and the fiscal balance (as a share of GDP), the lower the spreads

---

[12] While one could increase the number of emerging markets by accepting a shorter sample period, it seems important to work with the longest available sample period, given that the historical sample period is already far longer than the modern period. A number of existing studies on modern data have used shorter sample periods with larger samples of countries, and have found broadly similar results for the macroeconomic variables.

Table 5.5 Spreads and News, Panel Regressions, 1994–2002

	Annual data				Quarterly data			
	Logs		Fractions		Logs		Fractions	
	No F.E.	With F.E.	No F.E.	With F.E.	No F.E.	With F.E.	No F.E.	With F.E.
Wars/Instability	0.166 (0.079)*	0.033 (0.086)	2.641 (0.699)*	1.683 (0.767)*	0.165 (0.056)*	0.041 (0.041)	1.155 (0.239)*	0.471 (0.177)*
Good/Neutral economic	0.397 (0.108)*	0.262 (0.102)*	2.665 (0.503)**	1.316 (0.496)*	0.251 (0.047)**	0.121 (0.033)*	1.481 (0.206)**	0.542 (0.148)*
Bad economic	0.235 (0.089)*	0.089 (0.086)	3.381 (0.684)**	1.722 (0.732)*	0.218 (0.051)*	0.071 (0.035)*	1.527 (0.234)**	0.514 (0.166)*
Reform	-0.331 (0.109)*	-0.125 (0.105)	-1.282 (0.814)	-0.147 (0.681)	-0.217 (0.061)*	-0.103 (0.041)*	-0.013 (0.264)	-0.016 (0.174)
Political	-0.107 (0.081)	0.024 (0.082)	0.922 (0.539)	0.578 (0.476)	-0.031 (0.045)	0.098 (0.032)*	0.755 (0.200)*	0.463 (0.138)*
Foreign	-0.27 (0.087)*	-0.033 (0.103)			-0.317 (0.053)**	-0.103 (0.039)*		
Portfolio spreads	0.798 (0.241)*	0.849 (0.184)*	0.799 (0.240)*	0.876 (0.184)*	0.869 (0.104)**	0.885 (0.068)**	0.878 (0.111)**	0.918 (0.071)**
Constant	1.653 (0.229)**	1.376 (0.290)*	-1.221 (0.648)	-0.763 (0.554)	0.017 (0.222)	-0.054 (0.146)	-0.748 (0.274)*	-0.318 (0.182)
Number of observations	72	72	72	72	282	282	263	263

Note: F.E. = Fixed Effects. Single asterisks indicate significance at the 5% level; double asterisks indicate significance at the 1% level. Standard errors in brackets.

Table 5.6. Spreads, Macroeconomic Variables, and News, Panel Regressions, 1994–2002

	Annual data				Quarterly data			
	Fixed effects	Fixed effects	Feasible generalized least squares	Feasible generalized least squares	Fixed effects	Fixed effects	Feasible generalized least squares	Arellano-Bond
Wars/Instability	-0.002 [0.085]	0.125 [0.048]*	0.083 [0.047]	0.153 [0.038]**	0.061 [0.045]	0.041 [0.049]	-0.005 [0.029]	0.037 [0.027]
Good/Neutral economic	0.288 [0.100]*	0.121 [0.061]	0.263 [0.064]**	0.191 [0.048]**	0.124 [0.036]*	0.076 [0.045]	0.036 [0.025]	0.014 [0.025]
Bad economic	0.077 [0.083]	0.016 [0.053]	0.161 [0.049]**	0.066 [0.044]	0.041 [0.039]	0.057 [0.045]	0.005 [0.024]	-0.004 [0.024]
Reform	-0.164 [0.106]	-0.223 [0.058]**	-0.270 [0.067]**	-0.282 [0.047]**	-0.064 [0.045]	-0.114 [0.053]*	-0.032 [0.026]	-0.066 [0.027]
Political	0.000 [0.081]	-0.022 [0.044]	0.015 [0.046]	-0.080 [0.036]*	0.084 [0.036]*	0.089 [0.042]*	0.046 [0.023]*	0.017 [0.022]
Foreign	0.058 [0.108]	-0.116 [0.055]*	-0.167 [0.063]**	-0.185 [0.044]**	-0.061 [0.045]	-0.079 [0.052]	-0.029 [0.025]	-0.025 [0.028]
Exports	-0.438 [0.218]	-0.535 [0.220]*	-0.138 [0.063]*	-0.219 [0.077]**	-0.251 [0.091]*	-0.322 [0.108]**	-0.220 [0.046]**	-0.318 [0.100]
Fiscal surplus	-2.457 [1.921]	-2.381 [1.133]*	-2.295 [1.446]	-2.933 [0.857]**	0.000 [0.003]	0.000 [0.003]	-0.001 [0.002]	-0.001 [0.002]
Portfolio spreads	0.759 [0.192]**	0.720 [0.111]**	0.676 [0.137]**	0.745 [0.080]**	0.838 [0.073]*	0.839 [0.089]**	0.832 [0.077]**	0.521 [0.053]*
Debt/GDP	-0.317 [0.348]			-0.815 [0.224]**				
Growth real GDP	-1.034 [0.952]			-2.110 [0.818]**		-1.195 [0.270]**	-0.355 [0.135]**	-0.618 [0.135]*
Lagged spreads								0.411 [0.047]*
Number of observations	72	72	56	56	230	161	161	154

Note: News in logarithms. Single asterisks indicate significance at the 5% level; doubls asterisks indicate significance at the 1% level. Standard errors in brackets.

(Table 5.6). Other macroeconomic variables, such as the debt/GDP ratio do not seem to play much of a role and occasionally are found to have an impact contrary to expectations. Consistent with our theme of greater co-movement of spreads in modern times than in historical times (which will be discussed in detail in Chapter 6), we find the coefficient on (market-capitalization-weighted) average spreads to be 0.8 to 0.9 in modern times, compared with 0.4 to 0.5 in historical times.[13]

In interpreting our results for the importance of news about wars and other instances of politically motivated violence, and reforms, in the modern period compared with the historical period, a few caveats are in order. Regarding wars, there was certainly no shortage of major events in the modern sample, including political assassinations, coups, ethnically motivated unrest, and so on. Nevertheless, even if we do not have a precise way of comparing the importance of war news between the modern and historical periods (beyond the sheer number or share of news items), most people's intuition is that the number of major wars and all-out armed conflicts seem to have been less frequent in the modern sample than in the historical sample. Perhaps this is a factor underlying the result that war news seem to have had less impact on spreads in modern times than in historical times. Regarding reforms, the very notion of reforms seems to be fundamentally different in modern times from historical times. Indeed, classifying news about reforms seems to us to have been a somewhat easier exercise for the modern period than for the past. In modern times, there seems to be a considerable degree of consensus on what constitutes "market-friendly, investor-friendly" reforms. These are not only generally judged to be desirable, but are often reported as such in the financial press (including the *Financial Times*, our main source of news). In this light, the tentative evidence that reforms may help reduce spreads in modern times, though only in a few of our estimates, seems fairly consistent with modern notions of reform.

On the whole, investors today and in the past seem to pay attention to both macroeconomic fundamentals and information reflected in the news, especially news related to violent conflict.

---

[13] Including the lagged dependent variable among the regressors reduces the estimated coefficient on average spreads for both the historical sample and the modern sample; the result of higher co-movement in modern times than in historical times is thus maintained, as long as comparable techniques are used for both periods.

It seems, however, that country-specific fundamentals today play a less significant role in determining spreads than they did in the past: news matter somewhat less today than they did in the past; and while macroeconomic variables matter as much or almost as much today as they did in the past, it is important to bear in mind the higher quality of today's macroeconomic data. We conjecture that while investors in the past paid close attention to macroeconomic data, they were aware of the limitations of such data, and therefore focused even more closely on information that they obtained through the news.

Annex—Robustness of the Results

In this Annex, we check the robustness of our results to the use of a variety of estimation methods, as customary in those empirical studies in economics where there is no overwhelming presumption that a particular estimation method is the most appropriate. As in the baseline estimates reported in the main text, our key results remain that: war news are significantly and robustly associated with spreads; gold standard adherence and default history are statistically significant in many specifications; exports and, less frequently, fiscal measures are also significant in a number of cases (Tables 5.A.1 and 5.A.2). We include estimates based upon a variety of techniques, each of which has both advantages and drawbacks, as follows.

Pooled panel regressions with no individual country fixed effects make use of the cross-country information, but are subject to a well-known drawback: non-time varying country-specific features that are not included in the list of control variables may be driving the results. *Panel regressions with fixed effects* appropriately take into consideration individual country fixed effects, though a correction may be needed for persistence in the spreads. In some specifications, we include the lagged spreads. In a panel context, this introduces a bias in the coefficients, though such bias becomes smaller as the length of the time period increases. With more than 40 years of data, the bias is relatively small (Judson and Owen, 1999). *Seemingly Unrelated Regressions* (not reported for the sake of brevity) increase the efficiency of the estimates by taking into account the contemporaneous correlation of the residuals across countries. *Feasible Generalized Least Squares regressions* let the

Annex Table 5.A.1. Pooled and Fixed Effect Regressions, 1870–1913.

	No fixed effects						With fixed effects					
Wars	0.086 [0.020],	0.081 [0.019]**	0.142 [0.022]**	0.095 [0.021]**	0.081 [0.017]**	0.080 [0.019]**	0.054 [0.016]**	0.031 [0.016]	0.032 [0.016]*	0.027 [0.008]**	0.023 [0.009]**	0.029 [0.009]**
Good/Neutral economic	-0.119 [0.026]**,	-0.098 [0.025]**	-0.050 [0.028]	-0.024 [0.027]	-0.036 [0.023]	0.003 [0.026]	-0.110 [0.023]**	-0.016 [0.023]	-0.017 [0.024]	-0.010 [0.011]	-0.015 [0.013]	-0.017 [0.013]
Bad economic	0.057 [0.030]	0.053 [0.029]	0.019 [0.033]	0.031 [0.031]	0.051 [0.026]*	0.035 [0.029]	0.041 [0.023]	0.018 [0.022]	0.013 [0.022]	0.015 [0.011]	0.006 [0.012]	0.012 [0.012]
Reform	-0.006 [0.032]	0.018 [0.030]	0.028 [0.034]	0.049 [0.032]	0.010 [0.027]	0.022 [0.030]	-0.017 [0.025]	-0.013 [0.024]	-0.013 [0.024]	0.002 [0.012]	0.005 [0.014]	0.007 [0.013]
Political	-0.086 [0.002]**,	-0.118 [0.021]**	-0.123 [0.027]**	-0.088 [0.025]**	-0.138 [0.019]**	-0.092 [0.024]**	-0.013 [0.022]	0.025 [0.021]	0.025 [0.021]	0.003 [0.010]	0.006 [0.012]	0.005 [0.012]
Foreign	0.033 [0.021]	0.026 [0.020]	0.052 [0.022]*	-0.004 [0.021]	0.03 [0.018]	-0.032 [0.020]	0.019 [0.021]	0.034 [0.019]	0.043 [0.020]*	0.005 [0.010]	0.015 [0.011]	0.008 [0.011]
Gold standard	-0.450 [0.047]**,	-0.366 [0.046]**			-0.250 [0.043]**	-0.169 [0.050]**	-0.275 [0.044]**			-0.015 [0.022]	-0.004 [0.026]	-0.011 [0.025]
Default history		0.380 [0.044]**		0.380 [0.048]**	0.463 [0.041]**	0.427 [0.050]**	-0.213 [0.101]*		0.216 [0.116]		0.022 [0.065]	0.035 [0.064]
Exports			-0.216 [0.024]**	-0.185 [0.024]**		-0.125 [0.024]**		-0.468 [0.038]**	-0.479 [0.046]**		-0.074 [0.030]*	0.016 [0.035]
Fiscal surplus			-0.405 [0.093]**	-0.400 [0.087]**		-0.144 [0.087]		-0.142 [0.069]*	-0.134 [0.071]		-0.063 [0.041]	-0.035 [0.040]
Debt per capita			-0.120 [0.022]**	-0.120 [0.022]**		-0.072 [0.022]**		0.031	-0.026 [0.055]		-0.023 [0.031]	-0.010 [0.031]
Portfolio spreads					0.462 [0.040]**	0.350 [0.050]**				0.157 [0.022]**		0.151 [0.032]**
Lagged spreads										0.756 [0.023]**	0.786 [0.025]**	0.750 [0.025]**
Number of observations	627	627	531	522	627	522	627	531	522	600	508	508

Note: Single asterisks indicate significance at the 5% level; double asterisks indicate significance at the 1% level. Standard errors are in brackets. News indicators refer to the logarithm of the number of news for the category indicated.

Annex Table 5.A.2. Feasible Generalized Least Squares and Arellano-Bond Regressions, 1870–1913

	Feasible generalized least square			Arellano-Bond					
Wars	0.025 [0.006]**	0.024 [0.007]**	0.023 [0.007]**	0.030 [0.007]**	0.029 [0.007]**	0.029 [0.009]**	0.028 [0.008]**	0.028 [0.009]**	0.031 [0.007]*
Good/Neutral economic	-0.002 [0.009]	-0.004 [0.010]	-0.004 [0.010]	-0.002 [0.012]	-0.003 [0.012]	0.014 [0.013]	0.012 [0.013]	0.010 [0.013]	-0.002 [0.012]
Bad economic	0.011 [0.008]	0.011 [0.008]	0.010 [0.008]	0.030 [0.010]**	0.030 [0.010]**	0.030 [0.011]**	0.027 [0.011]*	0.028 [0.011]*	0.032 [0.010]**
Reform	-0.007 [0.009]	-0.006 [0.010]	-0.006 [0.010]	-0.016 [0.012]	-0.015 [0.012]	-0.014 [0.013]	-0.007 [0.013]	-0.007 [0.013]	-0.017 [0.012]
Political	-0.006 [0.008]	-0.004 [0.008]	-0.005 [0.008]	0.010 [0.011]	0.008 [0.010]	0.005 [0.012]	0.002 [0.012]	0.004 [0.012]	0.013 [0.011]
Foreign	-0.003 [0.007]	-0.005 [0.008]	-0.004 [0.008]	0.005 [0.009]	0.006 [0.009]	0.008 [0.011]	0.009 [0.011]	0.010 [0.011]	0.010 [0.009]
Gold standard	-0.191 [0.037]**	-0.115 [0.037]**	-0.108 [0.037]**	-0.135 [0.042]**	-0.129 [0.042]**	-0.127 [0.045]**	-0.127 [0.045]**	-0.130 [0.045]**	-0.152 [0.042]**
Default history		0.063 [0.084]	0.134 [0.096]	0.630 [0.163]**		0.456 [0.169]**	0.418 [0.171]*		0.684 [0.163]**
Exports		-0.216 [0.027]**	-0.211 [0.028]**			-0.153 [0.060]*	-0.106 [0.060]	-0.113 [0.061]	
Fiscal surplus		-0.031 [0.030]	-0.029 [0.030]			-0.026 [0.037]	-0.024 [0.037]	-0.020 [0.037]	
Debt per capita			-0.010 [0.031]					-0.043 [0.052]	
Portfolio spreads									0.239 [0.049]**
Lagged spreads				0.346 [0.034],	0.344 [0.034]**	0.437 [0.039]**	0.411 [0.039]**	0.413 [0.040]**	0.371 [0.034]**
Number of observations	627	531	522	568	568	482	482	477	568

Note: Single asterisks indicate significance at the 5% level; double asterisks indicate significance at the 1% level. Standard errors are in brackets. News indicators refer to the logarithm of the number of news for the category indicated.

residuals be autocorrelated with a country-specific AR(1), thus taking into account that of the persistence of spreads through the persistence of the residuals. *Arellano-Bond regressions* include the lagged dependent variable, but appropriately correct the bias that would result in a panel context, by using further lags of all the variables as instruments.

6

Co-movement of Spreads: Fundamentals or Investor Behavior?

6.1 Introduction

In previous chapters, we have focused on the determinants of borrowing costs. We have seen that economic characteristics of borrowing countries, as well as domestic and international instability had an impact on the perception of countries by foreign investors, as reflected in bond spreads. In this chapter, we turn to the co-movement of spreads across different countries, and to the frequency of crises shared by more than one country (a phenomenon sometimes called "contagion").[1]

Overall, we find that co-movement of spreads among emerging markets was far higher in the 1990s than during the pre-First World War era. Moreover, sharp changes in spreads (or crises, defined in a number of ways) during the 1990s typically affected many countries at the same time, whereas global crises were virtually nonexistent in the historical sample. However, the prevalence of high co-movement of spreads and contagious crises in modern times appear to be primarily a feature of the 1990s: co-movement of spreads ceases to be relatively high in the second half of 2001, with the onset of the debt crisis in Argentina (the country with the largest share in the Emerging Markets Bond Index (EMBI) index until then). Investors and financial markets of the twenty-first century would seem to be returning to the behavior they displayed before the First World War, although only time will tell whether this is a temporary or a more permanent return.

---

[1] Although there are a variety of definitions of "contagion" in the literature (e.g. Kaminsky and Reinhart 2000; and Kaminsky, Reinhart, and Vegh 2002), we will use the term in this chapter to describe crises that occur simultaneously in more than one country.

While our finding of greater co-movement in modern times (until recently) than historical times is based upon bond spreads, other studies corroborate this result for other asset prices. Based upon equity market returns, Goetzmann et al. (2002) show that cross-country co-movement of equity markets has increased over the past decades, thus requiring investors to hold equities in an ever-increasing number of (more and more similar) countries for their portfolios to be effectively diversified.

We begin this chapter by documenting the extent of co-movement using bond spreads (Section 6.2). We then ask whether greater co-movement of spreads today might be driven by greater co-movement of fundamentals (Section 6.3). We show that fundamentals co-move more strongly today, and analyze in detail one factor underlying such greater co-movement, namely today's lower degree of specialization in emerging markets' output and exports. Before the First World War, emerging market countries were highly specialized in production and exports: Argentina was largely about wheat and wool; Brazil was almost entirely about coffee and rubber. In contrast, today's borrowing countries are far more similar to each other than their historical peers: nowadays, both Argentina and Brazil are relatively well-diversified economies. Nevertheless, in Section 6.4, we show that not all of the greater co-movement of spreads today can be attributed to greater co-movement of fundamentals. Indeed, considering the portion of spreads that is unexplained by fundamentals (the residuals from running regressions of spreads on news and macroeconomic variables, as in Chapter 5), co-movement is still significantly higher in modern times than in historical times.

6.2 Co-movement and the Spread of Crises

We measure the co-movement of sovereign bonds issued by emerging markets using correlation coefficients, principal components analysis, and the share of sharp changes in spreads (crises) affecting more than one country at the same time.[2]

We begin with simple correlation coefficients for the spreads across pairs of emerging markets. The average correlation coefficient is 0.71

---

[2] Additional techniques to measure co-movement are reported in Mauro, Sussman, and Yafeh (2002).

for the modern period prior to Argentina's difficulties (November 1994–June 2001), compared with 0.47 in the historical period (May 1877–December 1913).[3] Nevertheless, if the modern sample is extended to 2004 (our data end in February), the average correlation coefficient falls to 0.39, primarily because the debt crisis in Argentina (and the rise in spreads on Argentinean bonds to extremely high levels) did not immediately affect other countries. To the extent that the Argentinean crisis spread to other countries, it did so with varying lags for different countries. If Argentina is excluded from the sample, the average correlation coefficient for 1994–2004 is 0.55, similar to the pre-First World War era, although not as high as in the 1990s.

Next, we compute another standard measure of co-movement, namely, the share of variation accounted for by the first principal component in the sovereign spread series for the various emerging market countries considered. This statistic is a measure of the percent of variation that is common to the different series—another way to describe how closely they co-move. The overall pattern of the results is similar to that for the average correlation coefficients. The proportion of variation in emerging market spreads accounted for by the first principal component is about ½ in 1877–1913, about ¾ in 1994–2001, and again about ½ if tests are carried out for the entire 1994–2004 period. More specifically, using monthly data for May 1877–December 1913, the share of variation accounted for by the first principal component is 54.1 percent (with a standard error of 1.8 percentage points).[4] The figures remain unchanged when other samples are used—for example, a sample excluding all countries experiencing payment difficulties. In modern times, the main sample considered is that of the eight emerging markets for which the EMBI spread data are available starting in November 1994. Monthly data are used for consistency with the estimates based upon historical data.[5] The share of

[3] Some of the techniques used in this section (notably principal components analysis) require a complete and balanced sample. To exclude observations for which the quality of the historical spreads data is less reliable, we need to drop the whole series for the country in question. Our baseline estimates are therefore conducted on the sample of countries for which the spreads are reliable throughout: we include Argentina, Brazil, Canada, Chile, China, Hungary, Japan, Portugal, Queensland, Russia, and Sweden. The exclusion of several countries that experienced (idiosyncratic) defaults would tend to lead us to find greater co-movement. Using different samples, including the full sample of countries, does not substantially alter any of our results.

[4] Details on the calculation of the standard errors appear in Mauro, Sussman, and Yafeh (2002). Egypt is excluded from this exercise because it was taken over by Britain in the middle of the period.

[5] The results at higher frequencies, such as daily or weekly, are not substantially different.

variation accounted for by the first principal component is about 74.6 percent (with a standard error of 3.4 percentage points) for the period ending in June 2001, the onset of Argentina's debt crisis. If the sample period is extended to February 2004, the share of variation accounted for by the first principal component falls to 54.6 percent (with a standard error of 3.9 percentage points), or to 62.2 percent (with a standard error of 3.7 percentage points) if Argentina is excluded.

These statistics come to life in Figures 6.1. and 6.2. (reproduced from Chapter 2 for the convenience of the reader) describing the co-movement of spreads in the two periods. Historical spreads have country-specific shapes and levels, whereas modern emerging market spreads tend to move together, especially prior to 2001.

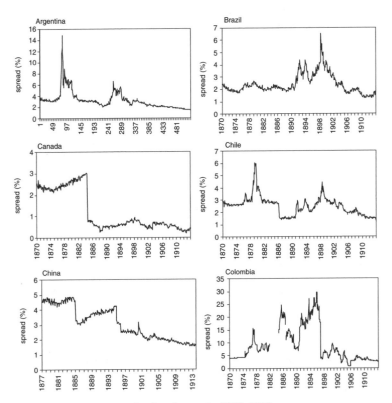

Figure 6.1. Emerging market bond spreads, 1870–1913

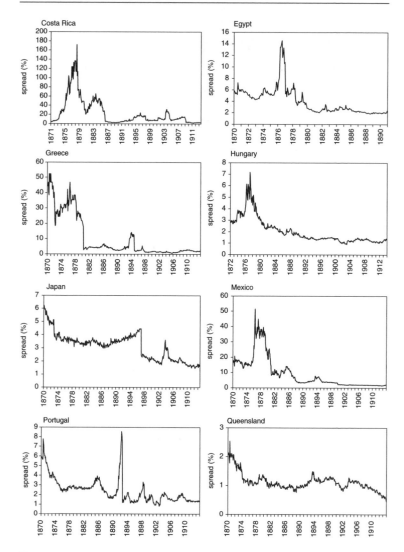

Figure 6.1. (*Continued*)

We conclude that prior to the crisis in Argentina, the modern period seemed very different from the historical period in terms of spread co-movement, but these differences have apparently diminished after 2001.

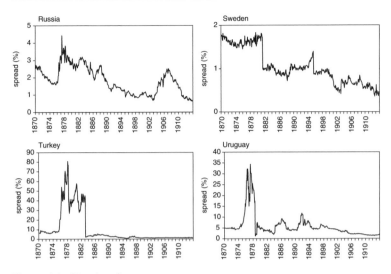

Figure 6.1. (*Continued*)

Table 6.1 reports sharp changes in spreads in the historical period and the modern period. "Sharp" changes in spreads in both periods are defined in three ways: first, as changes exceeding an absolute threshold (changes in basis points); second, as changes relative to existing spreads (changes in percent); and third, as changes exceeding two standard deviations. We then compute the proportion of such changes that affect more than one country at a time. We find that sharp changes in spreads common to more than one country at the same time are now more frequent, as a share of all sharp changes, than in the historical sample. Spreads rose sharply in all or nearly all emerging markets at the time of the Mexican crisis of late 1994 and early 1995, the Asian crisis of mid- and late 1997, and the Russian crisis of August 1998. Modern co-movement of spreads is not a phenomenon restricted to "similar" countries, or countries with close links. For example, during the Asian crisis, events in Indonesia (including news on then President Suharto's health problems) had a substantial impact on Korean spreads, even though the two countries differed considerably with respect to their economic fundamentals (see also Mauro, Sussman, and Yafeh, 2002; and especially Sussman and Yafeh, 1999a). In contrast, "contagion" (the rapid spread of crises across emerging markets) was a relatively rare phenomenon before the First

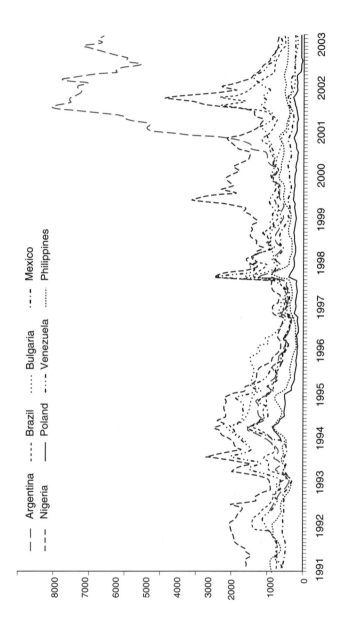

Figure 6.2. Emerging Market Bond Spreads, 1992–2003

Note: EMBI bonds spreads are in basis points.

Source: J. P. Morgan

114

Table 6.1 Common and Country-Specific Sharp Changes, 1877–1913, and 1994–2004

	Historical sample (15 countries, 1877:5–1913:12)			Modern sample (8 countries, 1994:11–2004:2)		
	200 basis points	20%	2 std. devtns.	200 basis points	20%	2 std. devtns.
Sharp changes in percent of total observations (%)	1.4	2.2	3.8	13.2	12.9	5.1
Number of months with characteristics listed:						
No sharp changes	374	327	302	48	49	84
Sharp changes in exactly one country	40	85	81	34	38	15
Sharp changes in exactly two countries	20	20	27	17	8	10
Sharp changes in three or more countries	4	6	28	12	16	2
Proportion of months with characteristics listed: (As a share of total months in sample period, in percent)						
No sharp changes	85.4	74.7	68.9	43.2	44.1	75.7
Sharp changes in exactly one country	9.1	19.4	18.5	30.6	34.2	13.5
Sharp changes in exactly two countries	4.6	4.6	6.2	15.3	7.2	9.0
Sharp changes in three or more countries	0.9	1.4	6.4	10.8	14.4	1.8
Ratio of months with sharp changes in *more than one* country to months with sharp changes in *at least one* country	37.5	23.4	40.4	46.0	38.7	44.4

Sources: *The Economist's Investor's Monthly Manual* and J. P. Morgan Web site. The historical sample consists of fifteen countries and the modern sample consists of eight countries, listed in the text. The sample periods were chosen to ensure that there are no missing observations. Standard deviations are defined using spread changes in basis points.

Box 6.1. THE BARING CRISIS AND (THE ABSENCE OF) CONTAGION

The coverage of the Baring crisis by the *Investor's Monthly Manual* provides a vivid account of the most well known financial crisis involving sovereign debt in the period under consideration in this book. The investment bank of Baring Brothers was heavily involved in Argentinian government securities. In July 1890 the central bank suspended specie payments, there was a minor revolt, and the government resigned in August. In September the central government assumed provincial debts, which were on verge of default, leading shortly thereafter to the default of the central government and the collapse of Baring's Bank.

The past month will long be remembered in the City. The downfall of ... Baring ... perhaps the greatest firm of merchant banking in the world ... but it will be even more distinguished by the fact that a crisis of the gravest character has been averted by the action of the Bank of England, aided by Joint-stock and other banks (*Investor's Monthly Manual*, 29 November, 1890, p. 564).

In the event, the banks provided liquidity to Baring, allowing it to liquidate some of its assets and negotiate with Argentina without affecting the market. A more detailed article examining developments on the London Stock Exchange shows that the collapse of Baring on 11 November had only a small impact on the Stock Exchange. Despite concerns suggesting that "speculators became alarmed at the prospect of stringent money for a lengthy period and ... that sooner or later great masses of securities must be liquidated" (*Investor's Monthly Manual*, 29 November, 1890, p. 564), the downturn was short-lived and the market rebounded immediately.

According to the *Investor's Monthly Manual*, the most important channel of potential contagion was insufficient liquidity of the financial market, exacerbated by sales of large quantities of bonds in search of liquidity. It also saluted the Bank of England for figuring this out and for supplying immediately the necessary liquidity to the market.

In a subsequent article it is noted that it was only "a small body of speculators who have suffered rather than the multitude of investors, who with commendable caution, ... diligently refused to be led on to dangerous ground ..." (*Investor's Monthly Manual*, 31 December, 1890, p. 616.) Thus, the provision of liquidity averted herd behavior and a major financial crisis.

Collapse and Recovery of Bonds Prices—11 November to 27 November, 1890 (Based on the *Investor's Monthly Manual*, 31 December, 1890)

Country/bond	Price on 11 November	Price on 19 November	Percent change	Price on 27 November	Percent change
Argentina 1884 5%	80	67.5	−15.6	75	+11.0
Brazil 1889 4%	89	77	−13.5	81	+5.2
Mexico 6%	91.5	86	−6.0	92	+7.0
Uruguay 5%	53	39	−26.4	54	+38.5
Greece 1881/1884 5%	89.25	86.5	−3.1	91	+5.2

Hungary Gold rentes	89.5	87.5	−2.2	89.5	+2.3
Italy 5 rentes	92	91	−1.1	92.5	+1.6
Portugal 3%	56.2	53.75	−4.5	56.2	+4.6
Russia 4%	97.5	96.75	−0.8	97	+0.3

As can be seen in the table, Argentina's immediate neighbors suffered the greatest price volatility, while European bonds moved much less. With the exception of Argentina and Brazil, all other bonds were traded on 27 November at prices that were no lower than on 11 November.

In the months that followed, spreads rose in a number of Argentina's neighbors. Should this be viewed as contagion? The *Investor's Monthly Manual* is careful to note that events in neighboring countries were independent of the financial crisis involving Baring's Bank. The Uruguayan (central) bank suspended payments before the outbreak of the Baring crisis (*Investor's Monthly Manual*, 31 December, 1890, p. 620). In Brazil, there was a ministerial crisis in January 1891, a problem of inconvertible paper money, allegations of vast corruption, and rumors that the Rothschilds were about to lose the role as underwriters for Brazilian debt, which resulted in a sharp decline in Brazilian bond prices (*Investor's Monthly Manual*, 31 January, 1891, pp. 2, 4). In Chile a revolution broke out in January 1891, causing a decline in bond prices (ibid.). Thus, what appeared like contagion in South America was actually the outcome of separate coinciding crises. It could be argued that the revolutionary spirit was contagious, but this is quite a departure from the concept of financial contagion as it is known today.

As noted by previous scholars, the Baring crisis bears a number of similarities with the crises of the 1990s. Eichengreen (1999b) compares it to the Mexican Tequila crisis of 1994–5. The Baring crisis also shares a number of features with the 1998 collapse of Long-Term Capital Management (LTCM), notably with respect to the magnitude of the crisis and the subsequent official intervention (by the US Federal Reserve, in the case of LTCM). While following the Fed's intervention, the consequences of the crisis were limited in advanced country financial markets, however, the Russia/LTCM crisis was followed by lastingly higher spreads in essentially all emerging market countries.

World War. Even the famous Baring crisis of 1890 was not obviously reflected in bond spreads of countries other than Argentina (Box 6.1).[6]

If, indeed, co-movement of spreads is greater today than in the past, to what extent is this attributable to greater co-movement of fundamentals today? Surely, while the impact of country-specific fundamentals on spreads may be lower in the modern period than in the historical

---

[6] See also Bordo and Murshid (2000, 2002) who consider the spread of crises between "core" countries and the periphery, and Kaminsky, Reinhart, and Vegh (2002) who point to the defaults of Peru and other Latin American countries in 1826–8 as a possible historical example of contagion.

period (as discussed in Chapter 5), fundamentals must have a considerable impact on spreads in both periods, and are therefore a potential factor underlying greater co-movement of spreads in the present than in the past. The next section analyzes the extent to which fundamentals co-move in each of the two periods.

6.3 Economic Fundamentals: Exports and Specialization, "Then" and Now

Is greater co-movement of spreads in the 1990s than in the past the result of changes in investor behavior, or the natural consequence of greater co-movement of economic fundamentals? The best summary measure of economic fundamentals that is available on a broadly comparable basis for emerging markets in both the historical and the modern periods is exports in common currency (US dollars).[7]

More specifically, we summarize the similarity of economic fundamentals by looking at the co-movement of export growth rates, where co-movement is measured by the magnitude of the first (common) factor in a principal components analysis. For 1870–1913, the first principal component accounts for 26.9 percent (with a standard error of 4.6 percentage points) of the variation in the growth rate of exports of the nine countries for which we have relatively reliable and complete data.[8] For 1968–2002, the first principal component accounts for a significantly higher proportion (53 percent, with a standard error of 6.4 percentage points) of the variation in the growth rate of exports of the seven countries in our EMBI sample for which we have good exports data.[9] Similarly, the average pairwise correlation of export growth was 0.13 in the historical sample, versus 0.43 in the modern one. This finding suggests that higher co-movement of

---

[7] As noted in previous chapters, modern measures of economic fundamentals such as gross domestic product or industrial production did not become popular until later in the twentieth century. GDP data are available for a very limited number of countries and usually not before the 1880s. Industrial production is available only for a smaller sample and is not representative of economic activity in emerging markets, which consisted largely of agriculture and natural resource extraction.

[8] Australia, Brazil, Canada, China, Egypt, Japan, Portugal, Russia, and Sweden.

[9] Argentina, Brazil, Mexico, Nigeria, Poland, the Philippines, and Venezuela. The results are robust to a number of variations in the estimation method, such as dropping one or two countries at a time (whether in the historical sample or in the modern sample), using more countries for a shorter historical sample period, or relying on other types of test statistics such as correlation coefficients.

Table 6.2. Composition of Exports by Product, Emerging Markets, 1900

Country	Export item 1	% of item 1 in total exports	Export item 2	% of item 2 in total exports	Export item 3	% of item 3 in total exports	% of top three in total exports	Herfindahl index of exports
Sample average		38		12		8	58	2195
Argentina	Wheat	32	Wool	18	Hides and skins	14	64	1544
Australia	Wool	27	Meat	5	Butter	4	36	770
Brazil	Coffee	57	Rubber	20	Cotton	3	80	3658
Canada	Lumber	13	Metals	10	Wheat	10	33	369
Chile	Nitrate soda	64	Copper	14	n.a.	0	78	4292
Egypt	Cotton	77	n.a.	0	n.a.	0	77	5929
Japan	Raw silk	21	Cotton	12	Silk products	9	42	666
Mexico	Silver	47	Copper	7	Coffee	4	58	2274
Turkey	Fruit	13	Raw silk	9	Wool	8	30	314
Uruguay	Wool	27	Hides, skins	27	Meat	26	80	2134

Source: Mitchell, B. R., *International Historical Statistics*, various issues.

fundamentals may tend to make today's spreads co-move more strongly than observed in the past.

In turn, today's greater co-movement of exports is likely to be related to the lower degree of specialization in the export structures of today's emerging markets compared with their predecessors in the pre-First World War era. Tables 6.2 and 6.3 shed further light on this hypothesis by listing the major export items of emerging markets in 1900 and 1999.

There is little doubt that emerging market countries in the previous era of globalization were far more specialized, with their top three exports accounting, on average, for close to 60 percent of total exports.[10] This figure is nearly twice as high as the corresponding statistic for emerging markets in the modern sample. The average Herfindahl Index for "concentration of exports" (in the top three

---

[10] The specialization figures remain virtually unchanged for the entire 1870–1913 period: there is no evidence that countries became more diversified over time.

Table 6.3. Composition of Exports by Product, Emerging Markets, 1999

Country	Export Item 1	% of item 1 in total exports	Export Item 2	% of item 2 in total exports	Export Item 3	% of item 3 in total exports	% of top 3 Items in total exports	Herfindahl Index of exports
Sample average				8.5		6.3	34.6	779
Argentina	423 Fixed vegetable oils	19.8	081 Animal Feed	8.8	333 Petroleum and crude oils	6.9	25.3	218
Brazil	281 Iron ore and concentrates	5.7	071 Coffee	5.1	061 Sugar and honey	4.0	14.9	75
Chile	682 Copper	27.2	287 Ores, metal concentrates	12.1	057 Fruit and nuts	7.1	46.5	938
China	894 Bady carriages and toys	4.4	851 Footwear	4.3	764 Telecom equipment	4.1	12.7	54
Colombia	333 Petroleum and crude oils	28.8	071 Coffee	12.3	322 Coal, lignite, and peat	7.2	48.3	1034
Czech Republic	781 Passenger motor cars	8.0	784 Part and accessories	5.5	778 Electrical equipment	3.7	17.1	107
Egypt	334 Refined petroleum products	27.4	333 Petroleum and crude oils	8.4	263 Cotton	6.8	42.6	869
Hungary	713 Internal combustion engines	10.8	752 Data processing equipment	8.9	781 Passenger motor cars	5.4	25.0	224
India	667 Pearls, precious stones	18.1	843 Women's outergarments	5.0	651 Textile yarn	4.4	27.6	373
Indonesia	333 Petroleum and crude oils	9.3	341 Gas	9.0	634 Wood	5.2	23.4	193
Israel	667 Pearls, precious stones	30.1	764 Telecom equipment	11.1	752 Data processing equipment	4.2	45.5	1049
Jordan	271 Fertilizers, crude	25.6	562 Fertilizers, manufactured	10.6	541 Pharmaceutical products	10.3	46.5	876
Kenya	074 Tea	28.4	071 Coffee	10.4	334 Refined petroleum products	8.2	47.0	984
Korea	776 Thermionic cells	15.2	781 Passenger motor cars	6.9	764 Telecom equipment	5.2	27.4	307
Malaysia	776 Thermionic cells	20.4	759 Parts of and accessories	12.5	752 Data processing equipment	7.6	40.5	630
Mexico	781 Passenger motor cars	9.1	333 Petroleum and crude oils	6.5	764 Telecom equipment	5.2	20.8	152
Morocco	843 Women's outergarments	10.9	842 Men's outergarments	9.0	522 Inorganic chemicals	7.8	27.8	262
Pakistan	658 Textile articles	14.5	652 Cotton fabrics, woven	14.1	651 Textile yarn	13.2	41.8	583
Peru	971 Gold, nonmonetary	20.1	682 Copper	12.2	287 Ores, metal concentrates	10.3	42.7	660
Philippines	931 Special transactions	51.2	776 Thermionic Cells	11.4	752 Data processing equipment	9.0	71.6	2830
Poland	821 Furniture	7.2	781 Passenger motor cars	4.0	793 Ships and boats	3.8	14.9	82
South Africa	681 Silver and platinum	9.5	667 Pears, precious stones	6.8	322 Coal, lignite, and peat	6.0	22.3	172
Taiwan P.O.C.	776 Thermionic cells	12.1	752 Data processing equipment	10.6	759 Parts of and accessories	9.6	32.3	350
Thailand	759 Parts of and accessories	10.3	776 Thermionic cells	6.9	037 Seafood	3.5	20.7	166
Turkey	845 Outergarments	7.1	846 Undergarments	6.4	843 Women's outergarments	5.3	18.8	120
Venezuela	333 Petroleum and crude oils	80.8	684 Aluminium	3.3	671 Various forms of iron	1.2	85.2	6535
Zimbabwe	121 Unmanufactured tobacco	33.4	671 Various forms of iron	6.8	263 Cotton	5.8	46.0	1195

Note: Three-digit numbers refer to Standard International Trade Classification (SITC) Codes, Revision 2.
Source: United Nations Conference on Trade and Development (UNCTAD), 2001.

sectors) is roughly three times higher for the historical sample than for the modern sample.[11]

A casual look at Tables 6.2 and 6.3 conveys two important messages regarding the export and production patterns of emerging markets in the historical period compared with the present. First, the typical emerging market was far more focused on a small number of export items. Second, its primary exports were much more likely to differ from those of other emerging market countries.

To see the second point more systematically, imagine that in each period, each of the existing N emerging countries is randomly assigned three primary export items out of a total of Y available products and commodities. What is the probability of at least one overlap in the top three exports of any two countries? This probability is equal to one minus the probability of no overlaps at all. This, in turn, can be derived as follows:

Probability of no overlap = [total number of possible combinations in which country i is assigned three export items out of the available Y products and country j is assigned three non-overlapping items out of the remaining $Y - 3$ products] divided by [total number of possible allocations of three export items out of the Y available to two countries].[12]

In the historical sample, fourteen export commodities are reported for the sample of ten countries for which data are available. The expected frequency of (random) overlaps (i.e. the frequency of country pairs with at least one common export items) is therefore about 0.55. One would thus expect to find about 25 country pairs (0.55 times forty-five possible country pairs) with at least one overlapping export item in the sample. In practice, the number is only 13. The standard deviation of the proportion of pairs with overlaps in the sample is $P/(N(N - 1)/2)$, where P is the expected proportion of overlaps and N is the number of countries. It is therefore easy to see that the actual proportion of overlaps is more than two standard deviations lower than its expected mean, under the null hypothesis that exports are randomly assigned. In other words, it is possible to

---

[11] The Herfindahl index, a standard measure of concentration, is defined here as the sum of the squares of the shares (in percentage points) of the top three products in total exports. In the extreme case of only one product accounting for all exports by a given country, the index would take the value of $100 \times 100 = 10,000$.

[12] Formally, if Y is the total number of available export items and X is the number of export items assigned to each country (in our case, $X = 3$), this is equal to $1 - [(Y - X)!(Y - X)!]/[(Y - 2X)!Y!]$.

reject the null hypothesis of random assignments of export items with a confidence level of over 95 percent.

In the modern data (with twenty-seven countries and thirty-four export items), the expected number of country pairs with at least one common export item is 88. The actual number in the data is 83, very close to (and statistically not different from) the number of overlaps one would expect to observe if export items were randomly assigned.

On the whole, we have shown that emerging markets in the past were more specialized in a few export commodities than are their counterparts today. To our knowledge, the present study is the first to show this result based on systematic data analysis. Our findings are consistent with the work by Imbs and Wacziarg (2003), who analyze the changing degree of specialization for a panel of countries at various stages of economic development, based upon post-Second World War data. They show that the typical pattern of development is for countries to be initially specialized at low levels of development, then to become gradually more diversified as their per capita incomes grow, and finally to return to being somewhat more specialized once they cross a per capita income threshold that would seem to characterize some of the higher-income emerging markets.

6.4 Do Fundamentals Explain the High Co-Movement of Spreads in the 1990s?

Despite the higher degree of co-movement of exports—and the greater similarity in the product structure of exports—in modern times than in historical times, probably only part of the explanation for the relatively high degree of co-movement in spreads in modern times (and in the 1990s in particular) has to do with fundamentals. In fact, our view is that fundamentals are unlikely to be the main part of the story: for example, the recent decline in co-movement of spreads that followed the Argentinean crisis is unlikely to be driven by changes in the degree of co-movement of fundamentals.

To assess more systematically whether fundamentals could be a substantial part of the story, we analyze the degree of co-movement of that portion of bond spreads that is not explained by fundamentals. More technically, we analyze the co-movement of the residuals from the regressions in Chapter 5 that sought to explain spreads on the basis of news indicators and macroeconomic variables.[13] Such residuals are the portion of bond spreads that cannot be explained by fundamentals. We now consider measures of co-movement for these residuals. The share of variation accounted for by the first principal component is 31.5 percent (standard deviation: 6.0 percentage points) for 1881–1913;[14] 67.3 percent (standard deviation: 7.7 percentage points) for 1996Q1–2001 Q2;[15] and 50.8 percent (standard deviation: 8.2 percentage points) for 1996Q1–2002Q4. Thus the results are broadly similar to those obtained in Section 6.2 without controlling for fundamentals: the degree of co-movement is greater in modern times than historical times; furthermore, in this exercise, even the extended modern series which includes the onset of the Argentinean crisis exhibits higher co-movement than the historical sample. This broad pattern of results is maintained using alternative measures of co-movement (omitted here for the sake of brevity). On the whole, this suggests that fundamentals are unlikely to be a major factor accounting for changes in the degree of co-movement of spreads over time.

An alternative, and perhaps more plausible, explanation for the high co-movement of spreads in modern times relates to differences between the modern and historical periods in the institutional arrangements for investing in emerging markets. However, it is not immediately obvious exactly what differences in institutional arrangements are relevant in this context. It might be argued that the presence of international financial institutions that seek to alleviate the consequences of financial crises could result in greater co-movement of spreads. If the international financial institutions are always going

[13] Specifically, we use the residuals from the regression in the 1st column in Table 5.3 for the historical period; and a regression as in the 6th column in Table 5.6, but omitting the portfolio spreads—the results on the other coefficients are quite similar—for the modern period.

[14] The principal components procedure requires a complete panel data set and computing the residuals requires that all the macroeconomic variables and news indicators be available for the whole sample period. Owing to data limitations, the sample thus needs to be restricted to the eight countries for which macro data are available and which did not experience payments difficulties that led us to question the quality of the spreads data in any single year (Argentina, Canada, Chile, Hungary, Japan, Portugal, Queensland, and Sweden), for 1881–1913. The observation for 1885 is dropped owing to lack of macro data for Queensland for that year.

[15] For the principal components procedure to be a sensible exercise, a sufficiently long time series is needed, making it necessary to use quarterly data in this case. Owing to data limitations, Nigeria is omitted from the sample, and the sample period has to be restricted to begin in 1996.

to come to the rescue of international investors, the argument might go, investors would be less likely to pay attention to individual country characteristics, helping explain why all spreads tend to move in unison. We find this hypothesis somewhat implausible, particularly in view of today's large spreads, which presumably reflect a high-perceived probability of default followed by investor losses. Nevertheless, this hypothesis has attracted considerable interest and we summarize the related studies in Box 6.2. It is important to note that the general tension between avoiding widespread financial crises and creating moral hazard problems existed in the previous era of globalization as well, as illustrated by the Baring Crisis (see Box 6.1 above). The intervention of the Bank of England in assistance of Baring's Bank could have reduced the incentives of investment banks, underwriters and investors to exert effort to gather information on borrowers and assess their creditworthiness. Investors in Argentinian bonds incurred heavy losses despite the bailout, but perhaps their losses would have been even higher without the Bank of England's intervention. With hindsight, it seems that the risk of opportunistic behavior did not materialize.

A more relevant difference in institutional arrangements, in our opinion, relates to the key role that individual investors played in the past. As noted in the previous chapter, Michie (1987) estimates that the number of individual investors on the London Stock Exchange in 1913 was about one million (see also Edelstein, 1982). This stands in sharp contrast with the role played today by large institutional investors (such as mutual funds, pension funds, and hedge funds), which—at least in the 1990s—invested in or divested from groups of emerging markets seemingly regardless of the varying strengths of the underlying economies' fundamentals. From the point of view of individuals, investing in foreign countries through funds may reduce monitoring and transaction costs. Yet when a crisis emerges, these funds tend to liquidate their holdings of securities in several emerging markets *en bloc*, apparently so as to maintain a given risk and liquidity profile. Hedge funds, for example, seem to operate in a way that forces them to sell their holdings in healthy economies when a crisis erupts elsewhere.[16] Another potential explanation is that "noise traders" or "herd behavior" (see a survey in Shleifer, 2000) might play a more

---

[16] See, for example, Eichengreen (1999a). Kaminsky and Reinhart (2000) discuss the behavior of investment funds more generally.

Box 6.2 SPREADS, CO-MOVEMENT, INTERNATIONAL FINANCIAL INSTITUTIONS, AND MORAL HAZARD—A LITERATURE REVIEW

A potential hypothesis is that the greater co-movement in spreads observed in the 1990s might be due in part to investor "moral hazard" resulting from the presence of the international financial institutions in today's environment. Indeed, a notable difference with respect to the pre-1914 era is the presence of international financial institutions, notably the International Monetary Fund, that in many cases lend to countries experiencing balance of payments difficulties. (This was emphasized in the earlier working paper title of Marc Flandreau's 2003b study: "Caveat Emptor: Coping with Sovereign Risk without the Multilaterals"). If the international financial institutions were always going to help countries in trouble, one might argue, today's international investors would have little incentive to monitor countries' fundamentals: in the end, regardless of countries' behavior, investors would nearly always be repaid. If that were the case, all countries would then have similar spreads at any point in time, and co-movement would indeed be expected to be greater today than in the past. Changes in country-specific risks would not be reflected in spreads, because the international financial institutions would provide insurance against such risks. Changes in spreads would only be driven by common shocks (such as changes in advanced country interest rates, or "risk appetite") affecting all emerging markets. (The international financial institutions are not large enough to protect all emerging markets at the same time against such common shocks).

This hypothesis has generated considerable interest in recent years, and some researchers have addressed it directly. (See Cordella, 2004 for a review.) The evidence supporting the hypothesis is mixed, though, admittedly, this is an especially difficult research objective, and existing studies often have methodological limitations. Several studies have found little impact of the IMF's presence on emerging market spreads. In regression analysis of the determinants of emerging market spreads before and after the Mexican "bailout," Zhang (1999) found the dummy variable for the post-Mexico period to have an insignificant and positive coefficient—the opposite of what one would find if moral hazard had increased after the crisis. Nevertheless, it has to be recognized that the main effect of the Mexican crisis of late 1994 and early 1995 must have been to increase investors' perceived probability of crisis; the IMF's rescue package would likely have been a less important, perhaps partially mitigating factor. Kamin (2004) finds that emerging market countries that could be considered to be "systemic," in view of their large economic size or other considerations, and that might therefore be viewed by some market participants as more likely to obtain an international rescue package, do not enjoy lower spreads than other countries. Lane and Phillips (2000) do not find a significant relationship between news regarding IMF packages and emerging market spreads. Brealey and Kaplanis (2004) find that most IMF-related news have little impact on spreads, although announcements that IMF support would not be forthcoming did lead to negative abnormal returns. Of course, studies (including our own in Chapter 4) seeking to identify the impact of news on spreads are subject to the possibility that "news" are in practice fully expected.

Perhaps the most careful test of this hypothesis to date is provided by a recent study by Dell'Ariccia, Schnabel, and Zettelmeyer (2002). The authors test for the existence of a moral hazard effect attributable to official crisis lending by analyzing the evolution of sovereign bond spreads in emerging markets before and after the Russian crisis. They interpret the "non-bailout" of Russia in August 1998 as an event that decreased the perceived probability of future crisis lending to emerging markets. In the presence of moral hazard, such an event should raise the cross-country variance of spreads, controlling for fundamentals. They find evidence consistent with this hypothesis. This is an interesting result, though an important caveat is in order. As seen in our own empirical analysis, the extent to which fundamentals explain spreads is limited. And emerging market spreads rose dramatically after the Russian crisis, for a variety of reasons, including large losses, and subsequent reduction in demand, by several specialized investors (notably hedge funds). Thus, an increased variance (as opposed to an increased coefficient of variation—the ratio of the variance to the mean) in the portion of emerging market spreads that is not explained by fundamentals is also consistent with the view that spreads rose in all emerging markets owing to other factors.

On the whole, our impression is that there is little evidence supporting the view that the greater spread of co-movement in the 1990s might be due to the presence of the international financial institutions. It is also important to note that spreads were much higher in the 1990s than in the pre-1914 era, suggesting that the perceived probability of default, and ensuing losses by international investors, was substantial in the modern period, despite the presence of the international financial institutions.

important role today than a hundred years ago, perhaps because large investment funds follow each other's strategies.[17] Yet another possible explanation (for which we have no specific evidence) is that the somewhat slower trading technologies of the past may have been advantageous in reducing panics and the spread of crises. For example, while news reports discussed in Box 6.1 suggest considerable concern among investors at the time of the Baring crisis of 1890, relatively slow trading technologies may have helped in inducing investors to "take a breather."

But if investor behavior is the main determinant of the degree of co-movement in spreads across countries, why does co-movement seem to have declined following the most recent crisis in Argentina? Are we arguing that institutional constraints led investors to behave in a seemingly irrational manner prior to 2001, but have suddenly been

---

[17] Somewhat related is the literature on the synchronicity of movements in stock prices in different countries (e.g. Morck, Yeung, and Yu, 2000; Li et al., 2004). In these studies co-movement of stocks (within a given market) is interpreted as evidence of inefficiency: investors are unable to distinguish between the fundamental values of different companies. We are not sure to what extent these arguments are applicable to the context of co-movement of spreads on bonds issued by different countries.

able to come to their senses and clearly distinguish between the economic fundamentals of Argentina and those of other countries?

While it may be too early to tell why the Argentinian crisis failed to cause immediate contagion, we conjecture that three factors may be at play. First, and most important, the Argentinian crisis was widely anticipated. Views on the country worsened gradually, with no obvious defining event or sudden surprise. Investors had time to get out of Argentina without panic and without sudden losses. Second, a technical factor may also have played a minor, though helpful role: Argentina's share of the EMBI was reduced by J. P. Morgan from 20 percent to 2 percent within a few months. (This reduction was prompted in large part by a debt swap whose characteristics implied that many of Argentina's bonds no longer met the requirements of international tradability for inclusion in the index.) Many emerging market institutional investors seek to mimic returns on the EMBI; they were thus able to reduce their exposure to Argentina selectively, rather than being forced to divest from emerging markets as a whole. Finally, to some extent, investors may have drawn lessons from the contagious crises of the 1990s and modified their behavior.

Based on these considerations, the future extent of spread co-movement is uncertain. On the one hand, greater similarities and co-movement of economic fundamentals across emerging markets may again tend to foster greater co-movement in the future. On the other hand, even in the 1990s, investor behavior (notably investment fund behavior) seems to have been a crucial factor behind the spread of crises (see also Kaminsky and Reinhart, 2000), and investor behavior may have changed following the recent crisis in Argentina. Comparing the 1990s and the early twenty-first century, it is too early to tell which will be the exception and which will be the rule.

7

Sovereign Defaults and the Corporation of Foreign Bondholders

7.1 Introduction

As we have seen in previous chapters, a substantial probability of default seems to be one of the defining characteristics of emerging market bonds. Having studied the determinants of the perceived likelihood of default, we now focus our attention squarely on times of crisis, and consider the mechanisms of default resolution in 1870–1913. To learn more about this issue, in the present chapter we analyze the workings of the Corporation of Foreign Bondholders (CFB), a London-based association of British investors holding bonds issued by foreign governments.[1] The CFB played a key role during the heyday of international bond finance, 1870–1913, and in the aftermath of the defaults of the 1930s.[2] It sought to protect the interests of its members by providing them with information about the borrowing countries and by fostering coordination among creditors, especially in

[1] While similar bondholders' associations were established in other countries at various times in history, the CFB was the longest-lived, best known, and most important among these institutions, in light of London's preeminence as the main financial center during the period we focus on. Other bondholders' associations included the Association Belge pour la Défense des Détenteurs de Fonds Public (Belgium), the Association Nationale des Porteurs Français de Valeurs Mobilières (France), the Association Suisse de Banquiers (Switzerland), the Caisse Commune des Porteurs des Dettes Publiques Autrichienne et Hongroise (France), the Committee of the Amsterdam Stock Exchange (Netherlands), the Conseil de la Dette Publique Répartie de l'Ancien Empire Ottoman (France), the Foreign Bondholders Protective Council (United States), and the League Loans Committee (United Kingdom) (Winkler, 1933, pp. 156–78).
[2] The CFB was formally set up in 1868 and was active until the early 1950s (the time of the last restructurings of international defaults that had taken place in the early 1930s).

cases of default. Indeed, the CFB's main objectives and core activities were related to default resolution.

To this day, sovereign defaults by emerging market countries remain a topical and thorny issue, as exemplified by the complex interaction between Argentina and its creditors in recent years. Improved creditor coordination in cases of sovereign default is a key objective of some proposals for reforming the international financial architecture, notably those related to a sovereign debt restructuring mechanism, more widespread use of collective action clauses, and a voluntary code of conduct for creditors and sovereign debtors.[3] In today's era of bond finance, creditor coordination is difficult—probably even more so than it was in the 1970s and 1980s, when the bulk of flows to emerging markets took the form of syndicated bank loans. Bondholders are more numerous, anonymous, and difficult to coordinate than are banks. Thus, once again, we search for potential lessons for improved creditor coordination today by going further back into the past and examining the experience of the most recent previous era of global financial integration and bond finance, 1870–1913.

To give a preview of our sense of the applicability of the CFB's experience to today's situation, our main conclusions may be summarized as follows: The CFB arranged successfully many important debt-restructuring agreements, though it failed persistently in a few cases. Yet, the CFB may have had an easier time than any comparable body would have today. While a revamped creditor association might once again help facilitate creditor coordination, the relative appeal of defection over coordination is greater today than it was in 1870–1913. Part of the original rationale for creditor associations seems to have disappeared, notably the need for creditors to coordinate in taking over collateral and tax revenues in defaulting countries. Moreover, a revamped creditor association may not be able to tackle challenges that existed to a far lesser extent in the past, such as avoiding lawsuits on the part of individual creditors.

Economists (Eichengreen and Portes, 2000; and Portes, 2000), lawyers (Macmillan, 1995b), and investment bankers (Buchanan, 2001) have pointed to the potential relevance of institutions such as the CFB in today's environment.[4] A few key bondholders have already

---

[3] See, for example, International Monetary Fund (2002), Krueger (2002), and Rogoff and Zettelmeyer (2002).

[4] The official sector has also considered the potential role of creditor committees (International Monetary Fund, 1999; Haldane, 1999, p. 186).

taken tentative steps in the direction of recreating a bondholders' association: the Emerging Markets Creditors Association (EMCA) was established in 2000, although it has thus far focused on issues of international financial architecture rather than playing an explicit role in country-specific cases.[5] Following Argentina's default in late 2001, and especially as the Argentine authorities held a series of meetings with private creditors in the summer of 2003 and announced the "Dubai guidelines" in September 2003, calling for a steep reduction in the nominal value of the defaulted bonds, a number of creditor groups and steering committees emerged, usually arranged by nationality, such as those representing bondholder representatives from the United States; German and Austrian retail bondholders; Italian banks in turn representing retail bondholders; and Japanese banks. In early 2004, several of these groups coalesced into a global committee of holders of Argentine bonds. Committees of this type played a significant role in the process that ultimately led to the debt exchange of early 2005.

Creditor associations are thus as relevant as ever. Could a revamped creditor association similar to the CFB provide a "private sector alternative," or at least a complement, to proposed reforms such as the more widespread use of collective action clauses or a sovereign debt restructuring mechanism? In what respect was the CFB successful in the past, and how successful would it be in the current environment? Which present-day problems are likely to be resolved through an association of this type? To address these questions, this chapter seeks to explore key similarities and differences in this context between today and 1870–1913, and to provide the most detailed and comprehensive description to date of the CFB's mode of operation.

As noted in the introduction, several previous studies, most notably Fishlow (1985) and Lindert and Morton (1989), provide excellent overviews of international default in the 1870–1913 globalization era. The CFB's importance in that context is well recognized, but its detailed workings remain relatively underexplored. Feis (1930), Borchard (1951), and Wynne (1951) provide early and fascinating treatments. More recent, and closely related to the present investigation, is a study by Kelly (1998), who discusses sovereign defaults and international trade in 1870–1913, but focuses on trade ties between borrowing countries and England as a major factor explaining

---

[5] See http://www.emta.org/ndevelop/emca.pdf.

defaults and willingness to pay. A series of impressive studies by Eichengreen and Portes (1986, 1988, 1989a, 1989b, and 2000) discusses sovereign debt, defaults, and workouts in the interwar period (with some reference to earlier cases and to the 1980s), and refers to the workings of the CFB in substantial detail. In particular, Eichengreen and Portes assess the CFB's effectiveness using two approaches. First, they compare the *ex post* returns on holdings of foreign bonds obtained by British bondholders to those obtained by American bondholders, who lacked a permanent organization to pursue their interests until the Foreign Bondholders Protective Council was created in 1933 (Eichengreen and Portes, 1989a). Second, they compare the typical delays between default, reorganization, and return to market access, before and after the establishment of the CFB (Eichengreen and Portes, 2000). They argue that the organization of British bondholders through the Corporation may have enabled them to realize high rates of returns on their holdings of foreign bonds, for example, in comparison with American creditors who were not as well organized.

Finally, Wright (2000) argues that the CFB's main role was to enforce collective behavior among creditors by disseminating information of members who "defected" and lent money to a defaulting country while it was embargoed; he presents a game-theoretic model that analyzes this function of the CFB. His study draws on the theoretical and empirical microeconomic literature that addresses the issue of collective action by creditors in periods when borrowing firms encounter payment difficulties. Studies such as Bolton and Scharfstein (1996), Gertner and Scharfstein (1991), and Hoshi, Kashyap, and Scharfstein (1990) all focus on firms in financial distress, their relations with creditors, and the importance of the number of creditors and other factors that determine their ability to act collectively.

Our analysis is mostly based on our own independent reading of the original sources (especially the *Annual Reports* of the CFB), but our interpretation is heavily influenced by what we have learned from previous studies on this topic. Our intended objective is not only to add important unearthed details to previous analyses of the CFB's mode of operation, but also to provide a single reference point to what is known about the CFB, which had previously been scattered around a number of different studies.

Our evaluation of the CFB and the potential lessons from its experience proceeds as follows. We first review the key differences between the need for creditor coordination in 1870–1913 and today, then analyze the CFB's success record and mode of operation, and finally draw potential lessons for today.

7.2 The Need for Creditor Coordination, 1870–1913 Versus Today

International lending was a risky business—and international defaults and renegotiations, messy business—during that first era of global financial integration, just as they are today. Nor are present-day proposals to set up a sovereign debt restructuring mechanism and to encourage more widespread use of collective action clauses in sovereign bonds by any means entirely novel. Indeed, the absence of a clear legal framework, let alone a sovereign debt restructuring mechanism, to deal with cases of international default was lamented as early as 1873, as evidenced by the quote reported below.

During the autumn of last year, a Conference of jurists and public men of various countries was held [. . .], having for one of its objects a discussion of the possibility of international agreements upon the principles of law which should determine the liability of Sovereign States and foreign subjects in their relations to one another. As a preliminary condition to the application of the moral force which is, after all, the sole ultimate sanction in such cases, there can be no question as to the advantage that would result from such an agreement (Corporation of Foreign Bondholders, Annual Report, 1874, London, p. 73. The Conference referred to was the Congress of International Law held in Geneva in 1873 and attended by Isidor Gerstenberg, Chairman of the Council of the CFB).

Even without a fully worked out legal framework to handle defaults and renegotiations, borrowing sovereign governments and private investors managed, with varying degrees of success, to give some structure to their often turbulent relationships and to find their own ways to deal with international defaults. The CFB emerged spontaneously as a, possibly insufficient, response by private creditors to the need to coordinate their actions.

Despite the similarities, however, in assessing the CFB's potential relevance for today, it is important to take into consideration a number of differences between 1870–1913 and the present. On balance, these differences suggest that the incentives for cooperation among creditors may have been greater in the past than they are today.

Extent of Sovereign Immunity

In the pre-First World War era, the doctrine of sovereign immunity made it almost impossible for individual creditors to sue sovereign debtors. As late as the early 1950s, Edwin Borchard concluded that as a general principle it was not possible to sue a foreign state on its public bonds (Borchard, 1951). For example, an English Court of Appeal denied an action to attach sales of Peruvian guano shipments designated as security for Peruvian loans in 1877, stating that "so-called bonds amount to nothing more than engagements of honour" that could not be enforced without the consent of the debtor country's government (cited in MacMillan 1995a, p. 336). Over the past few decades, there has been a gradual erosion of the principle of sovereign immunity. Beginning in the 1950s, the United States adopted a policy of restricted foreign immunity, whereby governmental activities that can also be conducted by private persons can be subject to standard domestic commercial law. This policy was formalized in the Foreign Sovereign Immunities Act of 1976. Britain adopted similar legislation—the State Immunity Act—in 1978. Lawsuits involving sovereign debtors have become rather common in recent years, as in the often-quoted case of Elliott Associates versus Peru.[6] The lack of scope for successful action on the part of individual creditors may have made creditor coordination easier to attain in the pre-First World War era than it is today.

Collateralized Bonds, Debt/Equity Swaps, Takeover of Tax Revenues, and (Rare) Use of Gunboats

The range of actions that could be conducted by a group of creditors in 1870–1913 was wider than it is today, making for a higher demand for a creditor association before First World War than it would be now. Bonds were often secured by collateral in the form of a railway or

---

[6] In 1995, Peru announced its Brady debt restructuring deal. One and a half years later, Elliott Associates, a "vulture fund," purchased some commercial loans that had been guaranteed by Peru. Elliott did not accept Brady bonds in exchange for the loans it had purchased; instead, it sued for the full value plus interest. In 2000 Elliott obtained a judgment against Peru and an attachment order against Peru's assets, which it used to delay Peru's payment of interest to its Brady bond creditors. Peru settled to avoid default on the Brady bond payments (International Monetary Fund, 2001, Box 2.6.). For a list of other notable lawsuits against sovereign governments, see Singh (2002). Lawsuits of this type have provided much of the impetus underlying proposals for a sovereign debt restructuring mechanism (see, for example, Krueger, 2002) and greater use of collective action clauses.

other easily identifiable assets, or even specific tax revenues. It was common for creditors to take over assets or even tax revenues (and, in extreme cases, the administration of tax revenues) of defaulting sovereigns. Even when the bonds were not formally collateralized, often they were used to finance a specific project, such as the construction of a railway, implying that the creditors had a natural choice for an asset to take over in lieu of debt repayments. As noted in Chapter 2, bonds used to finance railways (including both private and public) accounted for a substantial share of overall British holdings of overseas investment assets (Feis, 1930, p. 27; Fishlow, 1985, p. 392; Bordo, Eichengreen, and Kim, 1998, pp. 16–17). Taking over and monitoring a railway or a stream of tax revenues requires significant managerial resources, thus providing a strong incentive for creditor cooperation. At the same time, as we document below, conflicts often emerged regarding which investors had priority over the collateral, especially in cases where the same collateral was used to back up more than one bond. Finally, in extremely rare cases, gunboat diplomacy was resorted to. The extent to which the actual or potential use of force affected the relationship between international borrowers and lenders has been hotly debated. Tomz (forthcoming) reviews the experience of 300 years of international lending and borrowing and finds few cases in which the prospect of direct sanctions such as trade embargoes, the seizure of assets, or diplomatic/military pressure motivated countries to honor their debts and gave investors the confidence to lend. While the exact impact of the use of force in the past remains an open question, it seems clear that an association of bondholders was occasionally able to approach the creditor country authorities and attempt to persuade them to intervene on its behalf; by contrast, individual creditors would have been unlikely to be listened to. In today's environment, neither the seizure of collateral or tax receipts, nor military interventions are serious options, thus reducing the need for creditor cooperation in this respect.

Number of Financial Centers

Despite London's unchallenged preeminence as the main financial center for emerging bond market issuance in the past, emerging market bonds could be issued in several financial centers in 1870–1913, not unlike today. Russia issued bonds in various currencies (sterling, francs, florins, marks, and roubles—gold, silver, and paper) and financial centers (St. Petersburg, London, Paris, Amsterdam, Hamburg, Berlin, and Warsaw), often with exchange rate clauses or metallic clauses. It was common for emerging countries to issue a bond simultaneously in a number of centers, with coupons payable in a variety of currencies. For example, in 1913 China issued a bond with coupons payable—at the creditor's discretion—in sterling, roubles, marks, francs, or yen (Flandreau and Sussman, 2004). Although strictly comparable data are not available, the share of bonds issued on the four or five largest financial centers does not seem to be very different today from that observed in the past. Four countries accounted for 85 percent of the entire stock of international investment in 1914: the United Kingdom (44 percent), France (20 percent), Germany (13 percent), and the United States (8 percent) (Fishlow, 1985, p. 394).[7] The CFB reports mention only one other country—the Netherlands—that had lent significant amounts to emerging markets. Today, the four largest financial centers account for an even greater share of emerging market bond issues than was the case in the past. Becker, Richards, and Thaicharoen (2002) report that, out of a total of 2452 bonds issued by emerging market borrowers, 41 percent are issued under English law, 35 percent under New York law, 10 percent under Japanese law, 7 percent under German law, and the remainder in a variety of other laws (including those of Luxembourg, Italy, Spain, Switzerland, Hong Kong SAR, and Austria).[8] Thus, the number of financial centers where one could potentially issue today does not seem to be substantially different from the past.

Number and Variety of Bonds

The number of bonds issued by a given country tended to be somewhat lower in the past than it is today. In 1883, Russia, the largest borrower at the time, had twenty-three bonds (though there may have been multiple issues of the same bond, as some were perpetuities) traded in London and Paris (Flandreau and Sussman, 2004). By contrast, in late 2001 Argentina had more than 150 different bonds

---

[7] The percentage of Latin American external debt held by the four largest investor countries was similar, at 88 percent in 1914, though slightly more concentrated in British hands: Great Britain held 68 percent, France 14 percent, the United States 4 percent, and Germany 2 percent (United Nations, 1965, p. 16, cited in Lipson, 1985, p. 48).

[8] Type of law and location of the exchange are closely correlated.

outstanding, issued in several financial centers, in a variety of currencies and legal jurisdictions, and with different features. Disagreement over the relative treatment of different types of creditors is therefore an even more thorny issue today than it was in the past.

Degree of Diffusion of Bondholders

As noted by Olson (1965), the number of potential members of an organization is a key determinant of whether an organization emerges and operates successfully. There are substantial differences in the degree of diffusion of bondholders then and now, although it is not clear whether they ultimately make for easier or more difficult coordination among bondholders today than in the past. Despite lack of systematic evidence, it seems clear that the number of ultimate individual holders of sovereign bonds in 1870–1913 was far smaller than it is today. Based on the CFB reports, one could guess that the order of magnitude of holders of bonds of a typical emerging market in 1870–1913 was probably in the hundreds—clearly more than enough to present coordination challenges, but still a manageable number that could fit in a large room. By contrast, today there seem to be—at the very least—tens of thousands of individual investors. However, today's coordination problems are substantially mitigated as the majority of ultimate individual investors hold their bonds in mutual funds, whereas this was less common in the past.

International Financial Institutions

Finally, previous studies have emphasized that, in today's environment, international financial institutions are involved in an ongoing dialogue with member countries regarding their policies, through surveillance and—in the context of programs—conditionality. Researchers have also noted that the resolution of debt crises may be faster in today's environment partly because of the provision of new loans by the international financial institutions. In particular, Portes (2000) has argued that for the International Monetary Fund to "get out of the big bailout package business," appropriate institutions to deal with international debt problems would have to be in place, including revamped creditors' associations.

7.3 Effectiveness: Successes and Failures

It is difficult to provide a single measure of the CFB's degree of success, and in many respects the counterfactual is not clear—one can only speculate about what would have happened in the absence of the CFB. Nevertheless, several pieces of information related to the CFB's effectiveness are reported in this section, with the obvious caveat that different readers may interpret them differently.

The CFB was ultimately able to reach agreement in all renegotiations with important borrowers, such as Turkey, Spain, Greece, Portugal, Mexico, Argentina, and Brazil. The agreements proved to be acceptable to the bondholders, who otherwise would have been able to reject them. The CFB itself (obviously not an unbiased observer), seemed to be moderately happy with its ability to reach agreement with its large borrowers. In the early 1900s, the CFB stated that it had been able to manage "enlightened countries," none of which were in default any longer (1905–6 Report, pp. 1–2). In fact, the number of countries and total amounts in default declined dramatically between the 1870s (when the CFB began to operate) and the early twentienth century (Figure 7.1), although this may have been due in part to other factors such as improved macroeconomic conditions in the emerging markets of the day.

By early 1907, the only countries remaining in total default were three small Latin American countries: Costa Rica (since 1901), Guatemala (since 1899), and Honduras (since 1873). Despite the lower frequency of new defaults, the CFB lamented that by the early 1900s "the problem of effecting satisfactory settlements of debt remaining in default ha[d] increased in difficulty." The CFB recognized that in "small and backward" countries it had to either accept unsatisfactory settlements or face seemingly indefinite default (1905–6 Report, pp. 1–2). By 1913, only Honduras remained in default, in addition to several Southern US states (Louisiana, Mississippi, and West Virginia, plus the 1863 7 percent cotton loan of the former confederate states).

Debt repayment problems with some Latin American countries persisted for much of the period, especially with respect to smaller countries, which often reneged on their debt for decades and, when repaying, favored local or even US creditors. The following caricature from 14 August 1875 illustrates the way small Latin American borrowing countries may have been perceived:

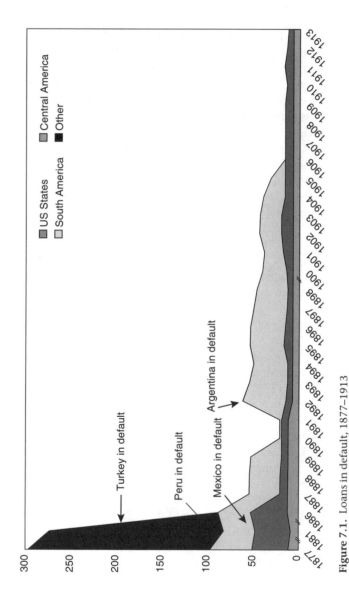

Figure 7.1. Loans in default, 1877–1913

Notes: Data are unavailable for 1878–80, 1882–5, and 1899. The prominent debt defaults of Argentina, Mexico, Peru, and Turkey are highlighted.

Source: Annual Reports of the Corporation of Foreign Bondholders.

PICKPOCKETS IN THE CITY.

ACCOMMODATION BILL AND FOREIGN-LOANS MO' "DOING BUSINESS."

Source: John Tenniel, 14 August 1875. Reproduced with the permission of Punch, Ltd.

Honduras, for example, was criticized as follows: "It is incredible that the Government should (reject a CFB offer and) prefer to enter its thirty-first year of unbroken total and disreputable default" (1901 Report, p. 23). Costa Rica, in default for 22 out of the preceding 39 years, tended to pay its internal obligations while defaulting on its external debt (1909 Report, p. 23): "The conduct of the Costa Rica Government in leaving its External Debt year after year in total default while regularly paying its internal obligations is deserving of the severest condemnation" (1903 Report p. 22). Ecuador completed a railway, while in default to its foreign bondholders, by investing a sum equal to its external debt. The CFB was less critical of Ecuador (1907 Report, p. 11) than it was of Honduras, possibly because it viewed investment in a railway as productive and ultimately leading to better ability to repay. Guatemala preferred to continue paying interest to American bondholders, but not to British ones (1909 Report, pp. 24–5), and so did Honduras and Ecuador. Guatemala even let an American syndicate possess coffee export duties. In Honduras, a railway was leased to an American company and in Ecuador, half of the export duties were given as security for an American loan.

Some of the Southern US states represented another consistent source of trouble for the CFB. Attempts to negotiate debts in arrears with Alabama, Virginia, and other states starting in the early 1870s were largely unsuccessful. One source of difficulty was that coordination was required with New York bondholders (see below). Moreover, the bondholders' ability to access US courts was severely limited, owing in part to a constitutional amendment that prevented individuals from taking legal action against states (1907 Report, p. 16). These defaulting US states also favored American creditors (1911 Report, pp. 11–3).

Why did the CFB eventually manage to find an acceptable agreement with the large borrowers, whereas it seemed to fail in its dealings with small Latin American borrowers and Southern US states? The answer seems to relate to international politics and the ability to borrow in the US markets (which were able to provide sufficient finance to the Southern US states and the small Latin American countries, but not to the larger emerging markets). Indeed, willingness to pay seems to have been more important than ability to pay (proxied by debt per capita or other macroeconomic indicators). The 1908 Annual Report of the CFB (pp. 11–5) contrasts Ecuador, which reached a settlement with its creditors, with other Latin American countries in this respect; it concludes that heavy debt burdens did not cause default. For example, Uruguay paid its debt even though on a per capita basis it was higher than for the three defaulters mentioned above. Venezuela's excellent repayment history (a few years after a military blockade by creditor countries) is praised as "a record in the history of the smaller Spanish-American republics." Salvador also had a very good record. By contrast, Guatemala was in default for 13 years and repudiated four negotiated agreements despite its relatively low debt burden (1911 Report, pp. 20–24).

Countries' willingness to repay their debts to British bondholders was probably determined by their relations with Britain as a trading partner (Kelly, 1998) and as an international superpower. Countries such as Argentina, which despite its location viewed Britain as a key partner, eventually came to terms with the British bondholders. By contrast, as explicitly recognized by the CFB itself, some of the smaller Latin American countries were evading payment by taking refuge behind the Monroe Doctrine, which regarded Latin America as the United States' "back yard" and sphere of influence (1911 Report, p. 26). One indication that this was a major factor is the significant decline in spreads for Latin American bonds between 1901 and 1905 following President Theodore Roosevelt's statement that he would not let Latin American countries use US protection to avoid debt repayment. This decline reflected investor optimism about the prospect of successful settlement negotiations with Latin American countries (1904 Report, p. 11). The CFB's failure and the American creditors' success with small Latin American countries and the Southern US states also show that trade links and international politics are far more important in this respect than is creditor coordination, as American bondholders did not have a permanent association during this period.

Eichengreen and Portes (2000) provide another evaluation of the CFB's success record. Relying on Suter (1992), they point out that the average duration of default periods (or the time required to arrive at a settlement) was shorter during the heyday of the CFB than it was in other periods. Defaults lasted on average about 6 years in the 1871–1925 period, a figure which may appear long by today's standards, but is substantially shorter than the comparable figures for 1821–70 (14 years) and for 1925–76 (over 10 years). Looking at bond prices of defaulting countries, one also gets the impression that despite the CFB's status as the "umbrella organization" representing British bond-holders, negotiations with defaulting countries were quite protracted, and that in many cases there was a long period of time in which bond prices of defaulting countries displayed a tendency to rise slowly, presumably in tandem with the (slow) progress in the restructuring negotiations.

In addition to examining the duration of default, Eichengreen and Portes (1989a), drawing on a large sample of bonds issued in

London and New York in the 1920s, show that British bondholders realized higher *ex post* rates of return on their holdings of foreign bonds than did American bondholders. They argue that this difference may have resulted in part from the organization of British bondholders through the CFB, and the lack of such a permanent association for American bondholders for much of the period they consider.

Finally, it would be interesting to know whether the presence of the CFB affected the frequency of defaults. Today, opponents of a sovereign debt restructuring mechanism or collective action clauses argue that arrangements aimed at facilitating the restructuring process might make defaults more frequent. While defaults in 1870–1914 were not especially frequent compared with other periods, unfortunately there are too many other determinants of defaults (and potential endogeneity problems—the CFB itself being a response to prior defaults) to say anything conclusive. In this context, the CFB at the time would probably have said that one of its objectives was to let borrowing countries know that if they defaulted they would have a tough negotiating counterpart, capable of coordinated action in seeking to punish them. In addition, it is interesting to note that, while providing investors with information on *all* borrowing countries, the CFB was primarily in the business of dealing with defaults after they occurred. However clearly the *ex ante* impact of the CFB on defaults remains an open question.

The record of the CFB could be viewed as an upper bound on what could be expected from a modern association of bondholders, for two reasons. First, the CFB was the most successful and longest surviving among the historical bondholders associations. Thus, in evaluating the record of associations of this kind, choosing the CFB (rather than another association) as the object of analysis implies a tendency to reach optimistic conclusions, resulting from a certain degree of "survivorship bias." Second, the incentives to deviate from cooperative arrangements among creditors are probably higher today than they were in the past. To summarize the assessment of its effectiveness, the CFB had a fairly impressive record overall, even though it was unable to guarantee successful debt settlements for those few defaulters that did not wish to regain access to the capital markets in London and Europe more generally. To analyze the sources of the CFB's successes and failures, we now turn to examining its mode of operation in detail.

7.4 The Corporation of Foreign Bondholders: Mode of Operation

The CFB's Objectives—Provision of Information and Creditor Coordination

The CFB's ultimate goal was the protection of the interests of the holders of foreign Government, State, or Municipal securities. That goal was pursued by providing information to bondholders about the borrowing countries (in particular, the less developed countries), and by fostering coordination among creditors, especially in cases of default. The information provided to bondholders included vast amounts of economic commentary and data, and analysis of political developments. For example, the CFB collected eighteen volumes of newspaper clips about Brazil in the period 1870–1913 and a total of over 500 volumes containing information and correspondence of the CFB regarding different countries. It also had agents in various countries providing "valuable and often confidential information," which it placed at the disposal of its members (1873 Report). The CFB's Annual Reports included a wealth of information on individual countries, such as a comprehensive history of debt and default, trade statistics, fiscal debt and expenditures, and the political environment.

Coordination among bondholders in taking action vis-à-vis borrowing countries was pursued in a number of ways as discussed in detail below. It may be argued that the provision of information itself facilitated coordination among creditors: creditors were more likely to agree on a common strategy if they based their decisions on similar data and analysis. Moreover, the CFB's reading room and library, and the lectures given at the CFB on topics of interest to its members, must have provided opportunities for members to exchange ideas and socialize. Finally, the CFB provided one simple but crucial piece of information that might not otherwise have been easily available to all bondholders, namely whether countries had defaulted to some bondholders. Wright (2000) suggests that this piece of information helped reduce the likelihood that other creditors might extend new credit to a defaulting country.

The CFB's Institutional History, Organization, and Officers' Incentives

The CFB was founded in 1868 and incorporated under License from the Board of Trade in 1873. In the first decades of its existence, the CFB was often criticized for being too willing to settle quickly for debt restructuring deals that were unfavorable to bondholders. Allegedly, this was because of the excessive influence within the CFB of banks that were involved in the bond underwriting business (Feis, 1930; Portes 2000, pp. 58–9).[9] The CFB was then reconstituted in 1898 (by Special Act of Parliament in 1897) and the influence of underwriting banks in it was greatly reduced, by revising the election mechanism. Starting in 1898, the Council (governing body) of the CFB consisted of twenty-one members, six of whom were appointed by the British Bankers Association, six by the London Chamber of Commerce, and nine co-opted by the Council as a whole (from among eligible "certificate holders"). The majority of the members after 1898 were therefore appointed by independent outside bodies, in contrast with the bank dominance in previous years. To help dissipate any remaining concerns, all annual reports starting in 1903 included a clear statement on the origins, functions, and procedures of the CFB.

The CFB was a nonprofit organization, and many of its officers were virtually unpaid: yearly stipends amounted to 1,000 pounds for the president, 500 pounds for the vice president, and 100 pounds for other members of the Council. CFB activities were funded by the interest proceeds on an initial fund of 115,000 pounds raised from members. Most of the CFB services to members were free of charge, although a "small fee" was sometimes awarded to committee members if a settlement was reached. Such fees were kept small to minimize the possibility that the committee members might be tempted to agree to an unfavorable restructuring deal just in order to secure a fee for themselves.

Country-specific committees were organized ad hoc, at the request of bondholders, to deal with loans to countries with repayment difficulties. A committee was organized if there was a "sufficient number" of interested bondholders. The President and Vice President of the Council of the CFB were members *ex-officio*; other members

---

[9] *The Economist* argued that "it is notorious that in all the negotiations for the re-arrangements of the debts of foreign States a powerful influence is exercised upon bondholders by the issuing houses, who find it practically impossible to do fresh business with the debtors while the default lasts, and who are, therefore, naturally anxious that some sort of settlement should be arrived at, more especially as settlements of the kind yield substantial pickings in the way of commissions, are frequently followed by new loans" (November 20, 1897, p. 1624). Similarly, "there are the financial houses interested in foreign loans, who, being only too well aware of the fact that business is altogether precluded while default exists, are also disposed to come to terms, self-interest being their only guide in the matter. But it was precisely because these evils were recognized that the Corporation was constituted" (20 February, 1897, p. 276).

were elected in a general meeting—they typically held bonds issued by the defaulting country but were otherwise essentially volunteers. Committees were able to act independently, without interference by the Council. The CFB provided the committees with housing, assistance, and advice; it was also responsible for some of the administrative and legal expenses. The vast majority of committee members were not members of the Council. In 1903 there were 20 separate Bondholders' Committees affiliated with the CFB, consisting of 215 members: of these, only 32 members (exclusive of the president and vice president) were also members of the CFB; and 17 out of those 32 had been appointed directly by the bondholders. Country-specific committees had a larger number of members, the larger the debt or the number of debt holders: for example, committees had more members for Spain and Portugal than for small Latin American countries.

Following default, committee members would travel to the defaulting country and meet with senior officials, often the country's chief executive or key ministers. The committee would conduct its own negotiations with the country authorities, return to London, and, in consultation with the Council, present a proposed restructuring deal to the membership of the CFB in the context of a general meeting of bondholders.

In a few cases, country-specific committees disagreed with the CFB Council regarding the desirable course of action. For example, in 1875 the Mexican committee tried to act independently of the CFB, though ultimately with little success (1875 Report, pp. 26–7). However, this seems to have been rare (1903 Report). Occasionally, the Council of the CFB also conducted some activities on its own initiative: examples include its appointing of the British representative on the Council of Administration of the Ottoman Public Debt and its occasional direct interventions on behalf of individuals whose rights had been "prejudiced" by the action of foreign governments. However, as a general rule the Council acted through the various country-specific committees associated with it.

Coordination among British Creditors

One of the key functions of the CFB was to coordinate creditors' actions. Indeed, to the extent possible, attempts were made to foster unanimity among bondholders: "every measure of the Council tends to promote that union of the bondholders which consists a real force against antagonists" (1873, p. 60). Although individual bondholders were not formally barred from taking independent action, "the advantages of co-operation are so great that there can seldom be sufficient ground for separate action" (1873 Report, p. 50). The CFB attempted to register the holders of bonds, even if deposited in banks or with brokers, to facilitate coordination in time of need.

One determinant of the ease with which creditors can coordinate their activities is the number of creditors; unfortunately, systematic evidence is not available on this point. Nevertheless, it appears that coordination under the auspices of the CFB typically involved hundreds of bondholders, representing a significant block, though not always the majority, of bondholders. For smaller bond issues, bondholders were often no more than a couple of hundred. About 200 bondholders were present at a general meeting regarding Costa Rica in 1874 (Minute Book, Costa Rica, 7 percent, 1874–85). A general meeting of holders of New Granada Bonds held on 18 November, 1872, was attended by seventy bondholders; a similar meeting in May 1873 was attended by about 150 bondholders (Minutes of the General Meetings of the Committee of Holders of New Granada and Colombia Bonds). Reports on other meetings of holders of bonds of small Latin American railway companies usually indicate the presence of twenty to eighty people.

Similarly, one determinant of the potential influence of a creditors' association in debt renegotiations is the share of total bonds held by creditors that it represents. Again, lack of systematic data makes it difficult to measure the CFB's influence in an accurate manner. It is clear, however, that the relative importance of CFB creditors varied substantially, ranging from cases where CFB bondholders had a very small share of the bonds, and where the CFB's involvement was minimal, to cases where the CFB spoke for the majority of outstanding bonds and was effectively the sole counterpart in the renegotiations. A number of specific cases and episodes illustrate this variation. In the case of Argentina's debt negotiated in 1889, about one-sixth of all holders of dollar-denominated debt were represented by the British CFB. In the case of Cedula Bonds issued by the Province of Buenos Aires, voters within the CFB held about a quarter of all bonds in 1903 (1903 Report, p. 13).[10] In the case of the

---

[10] A general meeting was poorly attended, so a "poll" was taken instead. Votes of holders of 23 million pounds (book value) were in favor of the proposed settlement; holders of 8.5 million pounds were against. The total value of outstanding Cedula Bonds at the time was 133 million pounds or more than 162 million pounds including various coupons and bonos certificados.

Pisco to Ica Railway (Peru), as of 1881, holders of 180 million pounds worth of bonds were registered with the CFB out of an original issue of 290 million pounds, of which 260 million pounds were unredeemed (National Pisco to Ica Railway Committee, 1878–92 Minutes). In the case of Ecuador, the amount of bonds represented by bondholders present at a "well attended" meeting in January 1907 was about 4 million pounds, a third of the total debt (1907 Report, pp. 140–2). In the case of Nicaragua, holders of 1 million pounds worth of bonds out of a total of 1.2 million attended a meeting in 1912, which, interestingly, was described as a "low turnout" (1912 Report, p. 12).

Mechanisms for Reaching Consensus within the CFB

All proposed deals (renegotiated agreements) with countries were brought to a vote in a public meeting of bondholders. For example, in 1874, a general meeting was convened to discuss overdue Spanish loans, where an overwhelming majority supported an agreement proposed by representatives of the CFB Spanish committee following their negotiations with the Spanish authorities. The renegotiated agreement did not let bondholders obtain their "full rights," but was enough to prevent outright Spanish default. "Dissentients were ultimately convinced" (1874 Report, p. 16). A debt restructuring proposal was occasionally brought to a general vote even if the country-specific committee itself did not have sufficient internal consensus on whether it should recommend the proposal (as was the case with the New Zealand Midland Railway in 1901, see 1902 Report, p. 14). A vote could also be taken by sending a "circular" to all bondholders—as indeed was done in the case of the New Zealand Midland Railway. Once a settlement was accepted, bondholders had to "lodge their securities for stamping in formal assent" (1903 Report, p. 13). If the proposed deal involved conversion or redemption of some of the bonds, a drawing would typically take place during the general meeting. Other payments to bondholders were also effected through the CFB.

Although the Council and the Committee played an extremely important coordinating role, the power to accept or reject a deal ultimately rested in the hands of the bondholders. For example, when Santo Domingo proposed to exchange its existing bonds for new bonds with a much lower face value, neither the Council nor the Committee accepted the offer, but the bondholders accepted it at a general meeting convened by the debtor (1886 Annual Report, p. 140).

147

Internal Disagreements and Coordination among Holders of
Different Bonds

While systematic evidence is hard to come by, the Reports of the CFB often refer to difficulties in reaching consensus among British creditors: "In cases of arrangements of Foreign Loans, there are generally some parties antagonistic to a settlement, and often either the negotiating Governments or some Bondholders wish to enforce their own peculiar views or terms upon the Council, which may be contrary to the general interest" (1874 Report, p. 8).

Internal conflict within the CFB membership often resulted from different interests among holders of different bonds issued by the same country. Therefore, one objective in negotiations with defaulting countries was the guarantee of "equal treatment" to all classes of bondholders. The settlement with Spain in 1876 involved a conversion of the old bonds with reduced interest payments at similar rates to all classes of creditors (1876 Report, pp. 44–50). In 1877, the CFB passed a decision providing that no arrangement with foreign governments would give preferential terms to any group of bondholders. This seems to have been in response to some cases in which individuals or groups of bondholders acted separately, particularly in the case of Turkey, where union among bondholders and concerted action proved hard to achieve (1878 Report, pp. 1–11). Nevertheless, it is not clear how frequently equal treatment across different classes of bondholders was attained in practice.

Internal conflict among holders of different bonds also often emerged when the same collateral was used to guarantee different bonds. Wynne (1951, p. 419) reports conflicts resulting from the use of the same securities to guarantee different bonds. Moreover, he reports instances in which bondholders with relatively easy access to the collateral guaranteeing their bonds pursued separate negotiations with a defaulting government. Following Turkey's default in the mid-1870s, for example, a group of British holders of Turkish bonds pursued separate negotiations because the debt they held was secured by Egyptian "tribute" payments, which were routinely channeled through London prior to the crisis, whereas the collateral securing most other bonds was held in Turkey.

As a general rule, the CFB made an effort to resolve conflicts among holders of different bonds and encourage joint action; the mechanism to reach consensus seems to have been, again, the general meeting.

Occasionally, the Council of the CFB or an independent arbitrator (as in the case of Chile, where more than one bond had been guaranteed by the same securities—Wynne, 1951, p. 164) would mediate among committees representing different classes of borrowers. In 1902 arbitration between bondholders and banks regarding a proposal to unify all Turkish bonds was tried first in Turkey (with no result), and then in England. In this case, arbitration seems to have been a mechanism to reconcile the interests of different claim holders within the CFB—in particular, banks versus individuals. (Continental bondholders supported individual British bondholders against a consortium of banks).

FORCEFUL COORDINATION AMONG CREDITORS

Lawsuits among Creditors

In rare instances, some bondholders appealed to the Courts against a deal reached by the CFB. Such disagreements often related to different treatment of different bonds. In the case of the default by Peru, the Peruvian Bondholders' Committee acted independently of the CFB, and the CFB only represented the interests of the holders of the bonds issued by the National Pisco to Ica Railway. An expensive and protracted litigation between these two groups resulted in an agreement confirmed by the High Court of Justice in 1885. One prominent bondholder, Mr Proctor, appealed this agreement but lost the subsequent lawsuit (Annual Report 1886, p. 106).

Dealing with Defectors

Wright (2000) argues that the CFB occasionally tried to put to shame those creditors who extended credit to countries in default to CFB members, and that the main function of the CFB was indeed to harm the reputation of defecting creditors. However, we have not found mention of this type of activity in the CFB reports.[11] Our own impression,

---

[11] Wright (2000) reports examples of this type of activity by creditor committees in the mid-1860s, prior to the establishment of the CFB. He also mentions a citation from the *Economist* in April 1897, stating that the intended function of the CFB was to safeguard against the evils of financial houses interested in issuing further loans. Our interpretation is different, however: at the time, there were widespread complaints against the issuing houses' excessive influence in the CFB, and their tendency to push for quick but unsatisfactory settlements in order to gain new business with countries emerging from default. As mentioned above, the CFB was restructured later that year to curb the influence of the issuing houses.

therefore, is that this may have been, at best, only one of a variety of ways in which the CFB attempted to foster creditor coordination and protect the bondholders' interests more generally.

Majority Action Clauses

In our research, we found no mention of majority action clauses (or collective action clauses). Previous research has shown that such clauses were introduced in corporate bonds in Britain by Francis Beaufort Palmer in 1879 (see Buchheit and Gulati, 2002, and Billyou, 1948) and rapidly gained popularity in corporate bond issues. It is not clear when these clauses gained prominence in sovereign bonds issued under UK law, where they have been common for a number of years.

Coordination with Bondholders in Other Countries

The CFB was well aware of the importance of coordination with creditors and stock markets in countries outside Britain: "It is the duty of the Bondholders of England and the Continent to remain united in their policy...and to preserve a common action, maintaining and promoting credit to the honest, and inflicting penalties on dishonest governments" (1873 Report, p. 43). Indeed, a major objective of the CFB was to "obtain unanimity of action among bondholders, and particularly with our influential allies in Holland" (1873 Report, p. 39). Since its early days, the CFB had constant relations with the Bourses of Amsterdam and Rotterdam "because of their high position in finance." It also cooperated with the Bourses of Frankfurt, Berlin, and Hamburg, and maintained correspondence with the Bourses of Paris and to some extent New York (1873 Report, pp. 51–2).

Coordination with bondholders based in other countries took place at various stages in the monitoring and renegotiation of debt contracts. International coordination during renegotiation was reported in many instances, such as the following. In 1875–6, negotiations with Spanish representatives in London by the English committee of the CFB were communicated "step by step to committees of Bondholders in Paris, Brussels, Amsterdam and Frankfurt..." (1876 Report, pp. 5–11). Coordination took place with creditors in Frankfurt in several instances, including overdue Alabama bonds in 1874 and Buenos Aires bonds in 1897. Separate committees formed in London, Paris, and Amsterdam to deal with Peruvian debt in 1877 seemed to coordinate their actions (1877 Report, p. 31). The committee of Egyptian bond-holders of 1876 included both French and British representatives. On April 24, 1873, a proposal to restructure the debt of New Granada was rejected by British bondholders, "with the concurrence of the Bondholders in Amsterdam" (Minutes of the General Meetings of the Committee of Holders of New Granada and Colombia Bonds). Coordination with creditors in other countries was also important in obtaining collateral and distributing the proceeds resulting from it: for example, British creditors and representatives of the French Société Générale coordinated the sales of Peruvian guano in 1876 and the division of the proceeds (1876 Report, pp. 34–40).

Coordination with bondholders in other countries was crucial in blocking defaulting countries' access to international capital markets, one of the most effective and important tools at the CFB's disposal—as shown in further detail in later sections. In 1874, "after consultation with the Bourses of the Continent it appeared desirable to make it known to the Mexican government that Mexico would no longer be allowed to avail herself directly or indirectly of European markets for the purpose of raising capital.... The effect of this intimation became immediately apparent..." (1874 report, p. 44) and the Mexican President sought settlement with the CFB. A similar boycott on Greek loans was enacted during negotiations with the Government of Greece in 1874, both in London and Amsterdam, in coordination with Dutch bondholders.

In cases where other countries' creditors had a greater share of the overall debt issued by a country in default, the CFB let others take the lead but lent its support in the negotiations. For example, the negotiation following Greece's default (dating back to 1860) is described as follows: "The holders in Holland, under the guidance of Mr. Louis Drucker, have taken a most active part in the vindication of the rights of the Bondholders, and the Council have given their hearty cooperation. Mr. Drucker himself visited Athens, and addressed the Ministers.... It has been determined to announce to the Greek Government that until the English loans in England and Holland are adjusted, no countenance shall be given to public or private enterprise connected with Greece. This policy is accepted by the Council, by the influential Bourse of Amsterdam, by that of Rotterdam, by Brussels, and by Antwerp. The declaration [... has been] published in English and French in the journals of Europe, and communicated to the leading papers in Greece, the diplomatic body in Europe and the East, and to others able to influence opinion" (1873 Report, p. 18).

Coordination with Continental European bondholders was usually smooth, but difficulties emerged in a few cases. For example, the Amsterdam-based bondholders accepted the conversion of the old New Grenada debt into new Colombian debt only when the deal involved cash payments instead of a land exchange that had been favored by the CFB bondholders (1873 Report, pp. 38–9). Similarly, disagreement arose between the British committee and the French and German committees with respect to a proposed settlement with Portugal in 1901, though eventually differences among the creditors were resolved (1901 Report, pp. 1–3).

The relationship with American bondholders was often far more confrontational, especially with respect to precedence in payments on Latin American debt. For example, the American Honduras Syndicate obstructed a settlement between British bondholders and the government of Honduras, and apparently demanded to be paid first (1903 Report, p. 233). There was also a dispute with US creditors regarding the debt of Santo Domingo (1904 Report, pp. 21–2), where British creditors eventually received substantially less than US creditors (and even Continental European creditors, who obtained separate deals in this case), leading the CFB to appeal to the US government (1908 Report, p. 15). In the case of the Guayaquil–Quito Railway in 1907, the origin of the differences between British and American investors was that the Americans held stock (equity) while the CFB represented (British) holders of debt. More generally, Eichengreen and Portes (1989, p. 16) point out that sterling and dollar covenants often differed significantly in interest rates and security offered by the borrower. As a result, the British and American committees frequently disagreed on the appropriate treatment of different categories of bonds. American committees often settled unilaterally with the borrowers; the CFB was critical of its American counterpart; however, in several instances it had no choice but to accept American terms.

Relationship with the British Government

The CFB kept in close touch with HM's Treasury and the Foreign Office, and in a few instances requested the support of HM's Government. Good relations with the Foreign Office may have been rendered easier by similarities in social background and by the involvement of some former diplomats in the CFB. Occasionally the CFB used these good relations to solicit diplomatic pressure on borrowing countries. The

CFB stated that "it is the endeavour of the Council to request as seldom as possible and in every case to the least possible extent the assistance of the Foreign Office. An employment of moral influence is all that is required for the solution of many of the most difficult cases that come before the Council, and it is the utmost that they can venture to solicit at the hands of H.M. Government." Indeed, the British government was usually reluctant to intervene on behalf of investors who had sought higher returns abroad, and usually regarded defaults as the consequence of imprudent investment (Lipson, 1985 p. 187).[12] Nevertheless, government intervention did take place on a number of occasions: diplomatic pressure was applied on countries such as Salvador (1875 Report, p. 28). In extreme cases, issues of foreign government defaults were brought to Parliament for examination, for example, the case of Honduras in 1875. In 1903, the CFB asked the British authorities not to recognize the new republic of Panama unless it assumed a fair share of the Colombian external debt. The continued default of Guatemala ultimately led to diplomatic pressure, which finally resulted in a renegotiated agreement in 1913—after approximately 14 years of default (1913 Report, pp. 12–13).

In many instances, British diplomats provided the CFB with some degree of cooperation perhaps with respect to more mundane tasks. They served as agents of the CFB in the country where they were posted (e.g. the consul and chargé d'affaires, and HM's minister resident in both Colombia and Guatemala—1873 Report, pp. 40–1, 50, and 54), received payments on behalf of the CFB, or supervised the collection of securities for the CFB (1873 Report, p. 49).

The Council members' social background greatly facilitated good relations with the British Government. In most cases, Council members had previously held high-level positions in government, parliament, the military, or finance. The 1938 Report contains a complete list of those who served as members of the Council of the CFB since its inception: of the 107 members, 13 had Lord as their main title, 12 Honorables or Right Honorables, 19 Sirs, 9 high-ranking military officers or judges, and 6 Earls or Viscounts; of the remaining Esquires, 3 had the title of Member of Parliament and many were well-known former diplomats.

Overall, the CFB seems to have had close relations with the British Government. At the same time, it could be argued that such relations

---

[12] Lipson (1985, p. 45) cites late nineteenth century socio-philosopher Herbert Spencer: "The ultimate result of shielding men from the effects of folly is to fill the world with fools."

between bondholders' associations and governments were at least as close in Continental European countries such as Germany and France, where bondholder committees occasionally seemed to be used as a foreign policy tool. For example, Wynne (1951, pp. 374–6) reports that, in the negotiations following Portugal's default in the early 1890s, the French and German creditors' associations sought to gain an active role in the collection and administration of some of Portugal's taxes at the behest of their respective governments. The CFB took a more conciliatory approach in this respect, in part because the British government at the time did not wish to infringe upon Portugal's sovereignty.

WHEN NEGOTIATIONS BETWEEN THE CFB AND THE BORROWING GOVERNMENT FAILED

Arbitration and Mediation

When direct negotiations with defaulting countries failed to lead to an agreement, the CFB occasionally sought arbitration or mediation. Arbitration took place in England between creditors and the Ecuador–Quito Railroad in 1897 and is described in great detail (twenty-two pages) in the 1897 Report. International arbitration was used in a few cases, including with respect to the debt owed by Santo Domingo. The CFB demanded (unsuccessfully) arbitration also in the cases of Guatemala and Honduras. Arbitration outcomes were not always favorable to the CFB: in the case of Venezuela, total bond-holder claims were around 10 million pounds, but the amount awarded by arbitrators was only 1.84 million (1907 Report, p. 22). Mediation was also occasionally used. For example, Lord Rothschild assisted in mediating between bondholders and the Brazilian Government regarding the debt of the Ituana Railway. Similarly, in the case of Venezuelan bonds, a "unification scheme" (of all bonds) was discussed under the auspices of the Banque de Paris et des Pays-Bas (1903 Report, p. 10, 14). However, these methods often failed to yield satisfactory outcomes.

Mechanisms for Punishment: Blocking access to capital markets

The CFB's main method for punishing defaulting countries was to attempt to block them from obtaining new credit. Formally, this method relied on the London Stock Exchange, which—following a practice adopted in 1827—would refuse quotation to new bonds to be issued by governments that were in default on existing obligations and had refused to negotiate in good faith with their creditors (Morgan and Thomas, 1969; Lipson, 1985, p. 154). In extreme instances, the Exchange would delist all loans of the offending government. However, the CFB played the key role in this process, as the Exchange relied on the CFB for information on the status of loans and renegotiations (Eichengreen and Portes, 1989, p. 15; and Feis, 1930, pp. 114–15).

This method seems to have had a powerful impact: "(The use of the) negative power of withholding money ... exercises its own effective influence ... (on defaulting governments).... Greece, Ecuador, the Southern States of the Union and other defaulting states ... find that it is not possible to find an open market when one has been closed" (1873 Report, pp. 60–1). A new bond issue by the government of Guatemala was prevented (with Amsterdam's cooperation) in 1873 because of "fallacious promises" to repay old loans. In 1875, the CFB reported that Colombia was unable to "appeal for foreign capital" until a settlement was reached regarding its outstanding debt in arrears (1875 Report, p. 32). A similar approach was successfully used in the cases of Turkey and Austria (1873 Report, p. 19).

While coordination with other stock exchanges usually prevented defaulting countries from tapping international capital markets, there were a few exceptions. For example, despite blacklisting by the CFB, Ecuador was able to obtain funds from French creditors and later US creditors (1911 Report cited in Kelly, 1998, p. 42). Guatemala was able to secure a German and an American loan despite defaulting on its British external debt (1895 and 1908 Reports, cited in Kelly, 1998, p. 34).

In the language of the day, blocking further access to international capital markets was viewed as a form of punishment, a sanction, a way to tarnish the defaulting country's reputation and to prevent diluting the claims of existing bondholders. In today's debate on the relative importance of sanctions versus reputation in international lending (Eaton and Gersovitz, 1981; Bulow and Rogoff, 1989), this would be labeled not as a sanction but rather as a formal manifestation of the fact that if borrowers default on their obligations, they will lose their reputation and therefore will not receive new lending.

Harsher ways of punishing countries

More extreme ways of punishing countries, such as diplomatic action or even military action by Britain, were used rarely. "Diplomatic intervention... would only be accorded under very exceptional circumstances.... Any expedient by which willfully defaulting States can in effect be 'posted' on the Stock Exchanges and Bourses of Europe, is likely to prove in the end the most practical vindication of the Bondholders' rights. The issue of 'certificates of default' is an expedient by which this end may ultimately be attained, and to which recourse has already been had with success" (1874 Report, p. 72).

Nevertheless, in a few famous instances, creditors succeeded in protecting their rights through their government's force, although British military intervention was typically also motivated by geopolitical considerations. The rather spectacular case of Egypt, where gradually increasing intervention in local affairs on the part of the European creditor powers culminated in Britain's military intervention in 1882, was only partially motivated by a desire to protect the interests of the bondholders (Feis, 1930). The blockade of Venezuela in 1902 by Britain, Germany, and Italy provides a similar example of successful use of force: by the end of 1906 "Venezuela ha[d] completed the whole of the payments to the three blockading Powers (1907 Report, p. 22). Again, intervention was partly caused by a longstanding dispute regarding the boundary between Venezuela and British Guiana (Kelly, 1998, p. 34). The Hague Peace Conference of 1906 accepted the legitimacy of the use of force in settling debt disputes, though only in cases where defaulters refused international arbitration or failed to comply with the terms of an international arbitration agreement (1907 Report, cited in Kelly, 1998, p. 43).

Lawsuits against countries

Legal action against foreign governments, though occasionally attempted, for example, in the cases of Costa Rica (1874), Brazil (1897), or the New Zealand Midland Railway (1901), was viewed as largely ineffective. Attempts were also made to use the US court system in resolving the defaults of the Southern states. The legal disputes vis à vis some of the defaulting Southern states (notably Virginia) were costly, complicated, and extremely protracted. They often took a particularly vicious nature (for example, at some point any lawyers who chose to represent the interests of the CFB in Virginia would be automatically disbarred). Occasionally, these disputes reached the US Supreme Court, which in some cases ruled in favor of the CFB. Nevertheless, the CFB generally failed to obtain significant payments from the Southern states.

THE NATURE OF SETTLEMENTS

The CFB usually operated under the principle that if a country could not meet its obligations, only mutually agreed (rather than unilateral) changes in the contracts were possible (e.g. 1874 Report, pp. 70–2). For example, Argentina's attempt to unilaterally redeem its dollar-denominated debt in 1889 prompted an immediate letter of protest by the CFB (1889 Report). Debt forgiveness was to be avoided, as a matter of principle, although it was sometimes considered. Eichengreen and Portes (1989a, p. 17) report that while the CFB opposed writing down principal (or interest arrears), in a few instances it displayed flexibility. Common ways of settling disputes included the following.

Debt/Equity Swaps

When possible, the CFB committees tried to take over assets in defaulting countries, subject to the goodwill of the local governments and courts. For example, in 1874, bondholders took over some land in Colombia instead of some unpaid bonds. In 1876, with the default of the Alabama Railroad, a sale was forced by the CFB. The bondholders purchased the railroad in exchange for a fraction of the debt due, and the bonds were converted to shares. The CFB appointed trustees to whom the possession of the railroad was surrendered in February 1876 (1876 Report, pp. 13–7). All of this was done under the auspices of US courts. In the 1870s, Peru offered guano to creditors as a security for its unpaid coupons (proceeds from its sale were divided among creditors), as well as some degree of control over state railways, customs, steamer lines on lake Titicaca, and plots of government land (Wynne, 1951, p. 171). In Paraguay, the CFB took over collateralized assets, railroads, and arable land, which were sold to repay the outstanding debt (1877 Report, pp. 29–31).

Taking over Customs and Tax Revenues

In more extreme cases, the foreign bondholders took over customs and tax revenues, most notably in Turkey, following the defaults of

157

the 1870s, and Greece in 1897—when the Great Powers enabled creditors to control state revenues pledged to bondholders. In both cases, this was a result of substantial diplomatic pressure and dire circumstances that forced local governments to accept a substantial degree of foreign financial control. Similarly, the Egyptian defaults of the 1870s resulted in foreign control of domestic finances, and eventually in the loss of Egypt's national sovereignty (Fishlow, 1985, also cited by Kelly, 1998, pp. 42–3). The dramatic events in Turkey are vividly described in *The Times*:

A Council of Administration was established at Constantinople, the bondholders to be mainly selected by the bondholders in each of the countries... and to this Council the Turkish Government conceded 'absolutely and irrevocably, and until the complete extinction of the debt' first the produce of the six indirect taxes on tobacco, salt, stamps, spirits, fisheries, and silk, which may be classed properly as fluctuating sources of revenue; secondly, certain fixed sums, stated as the tribute of Bulgaria, the revenues of Cyprus and Eastern Roumelia, and a specified part of the tax on Persian tobacco; and two further sources of revenue, the one dependent on any increase in customs duties . . ., and the other on any excess to be derived from a new license, or patent law... The Council was at the same time invested with the fullest powers of administration and collection, and with the entire control over the very large provincial and central establishments to be employed.... (*London Times*, 2 March, 1883, p. 3)

The Times cites a report by Mr Edgar Vincent, English member of the Council saying that

"(i)t is not the ordinary case of proceeds of certain revenues being handed over to foreign representatives. The decree of December gives to the Council the direct administration, receipt and encashment, by means of agents acting under its authority, of the revenues and other sources ceded to the service of the debt. It has the power to appoint and dismiss its emplyés who are considered as functionaries of the State in the performance of their duties... There is no instance in which powers so extended have been granted to a foreign organization in a Sovereign state" (ibid.).

The article goes on to describe the complexity of the task at hand. In the case of Turkey, half of the members of the board controlling the Ottoman revenues were from the CFB, and revenues were directed to a sinking fund for the payment of the bondholders. Given that the CFB's representatives were responsible for monitoring the tax revenues, the Annual Reports of the CFB provide an extraordinary amount of detail and analysis on the budget and the determinants of actual revenues (see, for example, the 1886 Report). In Uruguay, creditors took over the country's custom revenues in 1903. By 1906, Uruguay had pledged 75 percent of its customs revenues to pay its external debts, and the English bondholders' representative collected these receipts daily (1906 and 1907 Annual reports, cited by Kelly, 1998, p. 42). The management of customs revenues in defaulting countries was not always easy. In Turkey, a persistent problem was the distribution of proceeds between the Turkish government and various claim holders including banks and individual bondholders in different countries (1902 Report, pp. 15–18). Taking over other assets also occasionally proved difficult. For example, the CFB was unable to take over a railway, which had been pledged as security to the Honduras External Loans in 1901, because the government of Honduras preferred to let an American syndicate take it over. Probably for similar political reasons, the government of Liberia preferred an American-appointed Receiver General when it had to surrender its state revenues to creditors (1911 Report, p. 37).

"CONDITIONALITY"

On a number of occasions, the CFB offered advice regarding economic policies and, when it had sufficient bargaining power, sought to impose conditions on borrowing countries, much like what would be called today "conditionality." Not surprisingly, such advice and conditions were typically aimed at improving fiscal sustainability, the borrowing country's ability to repay its foreign creditors, and investors' ability to monitor developments in the borrowing country. Paraguay was encouraged to form a central bank in 1876 to regulate its finances (1876 Report, pp. 33–4). Turkey was able to obtain two new loans only after it allowed creditors to manage its customs revenues (during a period when British bondholders assumed the presidency of the Turkish Debt Council, 1904 Report, p. 26). Of course, debtor countries did not always comply with the CFB's advice and conditions. The CFB attempted to advise US Southern states on fiscal policies (1874 Report), and it urged the Greek authorities to enact legislation undertaking reforms in the financial and fiscal areas—essentially aimed at balancing the government's budget (1904 Report, p. 24)—but to no avail. On the whole, the CFB's attempts to impose conditionality seem to have been limited, and not very successful, except when they took an extreme form through the takeover of the administration of customs and other tax revenues. This is illustrated in a 1903 caricature describing how creditors attempted to induce reforms in the Ottoman Empire:

EVER READY TO OBLIGE!

Abdul Hamid. "DEAR ME! OUGHT I TO BE FRIGHTENED?"

Source: Bernard Partridge, 4 November1903. Reproduced with the permission of Punch, Ltd.

7.5 Assessment, Implications, and Open Questions

The CFB emerged in response to a wave of defaults in the 1800s, and the rationale for its existence gradually disappeared with the demise of the international bond market and the declining importance of British investors: the CFB was formally wound up more than a decade ago.[13] Today the market for sovereign debt issued by emerging countries is again large—and defaults frequent and potentially difficult to resolve. This has led to renewed interest in creditor associations, and the experience of the CFB may provide a number of relevant lessons for today. This analysis of the experience of the CFB leaves many questions open for further research, including the following.

Should official intervention attempt to foster the creation of a revamped creditors' association? Portes (2000) argues that advanced country

---

[13] *Financial Stability Review*, Bank of England, No. 8 (June 2000), p. 144.

authorities and international institutions should do so, through moral suasion. He points out that the United States' Foreign Bondholders Protective Council was set up thanks to the encouragement and support of the State Department. While the CFB emerged spontaneously from the private sector, it was recognized by the British authorities and often interacted with them. One might also note that the CFB was formed only decades after the initial wave of defaults in the 1820s and 1830s. Olson (1965) analyzes the tragedy of the commons with respect to setting up associations, especially those with a potentially diffuse membership: no individual has a sufficiently strong incentive to set up an association even though collectively its members would be all better off if the association were to be established. In practice, associations in a wide variety of domains have emerged both as the result of government intervention—such as the Farm Bureau, the longest lasting among farmers' associations (Olson, 1965, pp. 148–53)—and spontaneously—such as today's Emerging Markets Creditors Association.

Who would be the natural members of a revamped creditors' association today? Would the investor base be carved relying on nationality or size of the investors, location of the exchange, or type of bonds? MacMillan (1995b) argued that a resurrected Foreign Bondholders Protective Council could represent holders of government bonds issued under New York law and a resurrected Corporation of Foreign Bondholders could represent holders of government bonds issued under London law. However, many countries issue bonds under both types of law and many investors hold bonds issued under both types of law. The solution was clearly simpler in the past, when location of the exchange, type of law, and nationality of the investors tended to coincide.

Finally, would a creditor association provide appropriate balance of power between small and large bondholders? Today's debate on creditor coordination focuses on the need to prevent defection by "vulture funds," for which it makes sense to seek repayment in full (through lawsuits) because of their small relative size. In the past, however, one of the roles of the CFB may have been to protect small bondholders from large bondholders who might otherwise arrange for a separate, advantageous deal for themselves in exchange for the promise to provide the country with new lending.[14]

---

[14] This is somewhat related to the issue of protecting small shareholders who can be expropriated by large shareholders with controlling stakes (La Porta et al., 2000).

Overall, our impression is that the CFB may have had an easier time than any comparable body would have today. The CFB facilitated creditor coordination in the past, and it is likely that a club of bond-holders would also be helpful today. However, the CFB's track record was far from perfect, and a similar institution today would be unlikely to fare better. The CFB often faced difficulties in reaching consensus among creditors—especially among groups holding different types of assets. Such an institution would probably face even greater challenges today. In particular, it is hard to see how an association of bondhold-ers would be able to prevent lawsuits from dissenting creditors. Moreover, some of the rationale for creditor coordination in the past has essentially disappeared: few sovereign bonds today have tangible collateral for creditors to seize, and it is difficult to imagine a foreign creditor association taking over the tax administration of a defaulting country. In addition, the main bargaining strength of the CFB was its ability to block defaulting governments from accessing capital mar-kets. Replicating that aspect of the CFB's role in today's international financial environment might be difficult, given the possibility of issu-ing in a wide variety of markets. Moreover, an institution keeping track of which countries have defaulted and blocking them from access to exchanges around the world seems unnecessary. In fact, information is transmitted very efficiently, and reputational effects have made it impossible for defaulting countries to tap capital markets without previously settling their existing claims. Our main conclu-sion is therefore that the experience of the CFB provides modern-day observers with an "upper bound" on what could be achieved through a revamped creditor association.

8

A Few Lessons for the Future

The international financial environment in which today's emerging markets operate is characterized by high integration and considerable reliance on bond finance. The premise of this book is that, in order to learn more about this type of environment—which, in modern times, has been in place only since the early 1990s—it is useful to go back in history to the most recent period that witnessed these same characteristics, namely 1870–1913. During that past era, London—the world's main financial center at the time—saw massive amounts of bond issuance by emerging markets and very active trading by well-informed investors. In this book, we have focused on the determinants and behavior of spreads on emerging market bonds, and on some of the institutional features of the markets and their investor community, for the two periods, identifying both similarities and differences between them. In both the pre-First World War period and today, investors responded to events, news, and economic data, albeit in somewhat different ways, and a comparison yields interesting insights.

Three main themes are emphasized in this book. The first is that institutional and political reforms (such as the introduction of a constitution) or efficiency-enhancing structural reforms seldom reduce the cost of capital quickly. In a few instances, reforms of the monetary framework did have a rapid and substantial impact on spreads, especially when they were seen as the focal point of a concerted effort at buttressing the credibility of macroeconomic policies. Overall, however, other types of events—especially wars and episodes of politically motivated violence—have a far more immediate and pronounced impact on the cost of borrowing. In the short run, peace and stability seem to matter more for the ability of countries to borrow, then the establishment of investor-friendly institutions. While, there is little doubt that appropriate reforms can be beneficial in the long run, their benefits seem to accrue in a gradual manner, possibly because it takes time for investors to observe whether new *de jure* arrangements are respected *de facto*, in a durable manner. A lesson for today's emerging markets is therefore not to necessarily expect immediate rewards for the introduction of "good institutions." Political opposition to reforms seems somewhat more understandable if the financial benefits of reforms emerge only gradually and possibly with long lags. In making the case for reforms, expectations of the speed with which reforms may translate into beneficial reductions in the cost of capital should therefore be set at realistic levels.

Our evidence also confirms that sound macroeconomic policies help countries gain better access to bond finance. As long as such finance is put to productive use in the context of domestic and international peace, it may ultimately lead to more rapid economic growth. Indeed, there is some evidence suggesting that a few well-chosen, well-implemented, and fundamental macroeconomic changes have yielded considerable financial benefits for countries within a few years. For example, going beyond the relatively high-frequency evidence on modern spreads presented above, during the 1980s and 1990s emerging market countries such as Chile, Israel, Mexico, and Poland combined fiscal stabilization and a reduction in inflation to the single digits with reforms in the monetary area, such as the introduction of central bank independence or inflation targeting, as well as reforms in the fiscal area, such as pension reforms. As a result, these countries were able to improve their debt structures, making them less reliant on short-term or foreign-currency debt, and to reduce their cost of borrowing significantly, within a limited number of years (Borensztein et al., 2004, p. 20). In this context, it is important to note the role of narrowly defined monetary institutions such as the gold standard in the past or currency boards more recently. We find that these institutions, aimed at signaling commitment to stable policies and (to some extent) tying the government's own hands, can sometimes affect the creditworthiness of a borrowing country (the example of the adoption of the gold standard in 1897 Japan was discussed in detail in Chapter 3). Nevertheless, if policies turn out to be inconsistent with the commitment implied by the monetary institutions, the resulting loss of credibility and rising spreads may precipitate a crisis.

More generally, despite the apparent consensus today regarding the appropriate set of institutions and policies a country should adopt, similar institutions (e.g. a *de facto* independent central bank today, or the gold standard in the past) do not always involve the same degree of commitment across countries: the likelihood of suspension of the gold standard or of central bank independence depends on a deeper institutional structure, which is not always easy to gauge. We are therefore not surprised by the generally slow assessment of institutional changes by financial markets. To evaluate a fundamental change, sufficient time has to pass—thus, even though some emerging markets occasionally herald the introduction of democratic, market-oriented institutions, there is little wonder why investors do not typically rush to invest in these countries.

The second theme emphasized in this study is that country-specific developments played a more important role in determining spreads in 1870–1913 than they did in the 1990s. This is reflected in both greater ability of country-specific fundamentals (both news and macroeconomic variables) to explain historical spreads, and in the higher co-movement of spreads across emerging markets in the 1990s. We have also seen that economic fundamentals, measured by exports, co-move to a greater extent today than they did in the pre-First World War era, a feature which is consistent with the greater similarity of export product composition across emerging market countries today than in the past. However, the higher co-movement of emerging market bond spreads in the 1990s relative to 1870–1913 can only partially be explained by higher co-movement of economic fundamentals. We conjecture that the arrangements underlying institutional investor behavior have important consequences for the behavior of bond spreads. Argentina's massive default in 2001 seems to have been followed by a decline in co-movement of spreads across emerging markets, but it remains to be seen whether this is simply a temporary reversal or a more permanent return to the distant past. It is therefore important to remain alert to the possibility of high co-movement in financial variables across emerging markets in the future, and to crises that may affect several emerging markets simultaneously, regardless of fundamentals. Even though the recent crisis in Argentina did not immediately spill over to other emerging markets as had been the case for the Mexican, Asian, and Russian crises, our impression is that rapid international contagion is still a likely possibility. It would therefore be desirable to continue considering policies and mechanisms (both at the national level and in the international architecture) aimed at reducing the possibility and alleviating the consequences of such contagion. Our view from the past suggests that contagion is not endemic to global finance—even the Baring crisis did not result in global contagion—and this objective is therefore attainable.

The third theme is related to the resolution of sovereign debt crises in the two periods. We conjecture that the existence of institutions aimed at resolving debt crises may be seen as part of the financial market architecture that enabled the continuous expansion of the international bond market in the nineteenth century, despite large defaults. At the same time, the achievements of the Corporation of Foreign Bondholders should be viewed as an upper limit on what might be achieved through creditor coordination. Thus, while a revamped association of creditors might help improve the functioning of the international market for sovereign debt in the twenty-first century, it would seem unlikely to alleviate the costs of debt crises in emerging markets in a major way.

More generally, we hope to have helped make the case that a better understanding of today's international financial environment can be gained by studying both the similarities and the differences between the two eras of globalization and bond finance. Despite the difficulties and caveats involved in the construction of some of the historical variables, we feel that the information and data sets we have put together in the process are reliable and exciting enough to serve as a stimulus and a helpful tool for the efforts of other researchers.

APPENDIX 1

BONDS USED IN COMPUTATION
OF HISTORICAL SPREADS

	Starting date	Ending date	Bond name	Coupon	Issue date	Issue price	Redemption date	Sinking fund (%)	Coupons paid	Underwriter	Remarks
Argentina											
1	Jan 1870	Apr 1871	6%	6.0	1866	72.5	1890	2.5	January, July	Baring	
2	May 1871	Mar 1886	Public works	6.0	1871	88.5	1892	2.5	March, September	Murrieta	
3	Apr 1886	Dec 1913	5%	5.0	1886	80.0	1919	1	January, July	Baring	Redemption suspended in January 1894. Redemption moved to 1922 on January 1904. Coupon reduced to 4% from 1893 to 1898
Canada											
1	Jan 1870	May 1873	6%	6.0	1870	n.a.	1877–84		1 January, 1 July	Glyns, Baring	Redeemable in 81–84
	Jun 1873	Dec 1881	6%	6.0	1870	n.a.	1877–84		1 January, 1 July	Glyns, Baring	Redeemable in 82–84
	Dec 1881	Jul 1884	6%	6.0	1870	n.a.	1877–84		1 January, 1 July	Glyns, Baring	
2	Aug 1884	Dec 1913	3.5%	3.5	1884	91.0	1909–1934	0.5	1 June, 1 December	Baring	
Chile											
1	Jan 1870	Mar 1886	6%	6.0	1867	82.0	1891	2	1 January, 1 July	J. S. Morgan	Jan 1878 drawings suspended till 1884
2	Apr 1886	Jul 1907	4.5%	4.5	1885	89.0	Consol	0.5	January, July	City Bank	
3	Aug 1907	Dec 1913	4.5%	4.5	1886	98.5	Consol	0.5	January, July	Rothschild	
China											
1	May 1877	May 1885	8%	8.0	1877	98.0	1885		February, August	Hong Kong and Shanghai Bank	
2	Jun 1885	Mar 1895	Domestic 7% series A	7.0		n.a.	1895		February, August	Hong Kong and Shanghai Bank	
3	Apr 1895	Apr 1896	6% gold bonds	6.0	1895	96.8	no redemption date		June, December	n.a.	
4	May 1896	Dec 1913	5%	5.0	1896	98.8	1933		April, October	Hong Kong Bank	
Colombia											
1	Jan 1870	Jun 1874	6%	6.0	1863	86.0	1874	7.5	April, October	London and Country Bank	
2	Jul 1874	Dec 1887	4.5%	4.5	1873	n.a.	no redemption date		January, April, July, October	London and Country Bank	Default since Aug 1879
3	Jan 1888	Dec 1896	New Granada debt converted	4.8	1873	n.a.					Converted 4.5% default
4	Jan 1897	Dec 1913	1.5–3%	1.5–3	1896	n.a.			January, July		Default in Aug 1899. Jan–Dec, 1906 2.5% paid. From Jan 1907—3%

Costa Rica											
1	Jun 1871	Dec 1871	6%	6.0	1871	72.0	2	1895	May, November	Goldsmith Knowles and Foster	Default in May 1874.
2	Jan 1872	Aug 1886	7%	7.0	1872	82.0	1	1903	April, October		
3	Sep 1886	Dec 1894	5% "B" Bonds	5.0		n.a.		Commencing June 1898	January, July	River Plate T. L. Agency	Aug 1887 to Aug 1889 4% paid
4	Jan 1895	Mar 1898	2.5% "B" Bonds	5.0		n.a.		from 1917	April, October		In default
5	Apr 1898	Jan 1905	2.5% "B" Bonds	2.5		n.a.		from 1917	January, July	Glyn Mills	Default since November 1901
6	Feb 1905	Dec 1911	5% "B" Bonds	5.0		n.a.			January, July	Glyn Mills	Default until Aug 1909
7	Jan 1912	Dec 1913	4% Refund Bonds	4.0	1911	n.a.		None till 1921	April, October	Glyn Mills	
Egypt											
1	Jan 1870	Dec 1876	7%	7.0	1868	n.a.	1	1892	January, July	Imperial Ottoman Bank	
2	Jan 1877	Dec 1890	5% preferred	5.0	1877	n.a.			January, July	Comptoir d'escomptes Paris	
Greece											
1	Jan 1870	May 1880	5%	5.0	1824	n.a.		1891		Ionian Bank	In default
2	Jun 1880	Jul 1881	consolidated 5%	5.0	1879	n.a.		1899	January, July	Hambro	
3	Aug 1881	May 1893	5%	5.0	1881	74.0	1.25	1921	January, July		In default
	Jun 1893	Nov 1894	5%	5.0	1893	n.a.					
	Dec 1894	Dec 1898	5%	1.5	1893	n.a.					
	Jan 1899	Dec 1899	5%	1.7	1893	n.a.					
	Jan 1900	Jan 1901	5%	1.8	1893	n.a.					
	Feb 1901	Dec 1901	5%	1.7	1893	n.a.					
	Jan 1902	Dec 1902	5%	1.8	1893	n.a.					
	Jan 1903	Dec 1903	5%	1.7	1893	n.a.					
	Jan 1904	Dec 1905	5%	1.9	1893	n.a.					
	Jan 1906	Dec 1906	5%	2.1	1893	n.a.					
	Jan 1907	Dec 1907	5%	2.2	1893	n.a.					
	Jan 1908	Dec 1908	5%	2.6	1893	n.a.					
	Jan 1909	Dec 1909	5%	2.8	1893	n.a.					
	Jan 1910	Dec 1911	5%	3.0	1893	n.a.					
	Jan 1912	Dec 1912	5%	3.1	1893	n.a.					
	Jan 1913	Dec 1913	5%	3.2	1893	n.a.					

	Starting date	Ending date	Bond name	Coupon	Issue date	Issue price	Redemption date	Sinking fund (%)	Coupons paid	Underwriter	Remarks
Hungary											
1	Jan 1870	Dec 1871	6%	6.0	1867	n.a.	1891		April, October	R. Raphael and Sons	
2	Jan 1872	Dec 1881	5%	5.0	1871	81.0	1904	1.5	January, July	Rothschild	
3	Jan 1882	Dec 1913	4% gold rents	4.0	1881	n.a.	No redemption date		January, July		
Japan											
1	Jun 1870	Mar 1873	9% customs loan	9.0	1870	98.0	1882	10	February, August	Schroder	
2	Apr 1874	Jul 1897	7%	7.0	1870	92.5	1898	2	January, July	Oriental Bank and Glyn Mills	
3	Aug 1897	Dec 1913	5%	5.0	1897	n.a.	No redemption date		June, December	Yokohama Special Bank	
Mexico											
1	Jan 1870	Aug 1888	3%	3.0	1846	n.a.	Consol		January, April, July, October	Baring	In default
2	Sep 1888	Dec 1899	6%	6.0	n.a.	n.a.	Consol	0.5		Gibbs	
3	Jan 1900	Dec 1913	5% domestic	5.0	1899	n.a.	Consol				
Portugal											
1	Jan 1870	May 1892	3%	3.0	1855–84	32.5–50	Consol		1 January, 1 July	Portuguese Financial	
	Jun 1892	Dec 1899	3%	1.0	1855–84	32.5–50	Consol		1 January, 1 July		
	Jan 1900	Dec 1900	3%	1.1	1855–84	32.5–50	Consol		1 January, 1 July	Agency, London,	
	Jan 1901	Oct 1901	3%	1.0	1855–84	32.5–50	Consol		1 January, 1 July	Paris, Lisbon	
	Nov 1901	Feb 1902	3%	1.2	1855–84	32.5–50	Consol		1 January, 1 July		
2	Mar 1902	Dec 1913	New 3%	3.0	1902		Consol		1 January, 1 July		
Queensland											
1	Jan 1870	Dec 1873	6%	6.0	1866	91.0	1891		January, July	Union Bank of Australia	
2	Jan 1874	Dec 1913	4%	4.0	1873–4	88.0	1913		January, July	Union Bank of Australia	Additional issues of bonds redemption changed to 1915
Russia											
1	Jan 1870	Dec 1913	5% consol	5.0	1822	n.a.	Consol		March, September	Rothschild	

										Purchase when below par

Sweden

#										
1	Jan 1870	May 1881	5%	5.0	1868	90.0		0.25	January, July	With various subscriptions into the series until 1888 reduced to 3.5% in 1894 and redemption date no longer quoted.
2	Jun 1881	Dec 1913	4%	4.0	1880	97.5–98.5 1930			April, October	

Turkey

#										
1	Jan 1870	Feb 1883	6%	6.0	1869	60.5	1902	1	April, October	Imperial Ottoman Bank	In default since Apr 1876
2	Mar 1883	Dec 1899	1% registered bonds	1.0		n.a.			March, September		Nov 1889—converted into C series bonds
3	Jan 1990	Aug 1903	4% priority loan	4.0	1890	n.a.	Consol		April, October	Dent and Palmer	
4	Sep 1903	Dec 1905	4% loan	4.0	1902	n.a.			January, July	Dent and Palmer	
5	Jan 1906	Dec 1913	4% unified English scripture	4.0		n.a.			March, September	Imperial Ottoman Bank	

Uruguay

#										
1	Jan 1870	Dec 1870	6%	6.0	1864	60.	Redeemable by purchase 1893	1	January, July	McGregor and Co.	
2	Jan 1871	Jul 1878	6%	6.0	1871	72.	1893	2.5	May, November	Thomson Bonar	Default since Feb 1876
	Aug 1878	Feb 1879	6%	1.3	1871	72.	1893	2.5	May, November	Thomson Bonar	
	Feb 1879	Nov 1883	6%	2.5	1871	72.	From 1883	2.5	May, November	Thomson Bonar	
	Dec 1883	Feb 1884	6%	3.0	1871	72.	From 1883	2.5	May, November	Thomas Bonar	
3	Mar 1884	Feb 1892	5%	5.0	1883	n.a.	1935	0.5	January, April, July, October	Thomson Bonar Robarts	
4	Mar 1893	Dec 1913	3.5% domestic	3.5	1893	n.a.		0.5	February, May, August, November	Baring Glynn Mills	

APPENDIX 2

MACROECONOMIC DATA SOURCES

Modern Sample, 1994–2002

Annual data for Argentina, Brazil, Bulgaria, Mexico, Nigeria, Philippines, Poland, and Venezuela were drawn from the International Monetary Fund's *International Financial Statistics* for the following variables: current account balance (in US dollars); exchange rate (period average) versus the US dollar; exports of goods and services in US dollars; fiscal balance in local currency; gross domestic product (GDP) in local currency current prices; GDP deflator; inflation (the rate of change of the consumer price index). In addition, central government debt was drawn from the World Bank's *Global Development Finance* database. Quarterly data for the same countries (except Nigeria), sample period, and variables are drawn from the International Monetary Fund (IMF)'s country desks (through the World Economic Outlook database).

Historical Sample, 1870–1913

Annual data for Argentina, Brazil, Canada, Chile, China, Colombia, Costa Rica, Egypt, Greece, Hungary, Japan, Mexico, Portugal, Queensland, Russia, Sweden, Turkey, and Venezuela were drawn from a variety of sources—mainly Mitchell's *Historical Statistics*, the *Investor's Monthly Manual* (*IMM*), and national publications (many collected by a host of previous researchers and kindly transmitted to us by Alan Taylor from the data set used for Obstfeld and Taylor, 2003a; 2003b). For national publications, we cite the original publications when we were able to check them. More specifically, we draw the variables we use from the following sources:

(1) Exchange rate versus the US dollar: Schneider *et al* (1991). Brazil from Ludwig (1985);

(2) Dates when countries in sample were on or off the gold standard taken from Larry Officer's data on Eh.net;

(3) Historical defaults (prior to 1870) taken from Beim and Calomiris (2001), Appendix to chapter 1;

(4) Fiscal Balance: expressed as the difference between government revenue and expenditures, as a ratio to revenues. Revenues and expenditures from Mitchell (1992, 1993, and 1995). Colombia, Costa Rica, and Queensland from the *IMM*;

(5) Exports: denominated in British pound sterling, from the collected volumes of Mitchell (1992, 1993, and 1995). Completed from the *IMM* for Chile in 1871–7, Queensland in 1871–1913, and Uruguay in 1870–1913. For Hungary we used Mitchell for the total combined exports of Hungary and Austria;

(6) Population: from the collected volumes of Mitchell (1992, 1993, and 1995). Completed from the *IMM* for Egypt in 1870–84, Mexico in 1872–1913, Queensland in 1870–1913, and Uruguay in 1872–99;

(7) Public Debt: total central government debt, from Bordo and Jonung (1996), except—Argentina: 1870–83 from the *IMM*, 1884–1913 from Della Paolera (1988); Brazil: 1870–9 from *IMM*, 1880–1910 consolidated (federal state and municipal) foreign debt in pounds sterling from IBGE (1990) and domestic debt in contos from Levy (1995); Canada 1870–1913 from Statistics Canada. Chile: 1870–1913 from Mamalakis (1978–89, vol. 6, 493, table 8.62), thence from United Nations, with appropriate conversions of some series from (gold) pesos of 6 pence (the interwar parity) to current pesos via the exchange rate series as above from Braun et al. (2000); China: 1882–1913 from the *IMM* (foreign debt only); Egypt: 1870–84 from Obstfeld and Taylor (2003b); Greece: 1871–1913 from the *IMM*; Japan: 1873–9 from the *IMM* and 1880–1913 from Bordo and Jonung (1996); Mexico: 1872–1913 from the *IMM*; Portugal: 1871–80 from *IMM* and Flandreau (2004) from 1881–1913; Queensland: 1870–1913 from the IMM; Russia: 1870–84 from the *IMM*, 1885–1913 from Flandreau (2004). Sweden: 1871–9 from the *IMM* and 1879–1913 from Obstfeld and Taylor (2003a, 2003b); Turkey: 1872–1913 from the *IMM*; Uruguay: 1872–1913 from the *IMM*. Foreign public debt for Argentina, Brazil, Chile, Colombia, Costa Rica, Mexico, Portugal, and Uruguay from the *IMM*.

173

References

Acemoglu, Daron and Simon Johnson, 2003, "Institutions, Corporate Governance, and Crises," in Peter Cornelius and Bruce Kogut (eds.), *Global Issues in Corporate Governance, Risk, and International Investment* (Oxford: Oxford University Press).

——2005, "Unbundling Institutions," forthcoming, *Journal of Political Economy.*

——and James Robinson, 2001, "The Colonial Origins of Comparative Development: An Empirical Investigation," *American Economic Review,* vol. 91, pp. 1369–401.

——2004, "Institutions, Volatility, and Crises," in Takatoshi Ito and Andrew R. Rose (eds.), *Growth and Productivity in East Asia* (Chicago: University of Chicago Press).

——2005a, "The Rise of Europe: Atlantic Trade, Institutional Change and Economic Growth," *American Economic Review,* vol. 95, pp. 546–79.

——2005b, "Institutions as the Fundamental Cause of Long-Run Growth," forthcoming in Philippe Aghion and Steven Durlauf (eds.), *Handbook of Economic Growth* (North Holland: Elsevier).

Alfaro, Laura, Sebnem Kalemli-Ozcan, and Vadym Lolosovych, 2004, "Why Doesn't Capital Flow from Rich to Poor Countries? An Empirical Investigation," Harvard Business School Working Paper Series, No. 04–040.

Arellano, Manuel, and Stephen Bond, 1991, "Some tests of specification for panel data: Monte Carlo evidence and an application to employment equations," *Review of Economic Studies,* vol. 58, pp. 277–97.

Becker, Torbjörn, Anthony Richards, and Yunyong Thaicharoen, 2003, "Bond Restructuring and Moral Hazard: Are Collective Action Clauses Costly?" *Journal of International Economics,* vol. 61, pp. 127–61.

Beim, David O. and Charles W. Calomiris, 2001, *Emerging Financial Markets* (Boston: McGraw-Hill).

Bénassy-Quéré, Agnès, Maylis Coupet, and Thierry Mayer, 2005, "Institutional Determinants of Foreign Investment," CEPII working paper No. 2005–05, Centre d'etudes prospectives et d'informations internationales, Paris.

Billyou, De Forest, 1948, "Corporate Mortgage Bonds and Majority Clauses," *Yale Law Journal,* vol. 57, pp. 595–611.

Bolton, Patrick and David Scharfstein, 1996, "Optimal Debt Structure and the Number of Creditors," *Journal of Political Economy*, vol. 104, pp. 1–25.

Borchard, Edwin M., 1951, *State Insolvency and Foreign Bondholders: Volume 1, General Principles* (New Haven: Yale University Press).

Bordo, Michael and Barry Eichengreen, 2002, "Crises Now and Then: What Lessons from the Last Era of Financial Globalization," NBER Working Paper No. 8716 (Cambridge, Massachusetts: National Bureau of Economic Research).

Bordo, Michael, Barry Eichengreen, and Jongwoo Kim, 1998, "Was There Really an Earlier Period of International Financial Integration Comparable to Today?" NBER Working Paper No. 6738 (Cambridge, Massachusetts: National Bureau of Economic Research).

Bordo, Michael, Barry Eichengreen, Daniel Kliengebiel, and Maria Soledad Martinez-Peria, 2001, "Is the Crisis Problem Becoming More Severe?" *Economic Policy*, pp. 51–82.

Bordo, Michael and Lars Jonung, 1996, "Monetary Regimes, Inflation, and Monetary Reform: An Essay in Honor of Axel Leijonhufvud," in Daniel Vaz and Kumaraswamy Velupillai (eds.), *Inflation, Institutions, and Information: Essays in Honor of Axel Leijonhufvud* (London: Macmillan).

Bordo, Michael and Antu Panini Murshid, 2000, "Are Financial Crises Becoming Increasingly More Contagious? What is the Historical Evidence on Contagion?" NBER Working Paper No. 7900 (Cambridge, Massachusetts: National Bureau of Economic Research).

—— 2002, "Globalization and Changing Patterns in the International Transmission of Shocks in Financial Markets," NBER Working Paper No. 9019 (Cambridge, Massachusetts: National Bureau of Economic Research).

Bordo, Michael and Hugh Rockoff, 1996, "The Gold Standard as a Good Housekeeping Seal of Approval," *Journal of Economic History*, vol. 56, pp. 389–428.

Borensztein, Eduardo, Marcos Chamon, Olivier Jeanne, Paolo Mauro, and Jeromin Zettelmeyer, 2004, "Sovereign Debt Structure for Crisis Prevention," IMF Occasional Paper No. 237 (Washington: International Monetary Fund).

Braun, Juan, Matías Braun, Ignacio Brones, José Diaz, Rolf Lüders, and Gert Wagner, 2000, "Economía Chilena, 1810–1995: Estadisticas Históricas, Documento de Trabajo No. 187, Pontifica Universidad Católica de Chile, Instituto de Economía.

Brealey, Richard A. and Evi Kaplanis, 2004, "The impact of IMF programs on asset values," *Journal of International Money and Finance*, vol. 23, pp. 253–70.

Buccheit, Lee C. and Gaurang Mitu Gulati, 2002, "Sovereign Bonds and the Collective Will," *Emory Law Journal*, Vol. 51, No. 4, pp. 1317–63.

Buchanan, Michael, 2001, "Emerging Market Financing: A Retrospective," *EMEA Economics Analyst*, Goldman Sachs, 16 November, pp. 4–10.

Bulow, Jeremy and Kenneth Rogoff, 1989, "Sovereign Debt: Is to Forgive to Forget?" *American Economic Review*, vol. 79, pp. 43–50.

References

Clemens, Michael and Jeffrey Williamson, 2004, "Wealth Bias in the First Global Capital Market Boom, 1870–1913," *Economic Journal*, vol. 114, pp. 304–37.

Cline, William R. and Kevin J. S. Barnes, 1997, "Spreads and Risk in Emerging Markets Lending," Research Paper No. 97 (Washington: Institute of International Finance).

Cordella, Tito, 2004, "Moral Hazard versus Real Hazard," *IMF Research Bulletin*, vol. 5, pp. 1–6.

Cutler, David, James Poterba, and Lawrence Summers, 1989, "What Moves Stock Price?" *Journal of Portfolio Management*, vol. 15, pp. 4–12.

Davis, Lance and Robert Huttenback, 1986, *Mammon and the Pursuit of Empire: The Political Economy of British Imperialism, 1860–1912* (Cambridge, Massachusetts: Cambridge University Press).

Dell'Ariccia, Giovanni, Isabel Schnabel, and Jeromin Zettelmeyer, 2002, "Moral Hazard and International Crisis Lending: A Test," IMF Working Paper No. 02/181.

Della Paolera, Gerardo, 1988, "How the Argentine Economy Performed during the International Gold Standard: A Reexamination," unpublished Ph.D. dissertation, University of Chicago.

Eaton, Jonathan and Mark Gersovitz, 1981, "Debt with Potential Repudiation: Theoretical and Empirical Analysis," *Review of Economic Studies*, vol. 48, pp. 289–309.

Edelstein, Michael, 1982, *Overseas Investment in the Age of High Imperialism: The United Kingdom, 1850–1914* (New York: Columbia University Press).

Eichengreen, Barry, 1999a, "The Regulatory Dilemma: Hedge Funds in the New International Financial Architecture," *International Finance*, vol. 2, no. 3, pp. 411–40.

——1999b, "The Baring Crisis in a Mexican Mirror," *International Political Science Review*, vol. 20, no. 3, pp. 249–70.

Eichengreen, Barry, and Ashoka Mody, 1998, "What Explains Changing Spreads on Emerging-Market Debt: Fundamentals or Market Sentiment?" in Sebastian Edwards (ed.), *The Economics of International Capital Flows* (Chicago: University of Chicago Press).

Eichengreen, Barry, and Richard Portes, 1986, "Debt and Default in the 1930s: Causes and Consequences," *European Economic Review*, vol. 30, pp. 599–640.

——1988, "Les prêts internationaux dans l'entre-deux-guerres: le point de vue des porteurs de titres," *Economie Appliquée*, vol. 41, pp. 741–71.

——1989a, "After the Deluge: Default, Negotiations and Readjustment During the Interwar Years," in Eichengreen, Barry and Peter Lindert (eds.) *The International Debt Crisis in Historical Perspective* (Massachusetts: MIT Press).

——1989b, "Settling Defaults in the Era of Bond Finance," *World Bank Economic Review*, vol. 3, pp. 211–39.

——2000, "Debt Restructuring with and without the IMF," unpublished manuscript, London Business School.

Elmendorf, Douglas, Mary Hirschfeld, and David Weil, 1996, "The Effect of News on Bond Prices: Evidence from the United Kingdom 1900–1920," *Review of Economics and Statistics*, vol. 78, pp. 341–4.

Faria, Andre and Paolo Mauro, 2004, "Institutions and the External Capital Structure of Countries," IMF Working Paper No. 04/236 (Washington: International Monetary Fund).

Feis, Herbert, 1930, *Europe, the World's Banker, 1870–1913* (New Haven, Connecticut: Yale University).

Ferguson, Niall, 2001, *The Cash Nexus: Money and Power in the Modern World* (London: Penguin).

Ferguson, Niall and Moritz Schularik, "The Empire Effect: The Determinants of Country Risk in the First Age of Globalization," forthcoming, *Journal of Economic History*.

——— 2005, "The Veil of Gold: Monetary Commitments and Risk Premia in the International Bond Market before the First World War," unpublished manuscript, Harvard University.

Fishlow, Albert, 1985, "Lessons from the Past: Capital Markets During the 19th Century and the Interwar Period," *International Organization*, vol. 39, pp. 383–439.

Flandreau, Marc, 2003a, *Money Doctors: The Experience of International Financial Advising, 1850–2000* (London: Routledge).

Flandreau, Marc, 2003b, "Caveat Emptor: Coping with Sovereign Risk under the International Gold Standard, 1871–1913," in Marc Flandreau, Carl-Ludwig Holtfrerich, and Harold James (eds.), *International Financial History in the Twentieth Century, System and Anarchy* (Cambridge: Cambridge University Press).

Flandreau, Marc, and Frederic Zumer, 2004, *The Making of Global Finance, 1880–1913* (Paris: Organization for Economic Cooperation and Development).

Flandreau, Marc and Nathan Sussman, 2004, "Old Sins: Exchange Clauses and European Foreign Lending in the 19th Century," in Eichengreen, Barry and Ricardo Haussman (eds.) *Debt Denomination and Financial Instability in Emerging Market Economies* (Chicago: University of Chicago Press).

Gertner, Robert and David Scharsftein, 1991, "A Theory of Workouts and the Effects of Reorganization Law," *Journal of Finance*, vol. 46, pp. 1189–222.

Goetzmann, William N. Lingfeng Li, and K. Geert Rouwenhorst, 2005, "Long-Term Global Market Correlations," *Journal of Business*, vol. 78, pp. 1–38.

Gregory, Paul, 1979, "The Russian Balance of Payments, the Gold Standard, and Monetary Policy: A Historical Example of Foreign Capital Movements," *Journal of Economic History*, vol. 39, pp. 379–99.

Haldane, Andy, 1999, "Private Sector Involvement in Financial Crisis: Analytics and Public Policy Approaches," *Financial Stability Review*, No. 7, pp. 184–202 (London: Bank of England).

References

Hoshi, Takeo, Anil Kashyap, and David Scharfstein, 1990, "The Role of Banks in Reducing the Costs of Financial Distress in Japan," *Journal of Financial Economics*, vol. 27, pp. 67–88.

IBGE (Fundacao Instituto Brasileiro de Geografia e Estatística), 1990, *Estatísticas históricas do Brasil: Séries económicas, demográficas e sociais de 1550 a 1988* (Rio de Janeiro: IBGE).

Imbs, Jean and Romain Wacziarg, 2003, "Stages of Diversification," *American Economic Review*, vol. 93, No. 1, pp. 63–86.

International Monetary Fund, 1999, 'Involving the Private Sector in Forestalling and Resolving Financial Crises—The Role of Creditor Committees—Preliminary Considerations', unpublished (Washington: International Monetary Fund).

——2001, "Involving the Private Sector in the Resolution of Financial Crises—Restructuring International Sovereign Bonds," http://www.imf.org.

——2002, "Strengthening the International Financial Architecture: Sovereign Debt Restructuring Mechanism (SDRM) A Factsheet," http://www.imf.org/external/np/exr/facts/sdrm.htm.

——2004, "Global Financial Stability Report," April. (Washington DC: International Monetary Fund).

Johnson, Simon, Peter Boone, Alasdair Breach, and Eric Friedman, 2000, "Corporate Governance in the Asian Financial Crisis," *Journal of Financial Economics*, vol. 58, pp. 141–86.

Judson, Ruth A. and Ann L. Owen, 1999, "Estimating Panel Data Models: A Guide for Macroeconomists," *Economics Letters*, vol. 65, pp. 9–15.

Kamin, Steven, 2004, "Identifying the Role of Moral Hazard in International Financial Markets," *International Finance*, vol. 7, pp. 25–59.

Kamin, Steven and Karsten von Kleist, 1999, "The Evolution and Determinants of Emerging Market Credit Spreads in the 1990s," BIS Working Paper No. 68 (Basle: Bank for International Settlements).

Kaminsky, G. and C. Reinhart, 2000, "On Crises, Contagion, and Confusion," *Journal of International Economics*, vol. 51, no. 1, pp. 145–68.

Kaminsky, Graciela and Sergio L. Schmukler, 1999, "What Triggers Market Jitters? A Chronicle of the Asian Crisis," *Journal of International Money and Finance*, vol. 18, pp. 537–60.

—— and C. Vegh, 2002, "Two Hundred Years of Contagion," unpublished manuscript, University of Maryland.

Kaufmann, Daniel, Aart Kraay, and Pablo Zoido-Lobatón, 1999, "Governance Matters," World Bank Policy Research Working Paper No. 216 (Washington: World Bank).

Kelly, Trish, 1998, "Ability to Pay in the Age of Pax Britannica, 1890–1914," *Explorations in Economic History*, vol. 35, pp. 31–58.

Keynes, John M., 1919, *The Economic Consequences of Peace* (London: Macmillan).

Klibanoff, Peter, Owen Lamont, and Thierry A. Witzman, 1998, "Investor Reaction to Salient News in Closed-End Country Funds," *Journal of Finance*, vol. 53, pp. 673–99.

Knack, Stephen and Philip Keefer, 1995, "Institutions and Economic Performance: Cross-Country Tests Using Alternative Institutional Measures," *Economics and Politics*, vol. 7, pp. 207–27.

Krueger, Anne O., 2002, "A New Approach to Sovereign Debt Restructuring," (Washington: International Monetary Fund).

Lane, Timothy and Steven Phillips, 2000, "Does IMF Financing Result in Moral Hazard?" IMF Working Paper No. 00/168 (Washington: International Monetary Fund).

La Porta, Rafael, Florencio Lopez-de-Silanes, Andrei Shleifer, and Robert Vishny, 2000, "Investor Protection and Corporate Governance," *Journal of Financial Economics*, vol. 58, pp. 3–27.

Levine, Ross, and Sara Zervos, 1998, "Stock markets, banks, and economic growth," *American Economic Review*, vol. 88, pp. 537–58.

Levy, Maria-B., 1995, "The Brazilian Public Debt: Domestic and Foreign, 1824–1913," in Reinhart Liehr (ed.), *The Public Debt in Latin America in Historical Perspective* (Frankfurt am Main: Vervuert).

Li, Kan, Randall Morck, Fan Yang, and Bernard Yeung, 2004, "Firm-specific Variation and Openness in Emerging Markets," *Review of Economics and Statistics*, vol. 86, pp. 658–69.

Lindert, Peter and Peter Morton, 1989, "How Sovereign Debt Has Worked," in Sachs, Jeffrey and Susan Collins (eds.) *Developing Country Debt and Economic Performance* (Chicago: University of Chicago Press).

Lipson, Charles, 1985, *Standing Guard*: Protecting Foreign Capital is the Nineteenth and Twentieth Centuries (University of California Press, Berkley CA).

Ludwig, Armin, 1985, *Brazil: A Handbook of Historical Statistics* (Boston, Massachusetts: G. K. Hall).

Macmillan, Rory, 1995a, "The Next Sovereign Debt Crisis," *Stanford Journal of International Law*, vol. 31, pp. 305–58.

Macmillan, Rory, 1995b, "New Lease of Life for Bondholder Councils," *Financial Times*, 15 August.

Mamalakis, Marcos, 1978–1989, *Historical Statistics of Chile* (6 vols.) (Westport, Conn: Greenwood Press).

Mauro, Paolo, 1995, "Corruption and Growth," *Quarterly Journal of Economics*, vol. 110, pp. 681–712.

Mauro, Paolo, 1998, "Corruption and the Composition of Government Expenditure", *Journal of Public Economics*, vol. 69, pp. 263–79.

Mauro, Paolo, Nathan Sussman, and Yishay Yafeh, 2000, "Emerging Market Spreads: Then Versus Now," IMF Working Paper 00/190.

——— 2002, "Emerging Market Spreads: Then Versus Now," *Quarterly Journal of Economics*, vol. 117, pp. 695–733.

References

Michie, Ranald, 1986, *The London and New York Stock Exchanges, 1850–1914* (London: Allen & Unwin).

Min, Hong, 1998, "Determinants of Emerging Market Bond Spreads: Do Economic Fundamentals Matter?" Policy Research Working Paper No. 1899 (Washington: World Bank).

Mitchell, Brian, 1992, *International Historical Statistics: Europe, 1750–1988* (New York: Stockton Press).

Mitchell, Brian, 1993, *International Historical Statistics: The Americas, 1750–1988* (New York: Stockton Press).

Mitchell, Brian, 1995, *International Historical Statistics: Africa, Asia and Oceania, 1750–1988* (New York: Stockton Press).

Morck, Randall, Bernard Yeung, and Wayne Yu, 2000, "The Information Contents of Stock Markets: Why Do Emerging Markets Have Comoving Stock Price Movements," *Journal of Financial Economics*, vol. 58, pp. 215–38.

Morgan, E. Victor, and W.A. Thomas, 1969, *The Stock Exchange: Its History and Functions*, 2nd edition (London: Elek Brooks).

North, Douglass, 1990, *Institutions, Institutional Change, and Economic Performance* (Cambridge, Massachusetts: Cambridge University Press).

North, Douglass and Barry Weingast, 1989, "Constitutions and Commitment: The Evolution of Institutions Governing Public Choice in Seventeenth-Century Britain," *Journal of Economic History*, vol. 49, pp. 803–32.

O'Rourke, Kevin and Jeffrey Williamson, 1998, *Globalization and History: The Evolution of a Nineteenth Century Atlantic Economy* (Cambridge, Massachusetts: MIT Press).

Obstfeld, Maurice, 1986, "Capital Mobility in the World Economy: Theory and Measurement," *Carnegie Rochester Series on Public Policy*, vol. 24, pp. 55–104.

Obstfeld, Maurice and Alan M. Taylor, 1998, "The Great Depression as a Watershed: International Capital Mobility Over the Long Run," in Bordo, Michael, Claudia Goldin, and Eugene White (eds.) *The Defining Moment: The Great Depression and the American Economy in the Twentieth Century* (Chicago: University of Chicago Press).

——2003a, "Globalization and Capital Markets," in Bordo, Michael, Alan Taylor and Jeffrey Williamson (eds.), *Globalization in Historical Perspective* (Chicago: University of Chicago Press).

——2003b, "Sovereign Risk, Credibility, and the Gold Standard, 1870–1913 Versus 1925–1931," *Economic Journal*, vol. 113, pp. 241–75.

——2004, *Global Capital Markets: Integration, Crisis, and Growth* (Cambridge, UK; New York: Cambridge University Press).

Offer, Avner, 1993, "The British Empire: A Waste of Money?" *Economic History Review*, vol. 46, pp. 215–32.

Olson, Mancur, 1965, *The Logic of Collective Action: Public Goods and the Theory of Groups* (Cambridge, Massachusetts: Harvard University Press).

Perron, Pierre, 1989 "The Great Crash, the Oil Price Shock, and the Unit Root Hypothesis," *Econometrica*, vol. 57, pp. 1361–401.

Platt, Desmond Christopher Martin (DCM), 1989, *Mickey Mouse Numbers in World History* (London: MacMillan).

Portes, Richard, 2000, "The Role of Institutions for Collective Action," in Adams, Charles, Robert Litan, and Michael Pomerleano (eds.) *Managing Financial and Corporate Distress: Lessons from Asia* (Washington: Brookings Institution).

Rogoff, Kenneth, and Jeromin Zettelmeyer, 2002, "Bankruptcy Procedures for Sovereigns: A History of Ideas, 1976–2001," *IMF Staff Papers*, vol. 49, pp. 470–507.

Sachs, Jeffrey and Andrew Warner, 1995, "Economic Reform and the Process of Global Integration," *Brookings Papers on Economic Activity*, vol. 1, pp. 1–118.

Schneider, Jurgen, Oskar Schwarzer, and Friedrich Zellfelder, 1991, *Wahrungen der Welt* (Stuttgart, Germany, F. Steiner Press).

Shleifer, Andrei, 2000, *Inefficient Markets: An Introduction to Behavioral Finance*, Clarendon Lectures in Economics (Oxford and New York: Oxford University Press).

Sinclair, John M., 1803, *The History of the Public Revenue of the British Empire*, Vol. II, Appendix 2, pp. 28–33 (London: A. Strahan).

Singh, Manmohan, 2002, "Recovery Rates from Distressed Debt—Empirical Evidence from Chapter 11 Filings, International Litigation, and Recent Sovereign Debt Restructurings," IMF Working Paper 03/161 (Washington: International Monetary Fund).

Stone, Irving, 1999, *The Global Export of Capital from Great Britain, 1865–1914: A Statistical Survey* (New York: St Martin's Press).

Sussman, Nathan and Yishay Yafeh, 1999a, "Contagion and Capital Market integration in Asia: Historical and Contemporary Evidence," *Seoul Journal of Economics*, vol. 12, pp. 391–417.

——1999b "The Gold Standard, the Cost of Foreign Borrowing, and Capital Market Integration: Historical Evidence from Japanese Sovereign Debt," A Century of International Financial Architecture, a Special Issue of *Economie Internationale*, vol. 78, pp. 85–103.

——2000, "Institutions, Reforms, and Country Risk: Lessons from Japanese Government Debt in the Meiji Period," *Journal of Economic History*, vol. 60, pp. 442–67.

——2004, "Constitutions and Commitment: Evidence on the Relation between Institutions and the Cost of Capital," CEPR Discussion Paper No. 4404 (London: Centre for Economic Policy Research).

Suter, Christian, 1992, *Debt Cycles in the World Economy: Foreign Loans, Financial Crises and Debt Settlements, 1820–1990* (Boulder, Colorado: Westview Press).

Suzuki, Toshio, 1994, *Japanese Government Loans on the London Capital Market, 1870–1913* (London: Athlone Press).

Sy, Amadou, 2002, "Emerging Market Bond Spreads and Sovereign Credit Ratings: Reconciling Market Views with Economic Fundamentals," *Emerging Markets Review*, vol. 3, pp. 380–408.

Tomz, Michael, 2005, Sovereign Debt and International Cooperation: Reputational Reasons for Lending and Repayment, unpublished book manuscript, Stanford University.

Wei, Shang-Jin, 2000, "How Taxing Is Corruption on International Investors?" *Review of Economics and Statistics*, vol. 82, pp. 1–11.

Wei, Shang-Jin and Yi Wu, 2002, "Negative Alchemy? Composition of Capital Flows, and Currency Crises," in Sebastian Edwards and Jeffrey Frankel (eds.), *Preventing Currency Crises in Emerging Markets* (Chicago: University of Chicago Press).

Winkler, Max, 1933, *Foreign Bonds: An Autopsy; A Study of Defaults and Repudations of Government Obligations* (Philadelphia: Roland Swain Company).

Wright, Mark, 2000, "Sovereign Risk and Creditor Coordination," unpublished manuscript, Stanford University.

Wynne, William, 1951, *State Insolvency and Foreign Bondholders: Vol. 2, Selected Case Histories of Governmental Foreign Defaults and Debt Readjustments* (New Haven, Connecticut: Yale University Press).

Zhang, Xiaoming Alan, 1999, "Testing for 'Moral Hazard' in Adjustment Lending," Institute for International Finance Research Paper No. 99-1 (Washington DC: Institute for International Finance).

Zweig, Stefan, 1943, *The World of Yesterday* (London, Cassell & Co.).

Index

Appendices, boxes, figures, notes and tables are indexed in bold as **app, b, f, n, t**, e.g. **47n**

Index